AKIRA IRIYE

University of Chicago

The Cold War in Asia

A HISTORICAL INTRODUCTION

Prentice-Hall, Inc.
Englewood Cliffs, New Jersey

Library of Congress Cataloging in Publication Data

IRIYE, AKIRA.
    The cold war in Asia.

    Bibliography: p.
    1. Asia—Foreign relations—United States.
    2. United States—Foreign relations—Asia. 3. Asia—
    Politics. 4. Asia—Foreign relations. I. Title.
DS33.4.U6174   327.5   73-16200
ISBN   0-13-139659-5
ISBN   0-13-139642-0 (pbk.)

© **1974 by Prentice-Hall, Inc., Englewood Cliffs, New Jersey**

PRINTED IN THE UNITED STATES OF AMERICA

10 9 8 7 6 5 4 3 2 1

PRENTICE-HALL INTERNATIONAL, INC., *London*
PRENTICE-HALL OF AUSTRALIA, PTY. LTD., *Sydney*
PRENTICE-HALL OF CANADA, LTD., *Toronto*
PRENTICE-HALL OF INDIA PRIVATE LIMITED, *New Delhi*
PRENTICE-HALL OF JAPAN, INC., *Tokyo*

For my daughters,
Keiko and Masumi

Contents

Contents   vii

CHAPTER FIVE

Toward a New Internationalism,   164

Necessity for a New World View, 164   The White Paper, 169
New American Perception of the Role of Japan, 173
Preserving Dominance in a Modified Yalta System: Korean War, 176
The San Francisco System, 182

Bibliography,   193

Index,   207

Preface

This is an interpretative history of the origins of the Cold War in Asia. The book tries to trace the story in the context of Asian-Pacific international relations and of United States-East Asian relations. The focus is on the 1940s, a decade that was of crucial importance in shaping the subsequent history of Asia and America's place in it. Today, in the 1970s, the world may be entering a new epoch of international politics. To understand the nature and possible direction of the change, it is essential to go back to the origins of the Asian-Pacific crisis and the roots of United States involvement.

I started working on a first draft of this book in 1969. In December of that year, the American Historical Association had its annual convention in Washington. On its program was a session on "The United States and East Asia," where Professor John K. Fairbank of Harvard University read a paper on "Sino-American Images." He called for a less ethnocentric approach to the study of American foreign relations, urging historians to recognize that the United States "is the most expansive power in history." He added that "expansion, sheer growth, is now the great enemy of us all, whether the expansion is at home or abroad, American, Soviet, Chinese or other." Listening to the paper, and reflecting on the mounting criticism on American involvement in Asia that was brought about by the Vietnam War, I felt there was a need to explore the recent past in the light of the traditional interactions between Americans and Asians.

It would have been a different book if I had finished it in 1970, as I had originally intended to do. The book would soon have been made out of date by the momentous changes that were to take place in American relations with the Soviet Union, the People's Republic of China, Japan, and the two Vietnams. There is always a risk in writing from the perspective of the present, especially when discussing international politics and diplomatic affairs. While the events of 1971 and 1972 have helped me raise some fresh questions about the Cold War, equally unanticipated turns and twists may occur in the near future, necessitating the search for yet another conceptual scheme. All that a historian can do is to try to avoid dogmatism and to examine as much documentary evidence as possible. In this connection, a delay in the completion of the manuscript was fortunate. Since 1971 the United States and Great Britain have begun to open up their public archives for the Second World War years, and the official American publication, *Foreign Relations of the United States*, has reached the year 1947 with respect to documents dealing with Asia. This book could not have been written without consulting these sources.

My intellectual indebtedness to professional colleagues and pioneering scholars is indicated, at least partially, in the footnotes and bibliography, so I shall not name them here. In writing this book I have particularly benefited from the scrutiny and criticism of my students, and I am especially grateful to Mitchell Serota and Franklin Ng for going over the entire manuscript with care. The officers of the National Archives, the Franklin D. Roosevelt Library (Hyde Park), and the Public Record Office (London) have been most courteous and efficient in extending to me their cooperation and assistance. For enabling me to make research trips, I would like to record my thanks to the Social Sciences Division and to the Committee on Far Eastern Studies, both of the University of Chicago. Mrs. Harriet Pearl has done the typing most expeditiously, and other secretaries of the Department of History have helped me in numerous ways. Finally, both my father and my father-in-law have provided inspiring examples of scholarly integrity and professional dedication, and I am indebted to them in more ways than I am conscious of.

Akira Iriye
June 1973

CHAPTER ONE

Introduction

February 27, 1972, was a memorable day in the annals of United States-Asian relations. President Richard M. Nixon and Premier Chou En-lai of the People's Republic of China put their signatures to a joint communiqué, expressing the two governments' readiness to put an end to the period of enmity and strive for restoration of normal relations between the two countries.

A key passage in this historic document asserted,

> Neither should seek hegemony in the Asia-Pacific region and each is opposed to the efforts by any other country or group of countries to establish such hegemony.

Furthermore, the Nixon-Chou statement declared that

> it would be against the interests of the peoples of the world for any major country to collude with another against other countries, or for major countries to divide up the world into spheres of interest.

1

In these two sentences were summed up the concepts and assumptions that had guided Chinese and American diplomacy over the years, which in turn were derived from their historical experiences in the modern world. Having now agreed on a common vocabulary to define their mutual attitudes, it remained to be seen to what extent it would serve to recreate a stable order in Asia and the Pacific.

Seven months later, on September 29, 1972, Chou En-lai, this time using a brush, signed another historic document, a joint statement between the People's Republic of China and Japan. The Sino-Japanese statement reiterated, almost word for word, the passage in the Nixon-Chou communiqué quoted at the beginning of the preceding paragraph. It is significant that the three powers found it possible and desirable to phrase their vision of a new Asian-Pacific international order in a way that was evocative of the past. It was as if the three governments were determined to search jointly for a new system of international affairs in that region of the world, and that in so doing they would be acutely conscious of the experiences of history.

These two crucial events of 1972, together with the signing of the Vietnam peace agreement on January 27, 1973, have marked the culmination of an era in Asian-Pacific international relations in general and United States-Asian relations in particular. A new, as yet undefined period is about to begin.

The time seems opportune to seek a fresh understanding of one of the basic themes of recent history: the Cold War in Asia. Whether the events of 1972 and 1973 usher in a new international order in the Asia-Pacific region, and in what way the role of the United States will change are questions that can be intelligently discussed only when one looks at them in a historical perspective. It is especially pertinent to examine the decade of the 1940s, which saw the coming of the Pacific War and the beginning of the Cold War. How the one was related to the other provides a clue to the history of the Cold War in Asia and to the understanding of subsequent decades.

Numerous histories of the Cold War have been written, and yet it is surprising how monotonous and at the same time how confusing the usually presented themes are. To cite one example, Gabriel A. Almond's influential book, *The American People and Foreign Policy*, was the first systematic study of public opinion in the mid-1940s. Written before the outbreak of the Korean War, it echoed the prevailing assumption that the

tension and the threat characteristic of the struggle of the Communists to impose their domination on the world has become a permanent part of the political environment of the era.[1]

[1] Gabriel Almond, *The American People and Foreign Policy* (New York: Harcourt, Brace & Jovanovich, 1950), p. 18.

The confrontation with the Communist challenge, the basic feature of the Cold War era according to Almond, determined not only the way the American people responded to international affairs but also the way a researcher asked questions. All were related to the fundamental phenomenon, and no question was raised as to the validity of the basic assumptions. There was no interest in ascertaining the historical origins of the Cold War, or whether the Cold War existed in reality.

In a new introduction to the 1960 edition of the above book, Almond touched on the first question. According to him, until about the middle of 1946 "we believed in the continuity of the World War II alliance" between the United States and the Soviet Union. This was a utopian age in American-Russian relations, which quickly gave way to the Cold War because of Soviet policies in Eastern Europe and Germany. While the wartime alliance turned into postwar enmity, Almond writes, the period 1946–49 was an "imaginative stage" of U.S. foreign policy, when the nation responded creatively and prudently to the challenges of the postwar world. But the alleged imaginativeness of Cold War diplomacy, according to this account, was essentially an automatic response to a changing balance of power:

> The Russian Communist threat to Western Europe—particularly to Greece and Turkey—and the withdrawal of England from her traditional position in the Mediterranean created a power vacuum in which we had no choice but to enter.[2]

These themes have been endlessly repeated by other writers, and there still persists a monotonous picture of a warm wartime friendship giving way to the Cold War because of the expansionism of Soviet Communism. The picture is monotonous, but it is also ambiguous because it fails to explain the timing of the alleged transformation in Soviet policy from one of amity with the United States to that of aggressive imperialism. Soviet policies in Eastern Europe and Germany were quite clear even before the end of the war, yet Almond would date the Cold War from mid-1946. If so, the transformation of American-Russian relations must be attributed at least in part to changes in United States policy. Could it be said that Soviet policy, however expansionist, had remained the same, and that it was American policy that brought about a sense of crisis and defined the crisis as a Cold War? If so, the type of interpretation presented by Almond would be little more than a reiteration of official American doctrine. It would be itself part of the ideology of the Cold War.

Such considerations have led some historians to reexamine postwar United States policy from a critical point of view. Instead of presenting it

[2] Ibid., revised edition (1960), pp. xii–xiii.

merely as a response to Communist expansion, they have sought to locate the origins of the Cold War by questioning the assumptions and perceptions held by American policy makers in the crucial months of 1945 and 1946. The basic premise here is that the Cold War was not inevitable, that a different perception of American-Russian relations at the end of the war might have brought about a more peaceful world order. Thomas G. Paterson's *Cold War Critics* (1971), for instance, has presented a study of those Americans who seriously questioned the inevitability thesis and tried, without much success, to propose alternative schemes of international relations. As Paterson writes,

> We cannot be certain that the alternatives were viable and would have made a difference in international relations, but adherents to the traditional account must now give attention to the alternatives and try to explain, not assume, that such options were unsound and unworkable.[3]

Some critics have gone further and accepted an inevitability thesis at the opposite end of the spectrum. Richard Freeland, for example, has argued, in his *The Truman Doctrine and the Origins of McCarthyism* (1972), that the Cold War psychology in the United States did not develop as an automatic reaction to Soviet policy, but that it was inspired by a government seeking to impose its view of postwar international commitments on an unwilling populace. It was necessary for the nation's leaders to do so because only in an atmosphere of crisis would the people and Congress be willing to authorize spectacular spending on armament and foreign aid, the two vital sinews of national existence. Thus it was the United States government that led the way in the making of the Cold War, which was not so much a description of the reality of international affairs as a perception of American-Russian relations created for domestic consumption.[4]

These revisionist writers have succeeded in unravelling many threads in the story of the Cold War which for so long remained tightly woven in only one pattern. The intensive questioning by recent historians has been such that even the epithet "Cold War" has come under attack. If it were merely a picture perceived by the official mind, it would make little sense to treat it as if it were the fundamental reality that defined the way nations behaved after the war. There must have been far more basic forces and factors which produced the fiction of the Cold War. As Joyce and Gabriel Kolko have written, the term

> burdens one's comprehension of the postwar era with oversimplifications and evokes the wrong questions. At best, the unfortunate phrase describes United

[3] Thomas G. Paterson, *Cold War Critics* (Chicago: Quadrangle, 1971), p. 12.
[4] Richard Freeland, *The Truman Doctrine and the Origins of McCarthyism* (New York: Knopf, 1972).

States-Soviet diplomacy in the narrowest context, as if the relationship subsumes most that is crucial in the history of our times.[5]

The Kolkos rightly point out that the American-Russian rivalry has been only one aspect and perhaps not even the most significant feature, of postwar international history. But their alternative framework is just as subjective and myopic as those whose interpretations they criticize. It is, the Kolkos argue,

the expansive interests of American capitalism as an economy with specific structural needs that guide the definition of foreign economic policy and the United States' larger global role and needs.[6]

Such a thesis is tantamount to looking at international affairs through the prism of American capitalism, the result of which tends to be a history no less American-centered than official and semiofficial Cold War accounts. For this reason revisionist writings have often been as monotonous and ambiguous as the rest.

There is obviously a need to develop a conceptual framework in which to comprehend recent world history, a framework that takes account of, but is not controlled by, the subjectivism of the participants in the drama. Admittedly it is a most difficult task, since there has been far more source material available on the American side than elsewhere, and writings by non-American authors have equally been unidimensional and distorted. They have also played their part in the evolution of the Cold War. If there is any hope for a fresh quest at this time, it is that the Second World War is now nearly thirty years old, and the historian has a much clearer perspective to look at the war and the immediate postwar years than was possible in the 1950s and the 1960s. Already in the late 1960s some began talking of the "decline of the Cold War," in Paul Seabury's phrase.[7] Whether the Cold War has ended and the world has ushered in a post-Cold War period are questions that divide observers and will be discussed elsewhere in this book. What is incontestable is the growing sense of distance from the early years, not simply physically but also mentally. As recently as 1965, a former President of the United States could write, discussing postwar foreign policy,

The United States lost no foot of the Free World to Communist aggression, made certain that the Soviets and China understood the adequacy of our military power, and dealt with them firmly but not arrogantly. We regarded our friends as respected partners and valued partners and tried always to create

[5] Joyce and Gabriel Kolko, *The Limits of Power* (New York: Harper & Row, 1972), p. 6.
[6] Ibid., p. 8.
[7] Paul Seabury, *The Rise and Decline of the Cold War* (New York: Basic Books, 1967).

mutual confidence and trust, well knowing that without these ingredients
alliances would be of little enduring value.[8]

One suspects that the writer of such a statement was intellectually closer to
the atmosphere of the late 1940s and 1950s than he was to today's mentality.
Rapid and radical changes in international affairs and within American
society have brought into being a new questioning generation which does not
share the psychology of the earlier generations. If, in the meantime, the
various governments relax their policies regarding the release of public
documents, it may be confidently expected that more satisfactory studies of
the Cold War will begin to appear.

Despite the staggering volume of works dealing with the Cold War,
there has not been written a comprehensive history of the Cold War in Asia,
giving the subject a specific geographical focus. In general studies Asia is
discussed only in passing, as another arena for the struggle for supremacy
between the Big Two. Most discussions of the origins of the Cold War point to
such areas as Germany, Iran, Turkey, Greece, and Eastern Europe as the
crucial theaters of American-Russian rivalry, and have difficulty fitting the
Asian picture into an overall framework. Two recent histories of the Cold
War—John Lewis Gaddis, *The United States and the Origins of the Cold War
1941–1947* (1972), and Walter LaFeber, *America, Russia, and the Cold War,
1945–1971* (second edition, 1972)—while excellent in many respects, are no
exception in that they do not deal extensively with Asia and the Pacific in the
immediate postwar years.

In the meantime, specialists in Asian international relations in general
and in Soviet, Chinese, or Japanese foreign policy in particular have
produced a sizable body of literature on these years. But unfortunately, there
has not been sufficient intellectual interchange between these writers and
specialists in United States diplomatic history who write on the Cold War.
This is due in part to the fact that the bulk of the writings by the former
group has not been translated into English, and with notable exceptions such
as Tang Tsou's *America's Failure in China* (1963), their contributions have
made little impact upon American historiography. On the other hand,
because American historians address their works primarily to their colleagues
studying various aspects of domestic history, their findings have not always
been taken by others with the seriousness which they deserve. To the extent
that it is essential to avoid intellectual parochialism, one must try somehow to
fill this gap so that one may have a balanced view of the origins of the Cold
War in Asia, both in terms of its geographical setting and of the role of the
United States.

[8] Dwight D. Eisenhower, *The White House Years: Waging Peace, 1956–1961* (Garden City,
N.Y.: Doubleday, 1965), p. 624.

"The Cold War in Asia" is a shorthand for describing the changes that took place in the Asia-Pacific international system and in America's role in it. To understand these changes, it is important to trace the subject in historical perspective. The following chapter will provide the background to 1940 in order to set a stage for a more detailed discussion of the Pacific War and the rest of the 1940s, which comprise the main part of this book.

CHAPTER
TWO

The
Historical
Background

THE ASIAN INTERNATIONAL SYSTEM

"Neither should seek hegemony in the Asia-Pacific region," declared the United States and the Chinese governments in February 1972, marking the beginning of the end of the Cold War in Asia. Since China had not sought such hegemony, the obvious inference was that the United States would retrench its power in the Asia-Pacific region. A further inference was that the two governments were now determined to define a new order in the area on the basis not of the preponderance of one power but of an equilibrium among nations.

In order better to understand the implications of this, probably the most significant passage in the Shanghai communiqué, it is necessary to go back to the earlier history of Asian-Pacific international relations. American presence in postwar Asia was a consequence of the Second World War, which in turn had been brought about by developments in Asia and the Pacific during the 1930s. Ultimately, one has to go back to the nineteenth century and trace, however briefly, the evolution of international relations over the years. The Pacific War and the Cold War, in such a perspective, were stages in the long search for an international order in that part of the world after the collapse of the two thousand year old system that had been sustained by the state and civilization of China.

Opening of the East

It was in the mid-nineteenth century that China and Japan "entered the family of nations"—a convenient expression to describe the merging of the Asian and the European international systems. Before that time the European nations had extended their power as well as economic and cultural activities to India, Southeast Asia, the Southwestern Pacific, and Siberia; these regions had been integrated into the European state system. But they were essentially colonies, supplying the metropolitan countries with gold, raw materials, and foodstuffs; they did not contribute to creating a new pattern of international relations in that part of the world. Colonial rivalries were reflections of European politics, and they had little bearing upon the traditional supremacy of China in East Asia. The two systems of "international" relations existed side by side, and their contact was limited to commercial interchanges, an undertaking for which no formal diplomatic arrangements seemed needed.

The 1840s saw the breakdown of this uneasy equilibrium and the beginning of the search for an alternative arrangement in the Asia-Pacific region. The basic framework of the new order, which was to last for over a century, was "the treaty system," which was somewhere between the European-style international relations and the outright colonial arrangements. The Western powers, more often collectively than singly, acted together to enter into treaty relations with China, Japan, Korea, and others and to safeguard their interests jointly. The fact that the governments of Western countries signed treaties with their equivalents in Asia indicated that at least in terms of international law the former recognized the sovereignty and independence of the latter. China, for instance, was not going to be an object of European colonization or partition. It was to be opened up, at least partially, to foreigners, but the Chinese government would continue to be responsible for maintaining law and order internally. The Asian international system, in other words, would become part of the Western international system, but not be absorbed by it. China was technically still a sovereign entity, like Sweden or Turkey, and it was expected to behave like one. This may have given the government, the reigning Ch'ing dynasty, real trouble, as it was called upon to exchange ambassadors, protect foreigners, and regulate foreign trade just as did other members of the international community. In reality the Chinese regime was neither willing nor capable of doing all these things, but its sovereign status in international law was, paradoxically, forced upon it by the West.

In the final analysis, what sustained this system was Western, in particular British, power, both in reality and in appearance. Britain's major source of power was the land force based in India and the navy with its bases in Gibraltar, Singapore, Hong Kong, and elsewhere. All this was far from sufficient in establishing military control over the whole of China, but Chinese officials were apt to be impressed by a quick and decisive show of small force, as happened during the Opium War and again during the Arrow War (1856–59). Several hundred British soldiers, many of them from India, coming ashore from some gunboats, were usually enough to demonstrate British superiority and exact concessions from China. And the British never hesitated to use force. Said Lord Clarendon in 1857,

> I fear that we must come to the conclusion that in dealing with a nation like the Chinese, if we intend to preserve any amicable or useful relations with them, we must make them sensible of the law of force, and must appeal to them in the manner which alone they can appreciate.[1]

Whenever a Chinese official seemed unwilling to abide by a treaty agreement, or a mob attacked a foreign resident without restraint from the local gentry, the Western response followed this philosophy. Their actual strength was less important than their determination. Moreover, the Western countries were united as "treaty powers." They could present a common front and join their forces, giving the appearance of Western unity. An image of Western military superiority was shared by the Chinese. They were especially influenced by the idea during the great Taiping upheaval (1850–64), which plunged China into administrative chaos and political crisis. It is interesting to note that during this civil war both the Taiping rebels and the Ch'ing dynasty turned to the West as a model of military power and a supplier of arms and strategists. While driven by traditional ideologies and massacring one another with little thought of the welfare of the Chinese nation as a whole, the factions were consciously or unconsciously adopting Western weaponry and confirming the image of Western superiority. These became leading features of Chinese foreign affairs after the suppression of the Taipings. The West was strong and not to be easily trifled with. In the meantime China, too, would undertake to strengthen itself militarily.

[1] Douglas Hurd, *The Arrow War: An Anglo-Chinese Confusion, 1856–1860* (London: Collins, 1967), pp. 57–58.

There existed, then, a system of Chinese-Western relations in which the fiction of Chinese sovereignty was upheld through the reality and appearance of Western power. Such a system was conducive to the West's more or less informal expansion at minimum cost, and to a degree of stability among the various countries in East Asia, China included. No one power or group of powers was strong enough to impose its imperial will on the scene.

This period of the treaty system coincided with the opening of Japan and its development as a modern state, and with the trans-Pacific expansion of the United States. Thus, just as an Asian scheme of international relations developed on the continent, the Pacific Ocean came to have a regional order of its own. While both Japan and the United States participated in the Chinese treaty system, it is well to keep in mind that they were also Pacific countries, and that international relations in East Asia and the western Pacific did not always develop in parallel fashion.

Japan, like China, became a member of the international community through unequal treaties with Western countries. The latter stationed troops and gunboats to see to it that the treaties were observed. Like China, Japan was not turned into a colony and, despite the internal chaos of the 1860s, the Western powers were on the whole satisfied with letting Japanese authorities maintain law and order. In one respect, however, the Japanese differed from their continental neighbors. They were far more nimble in adapting themselves to the idea of an international system both in Asia and the Pacific, and from the earliest moment tried to stake out Japan's position in it, rather than passively accepting a status quo imposed from the outside. They were willing and even eager to see their country incorporated into the community of nations, and then to view developments in Asia through this new perspective. On the continent of Asia, the Japanese government after the Meiji Restoration (1868) sought a treaty relationship with China and Korea, approximating the status achieved by the Western powers. In the Pacific, Japan asserted its claims to the Bonins, the Kuriles, and the Ryukyus, while eyeing other island territories as possible areas for expansion. Considering the fact that the unequal treaties with the West were never fully abrogated until 1911, it is quite remarkable that this did not deter the Japanese from defining their nation as an expansive power. Expansion at first was visualized as more commercial than territorial, but it was a conceptual framework which enabled them to envision their role in Asian and Pacific international affairs.

On such a system of Asian-Western contact was superimposed a diplomacy of imperialism which defined the power politics of the area after the 1890s. What this entailed was twofold: the partitioning of the Asia-Pacific region into colonies and spheres of influence, and a series of agreements and ententes among the imperialist countries.

Imperialism and Nationalism

The first to take away Chinese territory was Japan, which obtained Taiwan as a result of victory in the Sino-Japanese War (1894–95). The war was essentially a test of will between Japan, intent upon emerging as an Asian-Pacific power, and China, determined to maintain its status on the continent of Asia. It was symbolic that Japan's success involved tangible gains in the Pacific (the cession of Taiwan) and on the continent (detaching Korea from Chinese suzerainty). Japan was now accorded the status of a great regional power with a respectable and growing army and navy. Because the island operated from the home base, its military strength could be rapidly mobilized and utilized as a tool of diplomacy. It is interesting to note, however, that for a while after the Chinese war the Japanese were more interested in expanding eastward and southward, in the direction of Hawaii and the Philippines, than westward to the Asian continent. Publicists wrote of Japan as a Pacific power, and some dreamed not of Asian empire but of Pacific empire. But this was not to be, because of the rapid turn of events after 1897.

That year saw the German seizure of Kiaochow Bay and the beginning of the "slicing of the Chinese melon." Within a short span of time China was forced to grant bases and leases to the foreign powers, to obtain loans on the security of imperial revenues and in exchange for economic concessions, to agree to foreign capital investments in railways and mines, and to be a passive observer of the partitioning of the land into spheres of influence. The fiction that Chinese sovereignty remained more or less unimpaired now gave way to a sense of an inevitable break-up of China. Informal empire seemed about to be replaced by formal empire.

Why such a shift came about at this time has often been debated in the context of the theories of imperialism. Yet most interpretations of imperialism have focused on Africa and the Middle East, and East Asia is usually mentioned, if at all, only casually and superficially. This is understandable, since none of the usual theories really fits the East Asian scene.[2] In the discussion of the Asian international system, however, the period of the diplomacy of imperialism becomes comprehensible as an attempt at erecting a new framework of international relations after the Sino-Japanese War revealed China's weakness. At the same time, the war also gave rise to the first generation of Chinese nationalists. These two factors combined to destabilize conditions in East Asia and led the powers to restructure the treaty system to make it conform to the demands of the new age.

[2] See Akira Iriye, "Imperialism in East Asia," in James B. Crowley, ed., *Modern East Asia: Essays in Interpretation* (New York: Harcourt, Brace & Jovanovich, 1970), pp. 122–50.

The Sino-Japanese War shattered the key assumption on which the treaty system had been based, that there was a central government of China capable of speaking for the whole of the country and of regulating foreign affairs. After 1895 the foreign powers became more and more interested in dealing with regional authorities and looked to provincial officials as sources of power. At the same time, the powers sought to entrench their own interests and influence in certain provinces. The result was dual control at the regional level. Germany, for instance, established a naval base in Tsingtao and a leasehold in Kiaochow Bay, and German naval and diplomatic personnel dealt directly with provincial Chinese officials in matters ranging from the administration of justice to improvements in sanitary conditions.[3] In similar ways Russia extended its power to Manchuria, Britain to the Yangtze River region of Central China, and France in the southern provinces bordering on Indochina. None of these spheres of influence became outright colonies; instead, government took the form of dual control by China and a foreign power. This was the way the powers responded to the revealed weakness of China after the war with Japan. They would henceforth stress regional arrangements without completely destroying the concept of Chinese sovereignty and unity.

Such a system created a degree of stability in Asian international relations, as the multiplicity of imperialist powers made it difficult for one power or group of powers to achieve hegemony. In fact no country wanted such hegemony, and all were interested in preventing chaos in their mutual relations. Thus from the beginning there was a tendency on their part to enter into bilateral and multilateral agreements in order to define the limits of their spheres of interest. Between 1898 and 1900, for instance, there were agreements between Russia and Britain, between Germany and Britain, between Japan and Russia, and between France and Britain. These pacts were intended to specify where a power had the right to build railways, open mines, and otherwise have prerogatives superior to those of the other nations. The multiplicity of such agreements ensured that an attempt on the part of a power to violate them would be met by a simultaneous and automatic response by all others.

If there was a degree of equilibrium among the imperialist powers, the stability of the new framework of Chinese foreign relations was threatened by the emergence of what can best be described as nationalistic public opinion in China. An increasing self-conscious generation of students, intellectuals, and officials began asserting their voice and calling for wholesale transformation of the country so as to combat foreign encroachment. Their determination grew the more they were frustrated by the inability of their government to resist imperialist demands. It was natural that they began seriously thinking

[3] See John Schrecker, *Imperialism and Chinese Nationalism: Germany in Shantung* (Cambridge, Mass.: Harvard University Press, 1971).

of the need to restructure Chinese government in order to deal more effectively with foreign affairs. They, too, were considering ways to restabilize Asian international relations, but on the basis of Chinese sovereignty.

This same period also saw a redefinition of international affairs in the western Pacific. The Spanish-American War of 1898 resulted in the transfer of the Philippines and Guam to the United States from Spain, causing the disappearance from East Asia of one of the oldest European colonial powers. Because Spanish rule in the Philippines had been tenuous and inefficient, giving rise to a formidable movement for autonomy and/or independence, its replacement by American rule removed one factor of instability in power politics in that part of the world. The major powers readily accepted the new situation, although the Japanese government was not unaware of the proximity of the islands to Taiwan and had entertained hopes of their eventual annexation to Japan. Now this ambition was frustrated, as was the hope, expressed by some officials and opinion leaders, that the Hawaiian Islands would in time fall to Japanese dominion. In 1898 the United States finally incorporated Hawaii as a territory, thus formalizing what had long been an accomplished fact.

The turn of the twentieth century thus ushered in an entirely new stage of international relations in the Asia-Pacific region. The whole area fell under the imperialistic control of a handful of powers. Russia, Germany, France, Britain, Japan, the United States, and the Netherlands held sway over the entire area embracing China, Southeast Asia, and the Southwestern Pacific. The destiny of this region was affected to a considerable extent by the friction and conflict as well as the cooperation among these powers.

The Anglo-Japanese Alliance

Of these powers, Britain and Japan emerged as the two strongest and most influential, and between 1902 and 1922 their formal alliance provided a basic framework of the international system in the area. Britain was essentially a status-quo power, interested in preserving its superior position in Chinese commerce, safeguarding its imperial rule in Burma and India, protecting the security and interests of Australia and New Zealand, and consolidating key naval bases such as Singapore and Hong Kong. These imperial assets had been obtained in the preceding centuries, and Britain had no far-reaching ambitions to extend its power and influence in Asia and the Pacific. But British officials were becoming less and less certain of their ability to preserve their position of supremacy in the face of competition from the other imperialist powers. The Foreign Office began to interest itself in a diplomatic framework in which British rights and interests would be safeguarded through a series of understandings with other countries. Most of all Britain counted on the Japanese alliance as a provider of stability in East Asia. By coordinating their imperialistic policies and pooling their naval resources in joint defense of these policies, Britain and Japan, it was hoped, would help one another as well as the cause of order and peace in China, India, and other regions of the East. A crucial assumption here was that the two powers would respect each other's prerogatives and spheres of influence. This would include, on Britain's part, its Imperial possessions and Dominions in South Asia and the Pacific, and its commercial interests in China, especially along the Yangtze. Japan in turn would be assured of its rights in Korea and Manchuria.

The Japanese were willing, even eager, to reciprocate British overtures to act as co-stabilizers of Asia and the Pacific. Such a scheme would not only guarantee British support of Japanese claims to a special position in Korea and, after the Russo-Japanese War (1904–5), Manchuria; it would also enhance national prestige and provide concrete evidence of Japan's status as an Asian-Pacific power.

Japan's imperialist thrust was aimed in the direction of the Pacific Ocean as well as the Asian continent. It is wrong to view Japanese imperialism purely as a continentalist phenomenon. There continued to exist a strong expansionist drive—by means of trade and emigration rather than of territorial annexation—toward the South Seas. For this reason, a British alliance meant that Japan would refrain from altering the status quo in the Southwestern Pacific, and that its Pacific expansion would be kept generally peaceful. When it was not, as happened during the First World War, there would be full consultation between the two governments as to a change in the imperial boundaries. In 1916 Tokyo and London secretly agreed that they would divide the German colonial possessions in the ocean between them, those lying north of the equator going to Japan, and those south going to Britain. Given wartime Japanese expansion in the Pacific, it is not at all surprising that Australia was among the staunchest supporters of the Anglo-Japanese alliance; in its view the alliance was vitally needed to keep Japan in check.

On the continent of Asia, the two countries had little cause for friction so long as Japanese continentalism was confined to southern Manchuria. This was the case until the outbreak of World War I. Britain loyally supported Japan against Russia and helped it during the Russo-Japanese War by all means short of war. After 1914, however, British power and prestige declined because of the war in Europe, and there was genuine alarm in London that the Japanese would take advantage of the European conflict to penetrate southward in China. The Japanese attack on the German leasehold in Shantung, and the presentation of the Twenty-One Demands (1915) confirmed such fears. Part of the demands, envisaging Japanese control over Chinese political and military affairs, went well beyond the limits of understanding between Britain and Japan. But Britain was helpless to check its ally because the latter's logistical and military support was needed in the war against Germany.

After 1917 the Asia-Pacific region became enveloped by the maelstrom of events resulting from the Russian revolution. Both London and Tokyo saw in the rise of the Bolsheviks a serious threat to their imperialist positions in China. Both favored the formation of an anti-Bolshevik second front in Russia, and they supported the idea of a Siberian expedition. The expedition, undertaken by Japan in the summer of 1918, was designed to entrench Japanese power in eastern Siberia. Since Japan had obtained the cession of southern Sakhalin after the Russo-Japanese War, there was a possibility that the whole northeastern Asian region would fall to Japanese domination. In 1918 the Tokyo government also extended large amounts of loans to the warlord regime in Peking with a view to coordinating the two countries' policies toward Bolshevik Russia. With Russian influence temporarily declining in Manchuria and Mongolia, it appeared that Japan would eventually establish hegemony over the whole of East Asia.

Japan's wartime expansion called forth a fierce response in China, whose nationalism now became focused on Japan to a greater extent than ever before. The May Fourth incident of 1919, triggering a nationwide movement of protest against Japan and the boycotting of Japanese goods and services, demonstrated that imperialistic diplomacy could no longer take China for granted. The latter's nationalism was also abetted by its participation in the World War. In 1917 it became a cobelligerent on the side of the allies. It did very little besides sending coolies to Europe to build railroads and work in factories, but far more significant was the fact that China declared war on Germany and Austria and proceeded to abrogate their extraterritorial rights. No other power protested, and thus the Chinese gained their first clearcut diplomatic victory in more than seventy years.

The Effect of the Washington Conference upon Postwar Relations

As one of the victorious allies, China was entitled to participation at the peace conference, and its delegates made the most of the opportunity. For the first time in history China participated as an equal in an international conference and demanded restoration of full sovereign status. In this effort the country had the support of the United States which was seeking to alter the system of international relations in East Asia by challenging the existing alliances and ententes. American policy aimed at replacing them, in particular the Anglo-Japanese alliance, with a new "concert of power" in which no single nation established hegemony and which encouraged the evolution of China as an independent state. The Chinese naturally welcomed American support, and the two acted closely during 1918–21 in order to undermine the diplomacy of imperialism on the continent of Asia.

The Soviet Union challenged the system in a different manner. Russia ceased to be a factor for a while after 1917, and the new Bolshevik leaders tried, as if to compensate for the fact, to influence the course of events in China through assiduous propaganda work. Their basic strategy was to call for an end not only to imperialist power politics but to the treaty system itself. The Moscow government expressed willingness to give up the old treaties and enter into new relations with China on the basis of equality. Such overtures were calculated to appeal to Chinese nationalism and turn it solidly against the imperialist powers, among which the Soviet leaders counted the United States as well as Japan and Britain. In the meantime, Comintern agents entered China, as they did India and other countries, in the hope of promoting anti-colonial, anti-feudal movements. Chinese opinion became decidedly more radicalized.

The war also brought about important changes in the power relationships of the Pacific Ocean. The European war had encouraged Japanese territorial and economic expansion in the South Seas, virtually eliminating Germany as a Pacific power, but it had also resulted in an increase in American naval strength. The Panama Canal had become operative in 1914, and the United States was now able to move its ships from one ocean to the other with relative ease and speed. It could thus station more ships in the western Pacific, and the Asiatic Fleet was consequently augmented. In the meantime, with Japan espousing the cause of racial equality, implying a right to migrate to racially white territories, the European colonial powers were impelled to seek a new definition of regional stability in the Pacific Ocean.

It was against this background that an international conference was convened in Washington in 1921 to redefine the politics of the Asia-Pacific region. The Washington Conference (1921–22) was an attempt on the part of the major countries involved in the area, except the Soviet Union, to come together and work out a structure of international relations to transform the diplomacy of imperialism. The resulting "Washington Conference system" was a compromise between the traditionalist concept, based on the Anglo-Japanese alliance, and the Sino-American insistence on a new order, looking to the abolition of spheres of influence and ultimate restoration of sovereignty to China. In the Pacific the polarity was between Japanese expansion and American expansion, either case involving an armament race. It was primarily because of the Pacific question that the Asian issue was settled by the abrogation of the Anglo-Japanese alliance. This was a price the Japanese government decided to pay in order to avoid a costly naval armament race with the United States. Japan sought an armament moratorium and the freezing of the oceanic status quo, which would enable the nation to retain its supremacy in the western Pacific without incurring American retaliation. Thus in the Pacific the Japanese were delimiting their own expansionism. Their position on the Asian continent would be weaker, too, now that they gave up the British alliance in accordance with America's wishes. Since the alliance had divided China up into spheres of influence, its termination necessitated a new formula for defining foreign rights in that country. Thus were produced the Nine Power Treaty and sundry other agreements, all asserting the principles of the Open Door and integrity of China, and specifying steps the signatory powers would take to restore rights to China in several stages. What these agreements amounted to was a new framework of Chinese-foreign relations which would take the place of the bilateral and particularistic arrangements of the diplomacy of imperialism and internationalize all efforts at protecting foreign rights and interests in China. Here again Japan was willing to retrench its imperialistic activities and abide by the new arrangements.

Japan's willingness to accept the Washington formula needs explanation, for the decision signified a change in the orientation of Japanese policy. There are two factors which accounted for the change. One was a substitution of economic for militaristic expansionism. Thus while territorial expansion would now be limited, its place would be taken by a policy of economic expansion in all directions. The feeling was that the country had bitten more than it could chew, and that territorial imperialism had proved to be costly and apt to arouse bitter enmities and armament rivalries abroad. It would be far better to concentrate on peaceful penetration of the world's markets for goods and capital. The ever-increasing surplus population, the awareness of which never abated after the war, could be settled overseas through emigration rather than outright colonization. Such was the thinking that provided the psychological and intellectual underpinning for Japan's acceptance of the Washington system. In 1922 Prime Minister Takahashi Korekiyo said,

> The war taught us that it is impossible to undertake national expansion through the use of force.

However, he went on, competition among nations still existed.

> While armed conflict has cooled off, economic competition is becoming more and more intense.

Under the circumstances, it was incumbent upon the Japanese to expand trade and build the foundation of their country's well-being.[4]

Another factor was the view that while the Anglo-Japanese alliance was

[4] *Asahi shinbun*, Jan. 1, 1922.

abrogated, big-power cooperation would not disappear from the scene. Japan would no longer be able to count on solid British support of its policy in China, but it would not be totally isolated inasmuch as the United States would now interest itself in maintaining a stable international order in East Asia. Thus in a sense tripartite understanding would replace bilateral imperialist collaboration. But there would still be some sort of cooperation among the major powers, in particular Japan, the United States, and Britain. It was hoped that such cooperation would serve to contribute to stabilizing conditions in Asia and safeguarding their respective interests. This was still power politics, but the Wilsonian rhetoric of the New Diplomacy and the abrogation of the Anglo-Japanese alliance gave the new framework of international relations an ideological, idealistic connotation. To the Japanese, certainly, "international cooperation" was as much an idea as a structure of politics. It seemed to be an attractive substitute both for the particularism of continental expansion and for the diplomacy of imperialism exemplified by the British alliance.

In actuality the new system based on the Washington Conference formula proved to be even less stable than the old regime of imperialist politics. To be sure the three major powers successfully redefined their power positions and spheres of predominance, and there was little occasion for Japan, the United States, and Britain to infringe seriously on each other's special rights and interests in the area. But systemic momentum was not enough to consolidate a new stable order in Asia. From the very beginning the Washington powers were challenged by China's revolutionary nationalism and by the Soviet Union's anti-imperialist propaganda. The challenge struck at the ideological foundation of the Washington Conference system.

From the nationalistic Chinese point of view, the world after the war was still dominated by the big powers. The Peking government, supported by some warlords, while being disappointed by the meager results of the conference, accepted the Washington formula which would at least open a way toward modification of the existing treaties. But the nationalists in China refused to accept the new formula and demanded more sweeping changes in Chinese foreign relations. Some of them followed the example of the Communist Party, organized in 1920, and declared that the Washington Conference had only ushered in a period of cooperative economic exploitation of China to replace competitive rivalry among the imperialists.[5]

Such a climate of opinion provided an ideal setting for Soviet influence. Russia reentered East Asian politics as a power standing outside the Washington Conference system, and, perhaps more importantly in terms of self-perception, as a country whose survival and strength would be vital to the welfare of the Chinese and other victims of imperialist oppression. Con-

[5] See Fujii Shōzō, *Sonbun no kenkyū* (Tokyo, Keisō shobō, 1966).

demning the Washington Conference, in which the Soviet government had vainly sought to be represented, as an imperialistic undertaking, Soviet policy in the 1920s challenged the Washington powers in terms both of structure and of power. First of all, in order to remove a threat to the existence of the Soviet regime, Russia recognized Mongolian independence and sought to perpetuate its rights in northern Manchuria. Second, Moscow approached Peking with a view to undermining the position of the United States, Britain, and Japan. This was done through bilateral negotiations with China for treaty revision, to put an end to the old treaty system. Finally, through the Comintern the Soviet leaders promoted radical movements which were directed not so much against the warlord regime in Peking as against foreign factories and concessions. By the middle of the decade there were revolutionary cells in these establishments, and strikes and sabotages occurred frequently. The May 30 incident, resulting from a clash between Chinese students and the Shanghai concession police in 1925, revealed the strength of Chinese nationalism, and gave impetus to the combined forces of the Nationalists (Kuomintang) and the Communists to undertake a "northern expedition" against the warlords. In this process the Kuomintang-Communist alliance disintegrated, but it did not affect revolutionary nationalism directed against the Washington powers. If anything, factions in China vied with one another to speak more loudly for sovereignty and independence. Even the warlords became infected and began mouthing anti-imperialistic slogans.

There were thus two radically different definitions of the postwar international order in East Asia. They existed side by side, and neither was successful in imposing its system upon the other. The Chinese pattern, initially supported by the Soviet Union, put the Washington powers on the defensive, but China could not really impose its will because of the persistence of domestic chaos and civil strife. Moreover, the Sino-Soviet axis turned out to be rather shaky in the second half of the 1920s because of various important causes: the Stalin-Trotsky struggle for power, making it impossible to have a consistent policy toward the Chinese Nationalist-Communist united front; the rise of Chiang Kai-shek and his rift with the Communists; continued Russian interest in preserving a position of influence in Mongolia and Manchuria.

Neither were the Washington powers prepared to cooperate in restoring stability and order to China. Britain and Japan, which remained the two strongest powers, economically and militarily, in East Asia, were never able or willing to coordinate action to safeguard their respective interests. Their economic-expansionist oriented policy made it difficult to conceive of a common stand to maintain the treaty rights. Each went its own way in the hope that by being patient it would encourage the Chinese to see the wisdom of close understanding with it. Britain, in particular, was anxious to avoid the use of force, except in cases where it was absolutely necessary to protect British lives, and to deflect Chinese nationalism away from Bolshevism toward a more moderate brand with which the British could live. As the governor of Hong Kong wrote in 1926,

> the time has gone by for warlike action to be undertaken by Great Britain alone, except at the risk of jeopardizing our future economic relations with China.[6]

Japan would have profited most from cooperation with Great Britain. Such cooperation would have provided one specific example of the workability of the postwar international system. The Japanese were fond of referring to the principle of international cooperation, but in East Asia there was little substance to the slogan. Not only were the British reluctant to coordinate action with their former allies, the Japanese, but the latter tended to the view that the nation's special position in China could best be preserved through some bilateral arrangements with China rather than through cooperation with Britain or the United States. It was only when this policy failed, and Japan undertook military expeditions to Shantung (1928), that it showed a serious interest in obtaining the understanding of the Washington powers. But they were certainly not interested in helping Japan entrench its influence in parts of China. Japan, it seemed, was intent on keeping China weak, a condition that was not conducive to expanding trade in that country.

At the same time, it should be noted that neither Britain nor the United States considered giving help to China against Japan, either in cooperation or unilaterally. In 1928, when the Japanese army occupied Tsinan, the capital of Shantung, and a group of Kwantung Army officers brought about the assassination of Chang Tso-lin, the Manchurian overlord, in order to bring about chaos in Manchuria and northern China, Britain and the United States assumed a neutral attitude, turning deaf ears to pleas from various groups in China to condemn Japanese action. If they did not like what Japan was doing, neither were they ready to challenge it in the name of the Washington Conference system, or of Chinese integrity, or of their respective national interests. There was a curious lack of determination to work towards building up a durable system of international relations in East Asia. The result was instability in the Asian international system to an extent never seen before. Cooperation became an empty word in East Asia.

In the Pacific Ocean, in contrast, there continued a pattern of big-power understanding. The Washington Conference had defined a new status quo, and on the whole it successfully balanced the potential rivals one against another. Japan, Britain, and the United States maintained their

---

[6] W. Roger Louis, *British Strategy in the Far East* (Oxford: Oxford University Press, 1971), p. 129.

naval forces within the limits set by the Washington disarmament treaty, but in the absence of a two-party alliance no one power was strong enough to menace the position of another. The Japanese and the American navies, it is true, continued to make war plans against each other, but there was no sense of imminent crisis. The British decision to strengthen the fortification of Singapore upset the Japanese, but this was within the Washington formula, and did not lead to any retaliation. The one potential agent of change in the Pacific status quo would have been a flood of Japanese emigrants. The government in Tokyo encouraged the people to undertake massive emigration to the Philippines, Malaya, and elsewhere, now that militaristic conquest had been ruled out. In 1925, for instance, there were only 34,660 Japanese in the Southwestern Pacific, compared with 232,140 in China and 346,208 in Hawaii and the Americas. In view of the anti-Japanese sentiment in China and Japanese exclusion in the United States, it seemed that the South Seas would be a good place for migration and settlement. If as many Japanese had decided to find their home in this area as had settled on the Chinese continent or the Western Hemisphere, the whole economic and political complexion of the Pacific Ocean would have been affected. No large-scale emigration in this direction took place, however, before the world economic crisis caused a redirection of Japanese expansion.

*The Manchurian Crisis
and the Sino-Japanese War*

By 1929, then, it was all too obvious that the much heralded coming of a new epoch of international cooperation had not materialized on the continent of Asia. The Washington Conference had frozen the Pacific but not China. It had succeeded neither in harmonizing relations among the powers nor in defining a stable relationship between them on one hand and Chinese nationalism on the other. With the Chinese vigorously pushing for a new order, and with the Washington powers unwilling and unable to respond to the challenge in unison, the only alternatives left were either for China to succeed in imposing its nationalistic diplomacy, or for one of the other powers to take the initiative once again to build up its own system of Asian politics.

That Japan took this course was related directly to the world economic crisis. Before 1929 the militaristic expansionists of Japan had been kept in check by the prevailing ideology of peaceful expansionism, and by the idea that Japan, as one of the major powers in the postwar world, must not do anything to disrupt it. There seemed to be a chance that Chinese nationalism and Japanese interests would be compatible, that a new order of Sino-Japanese coexistence and coprosperity might yet emerge. But the severe economic crisis after 1929 undermined such rationale for defending the spirit of the

Washington system. Japan's social and economic ills came to be blamed on the government's foreign policy that had allegedly failed to protect the national interests in Asia. It is illuminating that voices within Japan calling for vigorous policy attacked not only Chinese nationalism but also the Washington Conference formula. It seemed that the latter had encouraged the former, and that by subscribing to the Washington system the Japanese government had done nothing to stop China from violating Japan's rights and interests. The result was an erosion of Japanese influence in Asia and the dissipation of the special position which had been built up on the continent. The policy was a failure, and an alternative framework of international relations must be sought.

In this way, "international cooperation," which had not really existed, became an object of fierce attack in Japan, a symbol of a policy that had failed. This explains the stress on the need and the virtue of unilateralism that provided the justification for the revival of militaristic expansionism in the 1930s. Japan would cease to respect the status quo in Asia, in which they no longer felt secure and assured of continued protection of their rights. They would also challenge the ideological foundation of the status quo, exemplified by "international cooperation." Japan's speedy success in imposing a new order by force indicates the absence of an effective structure of international relations to take care of such a challenge. That is to say, the Japanese were right in judging that there would be no concerted attempt within the prevailing system to restrain its militaristic action. Because the system was weak and unstable, Japan sought to establish a new order; for the same reason, there was only feeble resistance to the Japanese initiative. Thus beginning with the Mukden incident of September 18, 1931, a premeditated attack on the Chinese in the city, the Japanese army successfully and speedily proceeded to conquer the whole of Manchuria. Within five months a puppet state of Manchukuo came into existence, whose military, diplomatic, and economic affairs were placed under close Japanese supervision.

Although the initial Japanese attack was on Chinese sovereignty, and although the Japanese government justified the use of force as an act of self-defense against Chinese violations of treaty rights, the Manchurian crisis did not develop into a war between these two countries. The Chinese leadership was unprepared to struggle with Japan singlehanded, and turned to the League and the other powers for help. The internationalization of the conflict was thus inevitable. Ironically, the very tendency of the time to internationalize such disputes was bound to ensure the success of unilateral action by a power determined to impose its will. To be sure the League of Nations provided a forum for discussing the Manchurian crisis. There was the feeling that the League was on trial, that it must demonstrate its strength to withstand the latest challenge to its principles. However, there was no thought of administering sanctions. The primary function of the organization was conceived to lie in its moral force as a representative of world public opinion. It would serve as a meeting place where antagonists would come together to try to solve their disputes peacefully. Such steps as the invocation of the Kellogg-Briand Pact and the sending of a commission of inquiry to East Asia were the types of action the League of Nations was ideally fitted to take.

Unfortunately, these acts were powerless to affect the course of Japan's militaristic expansion. But there was no other kind of international action that was ready at hand to be applicable to the situation. The three powers which, in some combination, might have restrained Japan failed to evolve a joint policy. The United States was the only country interested in the principle of collective security. Secretary of State Henry L. Stimson firmly believed that international pressure rather than independent action should be used to prod China and Japan to settle the dispute. Hence his extraordinary interest in collaboration with the League. When the latter failed to stop Japan, Stimson wanted to associate the United States with Britain so that the two could actively cooperate in East Asia.

Britain, however, was reluctant to countenance such cooperation. It would go as far as it could to associate itself with the League. In fact, from the British point of view, the international organization was the only viable mechanism through which to settle the Sino-Japanese dispute. There would be cooperation with the United States through the League, but outside of it, the British would be less prepared to undertake joint action. To British statesmen of the early 1930s such a proposal was hard to entertain, given their view that alliances and balance-of-power politics were antithetical to the League and to world peace. There was no assurance that Anglo-American cooperation, which would have to take place outside the League of Nations because the United States was not a member, would not end up undermining the League itself. Such drastic steps could be considered only when the nation contemplated war. But no British policy maker envisioned war with Japan on account of the Manchurian crisis. This was so because from the British point of view Japanese action in Manchuria could be seen as contributing to the stabilization of conditions in China.

Here was an interesting paradox. While the Japanese were penetrating Manchuria to define a new order in East Asia, the British came to see it as possibly an attempt to consolidate the Washington Conference system by creating a regime of stability. The Washington formula had envisioned cooperation among the powers which had not in fact taken place, but the new crisis could induce them to undertake such cooperation. Certainly this seemed a far better alternative to entertaining the possibility of an entirely different system on the basis of Anglo-American cooperation to help China against Japan. This would totally destroy the Washington system and substitute for it something which had never been tried before. Thus as long as

Japan refrained from openly attacking British treaty rights, London would try to conciliate, not antagonize, Japan. And the latter was ready to oblige, as could be seen during the early months of 1932, when Japanese forces in Shanghai agreed to a ceasefire under British pressure.

The Soviet Union would have been another power that might have stepped in to stop Japan; but for what purpose? The Sino-Soviet clash over the Chinese Eastern Railway in 1929 had resulted in a break between Nanking and Moscow, and there was no urgent reason why Russia should now come to the rescue of China. The Soviet leadership, moreover, was reluctant to get involved with Japan while the five-year plan, commenced in 1928, was being carried out. Such determination was reinforced by the fear that the United States and Britain were trying to turn Japan northward so as to weaken the Soviet Union. Premature conflict with Japan in such circumstances would only end up entrenching Western imperialism on the Asian continent. Consequently, Russian policy was passive, and went even so far as to offer the sale of the Russian rights in the Chinese Eastern Railway to Japan. The Soviet Union would remain passive until it could be sure of diplomatic cooperation with a group of powers against Japan.

Affairs in the East began to develop with dramatic speed after the outbreak of the Sino-Japanese War in 1937. After an initial period of hesitation, the Japanese army launched a full-scale attack on China proper, aimed at subjugation or elimination of the Chiang Kai-shek regime. It was also around this time that Japanese strategists began to conceive of a new order, not simply in China and Manchuria but also in the whole of Asia, including Southeast Asia and the Southwestern Pacific. The policy of establishing the new order under Japanese control was coupled with the ideology of pan-Asianism, asserting that Asians should set up their own rules of international politics and be guided by their own values and principles. Here was a challenge, though at first more potential than actual, to the West's power and influence in greater Asia.

The strategy of "southern advance," the term used to designate a policy of pursuing a new order in the Asia-Pacific region, was not formally adopted by Japan until 1940. But steps were taken already in 1938 and 1939 which steadily extended Japanese power southward. This was in part due to the military stalemate in China, where the Japanese army failed to win decisive victory. The stalemate was often blamed on British and French assistance to Chiang Kai-shek through Burma and Indochina, and the Japanese sought to cut off these routes to Chungking, the seat of the exiled Kuomintang government. This necessitated putting pressure on the colonial authorities so as to close off the channels of communication to southwestern China. But quite apart from this mode of southern expansion, there were more aggressive moves to extend the limits of Japanese power to the South Seas. As noted earlier, there had always been fascination with the idea of Pacific empire, and the "Fundamentals of National Policy" (1936), a government-approved memorandum setting forth strategic priorities, had spoken of southern as well as northern advances as future possibilities. The deteriorating conditions of international relations after 1938 impressed Japan's southern expansionists as a favorable opportunity to redefine the status quo in the Southwestern Pacific. The strategy gained steady acceptance among Japan's policymakers because of the abundance of raw materials in this region. There was a growing notion that the world was never again likely to revert to a system of free trade. Instead, it seemed that regional economic units would be forged, each trying to be as autonomous and self-sufficient as possible. Japan must also build such a bloc. This kind of reasoning lent support to naval expansionists, and the stage was being prepared for an assault on the Southwestern Pacific.

The international environment grew more and more favorable for undertaking a southern advance, and it was no accident that the initial moves in that direction coincided with Germany's spring offensive in 1940. The powers that had sustained a regional international system in the Pacific for centuries—Britain, France, the Netherlands—were forced to struggle for their very survival, and by the middle of 1940 only Britain remained free. None of these powers could afford to strengthen their defenses of the colonial territories. Great Britain, in particular, had to concentrate on the empire west of India as the immediate area of concern. And yet the French, Dutch, and British empires in the Pacific and Asia survived the German offensive in Europe, and they never came under Nazi domination. From the Japanese point of view, therefore, here was an opportunity not to be missed to extend their power and interests while the European colonies were in a state of crisis but before Germany would subjugate them.

The German-Japanese alliance of September 1940 was a product of such thinking, as was the Japanese-Soviet neutrality treaty of April 1941. The Axis alliance did not mean that Japan would automatically undertake to attack the European colonies in Asia, but was nevertheless tantamount to giving Japan a free hand—as far as Germany was concerned—if and when it should decide to strike south. In the meantime, while the Japanese prepared for a southern advance, they assumed that the nation's relationship with Russia would remain more or less stable. This was because of the view that Germany and the Soviet Union would remain in peace indefinitely, both intent on dividing the Eurasian continent into their spheres of influence. Japan, it seemed, should avail itself of the world situation to stake out its claims in the South Seas, and this could best be done by avoiding conflict with Russia. Hence the Japanese-Soviet neutrality treaty, in which the two governments pledged themselves to maintain neutrality in the event of a signatory's involvement in a war with a third party.

By 1941, then, it seemed that the map of Southeast Asia and the

Southwestern Pacific was about to be redrawn. The Japanese empire appeared poised for an attack southward to determine the future shape of international politics in this region. Whether and when the attack would take place, and if it would be successful depended on the policies and strategies of the other major powers, in particular Great Britain, long the dominant power in the Asia-Pacific area.

The British had eschewed outright resistance to Japan in China, but they were determined never to give up their interests and possessions in Southeast Asia and the Southwestern Pacific. The area was a vital link in the defense of the British empire. Not only natural resources but manpower of the Commonwealth countries were needed as essential parts of the global strategy. After 1940 troops from Australia were shipped in increasing numbers to the Middle East and the Mediterranean, and the British navy needed the oil and other resources of the Dutch East Indies as well as of Malaya. It was vital to deny them to Germany and to its ally, Japan. It was equally clear to British officials that they alone could not defend Southeast Asia. If Britain's power were to be preserved east of India, then the country must turn to friends and potential allies for cooperation and help. This could only mean assistance from the United States. Without America's help, it seemed that British status and interests in the East were doomed to be overrun by Japanese aggression. But the United States and Britain had never closely cooperated in the area, or for that matter anywhere else in Asia. Whether they could forge an alliance to preserve the status quo hinged on the attitudes and interests of the United States.

In this way, by 1941 the future of the Asia-Pacific region appeared dependent on two key factors: the timing and extent of Japan's southern advance, and the timing and extent of America's involvement in the Southwestern Pacific.

THE UNITED STATES
AS AN ASIAN-PACIFIC POWER

The preceding survey of the Asian international system indicates that prior to 1941 Japan and Great Britain were the two predominant members of the system. It was no accident that the two had for many years "cooperated" in order to stabilize international relations, but once that Japan appeared bent on far-reaching expansionism, confrontation between the two to determine the shape of the region became inevitable.

What role did the United States play in the development of the regional international system in Asia and the Pacific? This was the crucial question of 1941, as it is today. A glance at the history of American involvement in this region is essential for the understanding of the more recent years.

*Introduction
to the Spanish-American War*

Before the 1890s America's role in the politics of Asia and the Pacific was limited. Hawaii was the one area of special American concern; there was a fairly clear policy even in the 1850s and more so by the 1870s, of asserting the nation's superior economic rights and political influence over the islands, and of preventing European powers from annexing them. As Secretary of State James G. Blaine declared in 1881, the Hawaiian islands were "part of the American system of states." If they were not turned into outright colonies or territorial possessions of the United States, at least they would be closely integrated with it economically and politically. Beyond Hawaii, the United States became involved in Samoa in the south central Pacific in the 1880s, where the country established a sort of tripartite regime along with Germany and Britain. Such moves, however, were little related to international politics in the rest of the Pacific or Asia. They were more indicative of unilateral American initiatives in response to specific circumstances in the eastern half of the Pacific Ocean.

It should be noted, however, that there was always the concept of America as a Pacific nation. The Pacific Ocean was an arena of activity for traders, sailors, and whalers from the very beginning of the Republic. Even while the United States was confined to the Eastern states, explorers were assiduously making surveys along potential routes to the ocean. The Louisiana purchase facilitated the task, and as the national limits were extended westward, so was the national imagination. American communities came into existence in Oregon and California, and the West coast came to be seen as part of the American economic system, if not constitutionally part of the nation. The Mexican War, the annexation of New Mexico and California which the war brought about, and the settlement of the Northwest boundary dispute with Canada, all in a span of a few years in mid-century, made America a Pacific nation in name as well as in fact. Declared William H. Seward in 1860,

> It is a political law that empire has, for the last three thousand years . . . made its way constantly westward, and that it must continue to move on westward until the tides of the renewed and of the decaying civilizations of the world meet on the shores of the Pacific ocean.[7]

He was expressing a widespread belief that the destiny of the nation was bound up with the ocean, that the United States must continue to expand

[7] William H. Seward, *Works*, ed. George E. Baker (New York, 1889), IV, 319–20.

westward to "grasp the great commerce of the east." There is little doubt that this type of thinking, the conception of national development as oriented in the direction of the Pacific, provided intellectual and psychological justification for various activities in the wide ocean, ranging from sugar plantations in Hawaii to the opening of Japan.

That the United States took the lead in initiating commercial and diplomatic contact with the seclusionist regime of Tokugawa Japan, but merely followed Britain in China, is illuminating. Instead of waiting for the British initiative, as was the case in China in the 1840s, the United States was willing, in the 1850s, to take unilateral steps to establish contact with Japan. The island empire was also a Pacific country, and it seemed incumbent on America to expand its influence to the other side of the ocean. If Japan had been tropical islands without strong governmental organization, or a country rent by domestic strife, the United States might have become seriously involved in its internal affairs, politically and economically. That would have necessitated a larger military force than the nation possessed after the Civil War, and a more active diplomacy than the State Department, with its meager personnel, was willing to undertake. As it was, Japanese leaders were able to put their house in order and reorganize state institutions so as to preserve national autonomy and prevent foreign encroachment. Thus the United States, having opened Japan, did not have to follow up its initiative by a systematic foreign policy toward the western Pacific and East Asia. It remained one of the treaty powers in Japan, but it did not engage in power politics or imperialistic rivalries in the environs of Japan.

Although China was far more disunited and decentralized than Japan, the United States played little part in the domestic affairs of the Ch'ing empire. It followed the lead of Britain in obtaining trade concessions and residential privileges in China, but it did not concern itself with political or military affairs. American policy toward China in the nineteenth century can best be described as that of economic expansion. It may even be misleading to call this a policy, since the State Department took little initiative in formulating a specific approach toward increasing trade with China. The pursuit of profit was left largely in the hands of merchants who went about their business on their own, not as agents of American power. They were, of course, "extraterritorial" foreigners, enjoying special rights beyond the reach of Chinese jurisdiction. But their status did not depend on the presence of a large United States navy. As noted earlier, it was the reality and appearance of British power and of Chinese sovereignty that combined to tolerate activities by private merchants.

Only toward the end of the century did the United States bestir itself to formulate a policy in the East Asian-Western Pacific region, and become aware of the need to define the nature of its power and vision in the area. The transformation came about suddenly. Before 1895 it could hardly be said that the United States had an Asian policy. By 1900 officials were boasting of America's Asian empire and a unique approach to China. The Asia-Pacific region to be sure never became as important to American policy as the Caribbean, but at least for a while after the Spanish-American War there grew consciousness of the United States as an Asian-Pacific power.

This change must be explained at least in terms of three factors: domestic opinion, Asian international affairs, and specific occurrences in the Pacific. For some time before the 1890s American opinion had been increasingly concerned with questions of national security and power. Terms like "sovereignty" and "power" had begun to be used by men who sensed that the country was ready to assert its role in world politics and should have the means to do so. Such views were abetted by a public opinion that was becoming more and more interested in foreign affairs and receptive to nationalistic symbols. Nationalism after the Civil War had been directed internally; it signified the American people's adherence to the idea of one and indivisible nationhood, as against the idea that the nation derived its unity from a contract among its constituent elements. The nation was a natural, organic entity, the focal point of one's identity and loyalty. Gradually, however, external aspects of nationalism—the country's honor, prestige, and rights—came to be stressed, and America's greatness began to be seen not only in terms of domestic indexes of wealth and power but in relation to other countries. It is interesting that the word "power," which for long connoted domestic political rights and influence, came to be used in connection with foreign affairs. It signified the nation's concern with its role in foreign affairs and its determination to assert its voice in distant lands.

Developments in Asia after the Sino-Japanese War (1894–95) served to keep America's "foreign policy public" enlarged and interested in Asian affairs. A real turning point came toward the end of 1897, when Germany seized Kiaochow Bay, to be followed by similarly imperialistic moves by Russia, France, Britain, and Japan. Power politics in China made front-page headlines almost continuously from this time on, sometimes even eclipsing news on the impending Cuban crisis. Never before was such curiosity aroused concerning events outside the Western Hemisphere, and never before was there such an articulate foreign policy public defining its position toward China. The winter of 1897–98 saw the first formation of a public opinion relative to China, and it was instrumental in prodding the government to establish a specific and distinctive policy. Proclaimed the *New York Times*:

> Poor old China! Does she know what is happening? Does she care? Somebody really ought to ask her—not that it makes any difference, but just to gratify natural curiosity.[8]

[8] *New York Times*, Dec. 22, 1897.

But American concern with events in China was more than natural curiosity. There was widespread sentiment that the United States should not simply sit back and watch the unfolding drama in Asia. Rather, it was repeated in newspapers and magazines across the nation, the government in Washington should step in to protect American interests and be part of the drama.

New American Involvement in the East

How to define American interests, and what part to play in the drama, remained unresolved questions prior to April 1898, when the Spanish-American War broke out, influencing the whole subsequent course of American involvement in Asia. Origins of the war with Spain had nothing to do with Asia or the Pacific, but because of the aforementioned factors it ended up transforming the United States into an Asian-Pacific power.

Such an outcome was in part a product of military developments. Navy Department officers had prepared contingency plans in case of war with Spain over Cuba, and they had advocated the strategy of having the Asiatic squadron attack the Philippines to deny their use to the Spanish fleet during the war, in addition to launching an assault on Cuba and Puerto Rico.

Admiral George Dewey faithfully carried out this strategy. But the rousing public reception of the successful attack on Manila Bay revealed that the American people were ready to assert power thousands of miles away. It is no more likely that they had given careful thought to all the implications of such action, than that the naval authorities were prepared to cope with the logistical and diplomatic consequences of their war plan. But the public had developed a receptive mood, which now combined with the situation in Asia through the mediation of the Cuban crisis, ushering in the age of power politics for the United States.

While the initial attack on Manila was a consequence of military planning, the decision to retain the Philippines was a product of big-power consciousness. "There was nothing left for us to do but to take them all," declared President William McKinley in defense of the acquisition of the Philippines from Spain. The alternative of doing nothing was ruled out as ill-becoming a great power into which America was transforming itself. And this great-power status called for an active role to play in Asia and the Pacific. That is why many coupled the discussion of the Philippine question with that of China. Those who supported the new imperialism of the United States invariably argued that the possession of the islands would enhance America's power and prestige, and thus enable it to weigh more heavily in Asian affairs. America's commercial interests would be better protected, and the other powers would listen more deferentially to the United States. In order to have a positive policy in China, therefore, the nation must possess territory in the Pacific. And the United States must develop a foreign policy in Asia in order to count as a power. Similar reasoning rationalized the annexation of Hawaii as well as of Guam. As early as February 1898 the *American Review of Reviews* wrote:

> Our acquisition of Hawaii would be directly useful in helping to keep open Chinese Ports.[9]

Territorial imperialism, then, was considered an aspect of great-power status. It was never an end in itself, but an aspect of the new foreign policy of the United States emerging as a world power. Subsequent events were to show that once the consciousness of world power was implanted, possession of overseas territories ceased to matter that much; the United States would continue to be concerned with world affairs even while it would relinquish its colonial possessions.

It is evident, at any event, that the United States emerged as an Asian-Pacific power after the Spanish-American War. It joined the European countries and Japan as one of a handful of nations whose policies and armed forces would determine not only their mutual relations but also the destiny of China and other colonial and semi-colonial areas. In what way the United States would exercise its prestige and power became clear soon after the war. In the Pacific Ocean, the newly acquired or annexed territories would be retained and protected. This, of course, would necessitate the use of force and a demonstration of America's power to enforce its will. But these measures were part and parcel of the emergence of the United States as a Pacific power. It may be pointed out that the national debate of 1899–1900 regarding the retention of the Philippines boiled down to the question whether the United States should be a power in the Southwestern Pacific. Once the answer was given in the affirmative, then the establishment of a colonial regime sustained by force could be justified in any number of ways—by duty, honor, or civilization. What mattered was not so much rhetoric as power; it was *American* power that was being extended to the region, and to the imperialists it was clear that to deny this fact was tantamount to relinquishing a self-respecting role in the western Pacific.

The "Open Door" Policy

On the continent of Asia, however, the new self-consciousness of the United States as an Asian power did not result in military entrenchment, except during the Boxer uprising. Instead, American policy toward China came to be known as that of an Open Door. The meaning and implications of this

[9] *American Review of Reviews*, Feb. 1898, p. 146.

policy need examination, since it defined basic American approaches to East Asia, as separate from the western Pacific, throughout the first four decades of the twentieth century.

The term "Open Door policy" summed up a specific set of ideas which the United States government applied to East Asian international relations after the Spanish-American War. First, there was the assumption that the nation would play a role as an Asian power, instead of merely persisting in the traditional stress on private commercial enterprises. Second, the United States would not use military force in playing this role. Unlike the Philippine Islands, China would not be a theater for American military action. Since the term "Asian power" was thus divorced from the use of force, it had a different connotation from the term "Pacific power." But the United States sought to bridge the gap between the reality and pretensions of power by astutely conceiving of a policy that would turn military disadvantages into a political asset. Thus the third component of the Open Door policy stressed America's opposition to particularistic commercial practices on the part of the imperialist powers in China, and support of the idea of Chinese independence and integrity. In this way, the United States would stake out a special niche in East Asian imperialist politics by identifying itself as a champion of Chinese sovereignty. At a time when Britain, Japan, Russia, and other imperialists were openly seeking and obtaining bases, concessions, and exclusive privileges in China, America would refuse to follow their example but rather resist Chinese dismemberment.

The Open Door policy has been assailed from various angles, two of which stand out. One argument is that it espoused more than it practiced, that it was hypocritical. While the United States asserted its support of Chinese sovereignty, it has been pointed out, its merchants were bent on extending their trade and investment activities in China, whose cumulative effects could only mean further weakening of that country. The Open Door policy's emphasis on equal commercial opportunity for foreigners really was a formula for joint exploitation of the China market. Far from assisting China in any way, it provided a framework in which American capital could compete on favorable terms with European and Japanese capital. It is difficult to rebut such criticism on absolutist grounds; from the Chinese point of view, the Open Door was merely another mode of imperialist penetration. It was naturally a selfish policy, designed to promote American interests, and its supporters did not hide the fact. In terms of America's approaches to East Asia at that particular juncture, however, the Open Door assumes significance as an indication of economic as against militaristic modes of American expansionism. In contrast to the Philippines, American power would be primarily a function of economic enterprises, and the United States would perform its role as an East Asian power as a commercial expansionist. It should be added that to the contemporaries at the turn of the century such an approach seemed compatible with the interests of the Chinese themselves who, it was believed, were as opposed to European imperialism as the Americans and would welcome American economic activities as a more positive force. "Our interests in China," declared the *Memphis Commercial Appeal*, "are identical with the interests of the Chinese themselves." [10] It would be in the best interests of the two countries, said the *Cleveland Leader*, "if a united, progressive, independent, and popular government existed in China." [11] It was taken as axiomatic that the policy of the Open Door was well designed to achieve this aim.

Such rhetoric was expressed in 1900, at a time when the Ch'ing empire was in the throes of confusion and chaos because of the Boxer uprising. It is interesting that this type of idealistic language was used despite the reports of the anti-foreign rampage and administrative crisis in China. Why did the Americans begin talking of Chinese "independence" just at this time, when the country seemed reverting to the darkest days of the Taiping uprising? A key answer is that the Boxer crisis came about after the Spanish-American War, after a decision had been reached as to America's role in Asia and the Pacific. Since the United States was going to be an Asian power, it had to relate itself to events in China, instead of simply sitting back and professing unconcern save when American trade was involved. Commercial expansion remained the major national interest vis-à-vis China, but after 1899 it came to be put in the political framework of the Open Door. Something was being added to the traditional non-policy of seeking commerce wherever it could be found. Now the United States would more positively relate itself to China through the mediation of the policy which envisaged American-Chinese identity of interests.

The second criticism of the Open Door policy that is usually made is that it was never backed up by force. The principles of Chinese integrity and equal commercial opportunity, it has been argued, were high-sounding words that were never translated into practice. To do so would have involved the use of military force, and the United States was not prepared to provide it. Paradoxically, however, the absence of force was the very essence of the Open Door policy. The emphasis on the identity of interests between the two countries meant that the United States really did not have to enforce its will on China to promote its interests. At the same time, the espousal of Chinese integrity and equal opportunity was about the only thing American policy could do in the absence of military force. The inability and unwillingness to become militarily involved on the Asian continent were turned into a political advantage by an astute policy of emphasizing Chinese-American friendship and community of interests. Thus the principle of the Open Door from the very beginning implied that America had no militaristic intentions

[10] *Public Opinion*, June 21, 1900, p. 774.
[11] *Literary Digest*, July 28, 1900, p. 74.

in China, that it was in fact America's confession of its lack of military power in East Asia.

In a sense the United States was trying to play the role of an Asian power without military power. Ideologically, there seemed to be a coherence in such a strategy: there was a vision of American-Chinese relations, which in turn was based on an idealized image of China as a united and friendly country, capable of resisting the encroachment of the other imperialist countries and favorably disposed to reciprocate American overtures. It was not that the United States supported Chinese integrity as an expression of its traditional moralism, as has been alleged by historians. It was rather that Chinese independence was a *sine qua non* of America's aspirations as an Asian power. John Barrett best expressed this attitude when he wrote for *Independent* in July 1900,

> If China maintains her independence through our support, the United States in another decade will have greater material and moral influence than all other nations combined.[12]

John Hollady Latané, diplomatic historian at Johns Hopkins, wrote in his *America as a World Power* (1907) that

> the United States has now command not only of its own fortunes but of the fortunes of others, and cannot shirk the responsibilities that such a position brings with it.

After the turn of the century, these "responsibilities" were fairly clearly defined in Asia and the Pacific—in the former region, the maintenance of Chinese independence against imperialist encroachment, and in the latter, the governing and protection of the Filipinos. In both instances, there was a strain of what has been termed by historians American exceptionalism. As Latané wrote,

> In her role as a world power, armed with a mighty navy, which expansion in the Pacific and the cutting of a canal have made inevitable, it is to be hoped that America will not depart from her ancient ideals of peace or from the traditional frankness and fair dealing in diplomacy of which John Hay was one of the greatest exemplars.[13]

Moral Influence and New Diplomacy

Every country, of course, thinks it is unique and defends its foreign policy in exceptionalist language. American policy in the Asia-Pacific region, however,

---

[12] *Independent*, July 12, 1900, p. 1655.
[13] John H. Latané, *America as a World Power 1897–1907* (New York: Harper & Row, 1907), p. 319.

embodied the exceptionalist ethos in that it tended to dissociate itself from the policies of the other powers not only by word but also by deed. With rare exceptions, the United States rejected alliances and agreements with others, preferring to act alone and unwilling to combine its forces with theirs. While this unilateralism was a function of the Open Door policy, stressing America's stand as a friend of China, it was practiced in the Pacific Ocean as well, where the United States shunned formal agreements and alliances to protect its territorial possessions.

These were the circumstances and characteristic features which surrounded the United States as it emerged as an Asia-Pacific power at the turn of the twentieth century. America's role in the region in the period 1900–1921 reflected these same conditions, and it need not be chronicled in detail here. It will be recalled that at this time there was virtual Anglo-Japanese condominium in East Asia and the Southwestern Pacific, and as long as their alliance was in force, no third power could challenge the existing system of regional stability. But the period also saw America's power and influence grow, and by the end of World War I the country was already in a position to challenge the combined strength of Great Britain and Japan. In the Pacific Ocean, American power was primarily naval. Under President Theodore Roosevelt, the way was opened not only to expediting the construction of warships but also strengthening the defense of the Pacific by building an isthmian canal and fortifying some of the colonial possessions. By 1909, when Roosevelt was replaced by William Howard Taft, the United States navy had outstripped the navies of Japan, Russia, and France, and ranked third after Britain and Germany. Steps were being taken to turn Pearl Harbor into a major naval base, and the Pacific fleet had been organized to patrol the ocean together with the Asiatic squadron. After 1914 American power in the Pacific was augmented tremendously as the British and German navies cancelled each other off in their struggle in the Atlantic, and as the opening of the Panama Canal made possible the creation of a two-ocean navy for the United States. American naval planners were successful in persuading President Woodrow Wilson to undertake a construction program aimed at matching and ultimately surpassing the British navy.

American power in the Pacific, however, was still inadequate against the combined forces of the Japanese and British navies. So long as the Anglo-Japanese alliance was in effect, there was at least a theoretical possibility that the United States might have to defend its possessions and interests in the Pacific against the two navies. Because of the exceptionalist tradition and unilateralist orientation of foreign policy, the United States government did not seriously consider a formal alliance with Britain or with Japan for joint control of the region. Instead, it sought to destroy the Anglo-Japanese alliance so as to keep the two potential rivals of America separate. The pressure exerted in this direction resulted in the abrogation of the alliance at the Washington Conference (1921–22).

On the mainland of Asia, in the meantime, the United States continued to identify itself with Chinese sovereignty, both as the basic *raison d'être* for America's existence as an Asian power and as the best means for extending its economic interests. Inevitably, such a stand implied a challenge to the Anglo-Japanese entente in China. As these two powers dominated the trade and investment markets of China and, together with the other European countries, sustained a system of imperialist politics, the United States took upon itself a role as the one nation friendly to the Chinese. American policy was not always consistent or effective, not only because of resistance by the others to a basic change in the status quo, but also due to administrative decentralization and political polarization within China. Nevertheless, during the Wilson years, coinciding with the first phase of the Chinese republican revolution, American influence reached an unprecedented height.

This could best be seen in Japanese-American relations in China. For the United States Japan came to epitomize the old regime of imperialist politics, intent upon exploiting China. If America's self-appointed role as a champion of Chinese independence were to mean anything, therefore, it was necessary to develop a framework of Asian policy that opposed the United States to Japan. An image of Japan as an obstacle to Chinese sovereignty was thus an integral part of America's self-image as an Asian power. As Minister W. W. Rockhill reported, Japanese expansion in Manchuria after the Russo-Japanese War "viewed from the standpoint of the maintenance of China's integrity and sovereignty [is the] most dangerous feature" of Japanese-Chinese relations.[14] Lewis Einstein, chargé in the Peking legation, wrote in 1910 that

> the flood of Japanese settlers, the growth of Japanese industrial enterprise and the Japanese state-aided railways, public works, post offices and savings banks are continually sapping the remaining bases of Chinese sovereignty.[15]

No doubt these allegations were sincerely meant, although one must recall that "Chinese sovereignty" had long been compromised by the treaty system, in which the United States had participated. What is important is that such vocabulary reinforced the Open Door emphasis on the uniqueness of Chinese-American relations. For those who believed in America's role as a defender of Chinese independence, Japan's encroachment on it was tantamount to a challenge to the United States as an Asian power. That was why Japanese-American relations on the Asian continent tended to become an emotional issue; it seemed as if Japan was assailing the United States by expanding in China.

[14] Rockhill to Root, 1907, State Department archives, 5767/39.
[15] Einstein to Knox, 1910, State Department archives 793.94/150.

Thus in proportion as Japanese power and influence grew in China, the more self-conscious American policy became in East Asia. To do nothing would amount to giving up the nation's status as an Asian power. To use force was still out of the question. Between these two extremes there were various methods that could be employed to maintain America's integrity as a respectable and self-respecting power in East Asia. One was to use economic resources to assist the Chinese in their task of railway building, banking reform, and other programs of modernization. It was hoped that these enterprises would result in closer cooperation between the two countries, which in turn would have the effect of discouraging Japanese domination. Another method was more cultural, including such steps as inviting Chinese students to come to America and sending out American advisors to China. Finally, the doctrine of nonrecognition, asserting that the United States would not recognize any agreement involving China that violated the Open Door principle, was employed to stress America's difference from the other imperialists.

The cumulative effect of all these measures was such that by the end of the war the United States had emerged as the chief antagonist of Japan in China. The Chinese turned to America as their best friend, exactly as they came to regard Japan as their foe. The idea of Chinese-American cooperation not only in combating imperialism but also in transforming China gained currency. "Young China," noted Victor Wellesley, the British official, was "an Americanized China." [16]

Even so, the two countries would not have been able to alter drastically the politics of East Asia if the other powers, notably Japan and Britain, had been determined to resist such a trend and actively cooperated to do so. Actually, as sketched in the last section, the framework of imperialist politics crumbled because of mutual suspicion during wartime among the powers, the Bolshevik revolution, the defeat of Germany, and China's aggressive nationalism. American diplomacy under President Wilson provided an alternative scheme of Asian international relations by calling for the establishment of a cooperative order after the war. His New Diplomacy went beyond the Open Door policy of insisting on equal commercial opportunity and Chinese sovereignty; it sought to apply to East Asia the same principles of internationalism and equality under which the League of Nations was being erected. Instead of being an arena for big-power politics, East Asia would become part of the new world order where, as Wilson said, no special interest would override the "common interest of all" and no alliances and agreements would be permitted that were not sanctioned by the entire world.[17] In China this would mean substituting a universalistic scheme for extending loans for

[16] Louis, *British Strategy*, p. 27.
[17] Ray Stannard Baker and William E. Dodd, eds., *The Public Papers of Woodrow Wilson*, V, 254–58 (New York: Harper & Row, 1927).

the existing bilateral arrangements, and prodding the country's growth as a power.

Although the New Diplomacy was applied unevenly in different parts of the world, the major powers' deference to the United States at the end of the war meant that they would take its policies and principles in Asia much more seriously than earlier. While Wilson's pet scheme for a League of Nations never came to full fruition, and while his ideals foundered in Europe where they met fierce nationalistic opposition, in Asia they were more successful, and the United States emerged as the symbol of the new order. The achievements of the Washington Conference indicated that America had indeed grown to the status of a formidable Asian power.

Ironically, the United States failed to make good its enhanced prestige and power in the Asia-Pacific region after the Washington Conference. Despite all the efforts the country had made, and all the rhetoric it had employed, to justify its role in the international relations of this area, it never preserved the position of strength and influence it had achieved before 1922. During the next sixteen years or so, the United States reverted to a position of secondary importance. Whereas in 1922 the United States was a major power in East Asia and the Pacific, boldly challenging Japanese supremacy and proposing the construction of a new international order, fifteen years later it was a helpless witness to the rampage of Japanese militarism and continental imperialism. The decades of the 1920s and the 1930s were a period of retrenchment of American power in the Asia-Pacific region.

The situation was in part a by-product of the very system of new international relations which the United States had sought to create as a substitute for the Old Diplomacy. The New Diplomacy's emphasis on internationalizing the mechanism for protecting and promoting national interests, and on putting an end to big-power politics and militaristic expansionism, came to imply that no nation would take a leading political role in world affairs nor seek to be the stabilizer in maintaining a balance of power. The new politics cast doubt on the old practices of power politics backed up by military force, and it was assumed that peace and order would be maintained by means of increased exchanges of goods and capital among the nations of the world. International cooperation, the basic principle of the New Diplomacy, was not so much active collaboration among the major countries as abstention from such collaboration which gave the impression of the traditional imperialist collusion. Nor would the United States sanction the use of force as an instrument of foreign policy. There grew within the country revulsion against the use of military power to protect American interests overseas, and the Caribbean was the only region where the United States intervened militarily in the 1920s. Because there was relative stability in Asian-Pacific international relations for several years after the Washington Conference, Americans were not confronted with the question of how they proposed to defend the new system without force. It was assumed that peace and order would obtain for an indefinite period of time. In the meantime, the American government took steps to reduce its forces both in the Pacific and China. It seemed possible that no one power would establish hegemony over the area. It was no accident, therefore, that there was now less need to stress the traditional theme of Chinese-American cooperation. All this was tantamount to playing down America's own role as an Asia-Pacific power.

The complacency was shattered by Japan's assault on the Washington Conference, beginning in 1931. America's response to the renewal of Japanese militaristic imperialism shows that the crisis once again forced the country to define the extent and nature of its role as an Asia-Pacific power. One response was to say that the United States either had ceased or should cease to be a major country in the region and desist from meddling in Chinese-Japanese affairs. Such interference would only heighten tension between Japan and America without being of much assistance to China. Whatever pretensions the United States might have as a power in that part of the globe, the status was not worth the cost of military involvement and possibly conflict with Japan. Another argument was to revert to the traditional Open Door doctrine; the United States would stress friendship for China without, however, being prepared to use force. It was somehow hoped that through verbal attacks on Japanese aggression and by refusing to recognize any new arrangements that violated Chinese sovereignty, the United States might once again be in a position to influence the course of events in East Asia.

The Failure of International Cooperation

The official policy pursued by Secretary of State Henry L. Stimson was different from either of these approaches. He rejected the defeatist view that the United States should do nothing. It was not so much that America's national security or economic interests were at stake as a result of Japanese action. What disturbed him was that Japan had openly challenged the postwar international system in East Asia. To do nothing to resist was to ignore that Japanese aggression was a serious challenge to the structure of the peace which America had done much to erect. Neither was he satisfied with a simple reiteration of the traditional Open Door policy. To retain a viable amount of influence in Asia in the face of Japanese acts, old platitudes did not seem to suffice. The only effective alternative under the circumstances was to seek international cooperation so as to create enough pressure on Japan to retract. Stimson believed that the United States should act, not unilaterally as a nation whose interests were being menaced by another, but as a member of a coalition, presumably worldwide, that had a stake in the international order that was being undermined. As Stanley K. Hornbeck, chief of the Far Eastern division of the State Department, said,

> We should not permit attitudes or action of the American Government . . . as a manifestation of American Far Eastern policy; it should be made to appear as part of the international peace movement.[18]

Specifically, international pressure through cooperation meant recourse to the League of Nations. Though the United States was not a member of the organization, the State Department was willing to associate itself openly with it. A high point of American-League cooperation was reached when Stimson decided to let an American official, Prentiss Gilbert, sit at the League Council in October 1931. Unfortunately, the outcome of this cooperation was minimal, as Japan simply ignored League exhortations to withdraw from areas its troops had occupied. In the winter of 1931–32, then, Stimson became convinced that the only effective type of cooperation was one between the United States and Great Britain. He sought to associate Britain with his enunciation of the non-recognition principle and with measures taken to strengthen defenses of the Pacific. When the Shanghai incident broke out, Japanese forces fighting with stubbornly resistant Chinese in the city, the Secretary was eager to have the United States Asiatic fleet act together with the British squadron as a demonstration of Anglo-American solidarity.

For reasons discussed previously, however, no workable pattern of cooperation between the United States and Britain developed at this time. Nor did hopes in American-League cooperation long survive the shocks of 1931–32. As a result, American diplomacy in East Asia tended to revert to passivity. Since the United States alone was not capable of fighting Japan, and since no combination with other countries' forces seemed feasible, the avoidance of trouble with Japan became a cardinal principle of the officials in Washington. At the same time, the sentiment grew that Britain and others which might have helped had let America down. They appeared unwilling to join forces with the United States to protect world order. Such suspicions further hampered any effort at reviving cooperation, and for most of the time until after the outbreak of the Sino-Japanese War in 1937 the United States merely persisted in mouthing the Open Door doctrine without any thought of implementing it. In fact the State Department discouraged businessmen from giving financial assistance to the Chinese government, signifying the lack of will even to preserve the image of America as a major power on the Asian continent. In the Pacific, too, the Tydings-McDuffie Act of 1934, promising independence to the Filipinos within twelve years, signaled an approaching end of America's western Pacific empire. The United States alone was unable to challenge the ascendency of Japanese power in East Asia. When an

---

[18] Hornbeck memo, Sept. 20, 1931, State Department archives, 793.94/1889.

American ship, *Panay*, was sunk by the Japanese off Nanking in December 1937, there was the saddened recognition that such a humiliation could not be returned in kind because of lack of preparedness.

The very idea of international cooperation became a casualty of such a turn of events. It may be that even without the Manchurian crisis the tendency toward particularism and unilateralism might have come about, given the world economic situation which put a premium on nationalistic solutions. What the East Asian crisis did was to strengthen the trend toward unilateralism and further discourage any attempt at joint action with other nations to preserve the international order that looked more and more chimerical. The world was entering an era of high tariffs and managed currencies, replacing that of expanding mutual trade and freely exchangeable currencies based on gold. No one was sure what shape the coming world was to take, but it seemed more and more certain that it would not be a recreation of the Versailles or the Washington Conference system. Not knowing what to restore, the United States hesitated to lend its hand to stop the destruction of the old order.

Such an image of the changing world provided the intellectual basis of isolationism in the 1930s. A dominant strain of American thinking condemned acts of aggression by Japan and later by Italy and Germany, but it was opposed to intervention and involvement overseas, since such steps could eventuate in war. So long as the United States itself was not an object of foreign attack, its interests abroad seemed best safeguarded by avoiding external involvement. And it seemed as if there really was no fundamental national interest at stake in East Asia or the western Pacific. National security was not threatened in any immediate way. Nor was American trade of such importance that it deserved to be protected at the cost of war. If anything, purely in economic terms Japan was a better customer of American goods, and influential Americans in and out of the State Department were at last willing to recognize this fact.

Anglo-American Cooperation

In retrospect it appears that the year 1937 marked a turning point, at first barely perceptible, in American attitude toward the Asia-Pacific region. Underneath the dominant theme of isolationism and non-involvement, there grew a faint murmur for cooperative action. There was no departure from the abhorrence of military involvement overseas; but some began to believe that in order to preserve peace the United States must interest itself in world affairs instead of simply standing alone. Both in Europe and in Asia, such an interest could only mean greater readiness to cooperate with Great Britain. Earlier, Stimson's efforts at joint action with Britain had been frustrated, due fundamentally to the latter's unwillingness to entrust its fate to an American entente, which had never been tried before. The suspicion of the United States and the inclination to safeguard British interests through arrangements with Japan and Germany rather than through international cooperation persisted in London, where Prime Minister Neville Chamberlain said,

> It is always best and safest to count on nothing from the Americans but words.[19]

Nevertheless, such officials as Foreign Secretary Anthony Eden and his private secretary, Oliver Harvey, were convinced that only a firm stand jointly taken by Britain and the United States could stem the tide of aggression and instability in the world. They looked for signs in America that might give them hope, and in 1937 they were a little more encouraged than earlier by some slight indications of change in American public opinion and official thinking.

For instance, President Roosevelt's "quarantine speech," delivered in Chicago on October 5, talked of the need for collective action to contain the disease of aggression in the international community. The United States, in other words, must be willing to identify itself with the common interests of mankind and cooperate with others to discourage aggressors. In a similar vein, former Secretary of State Stimson began a letter-writing campaign, frequently writing to the *New York Times* about the importance of distinguishing between enemies and champions of world peace and freedom. He did not conceal his view that ultimately peace and order on the globe depended on active cooperation among a handful of key powers, especially Britain and America. In a book entitled *Is America Afraid?* (1937), the journalist Livingston Hartley expanded on the theme of Anglo-American community of interest. The book was among the first to harp on the theme, which would be heard more and more frequently until it came to be taken as almost axiomatic during the Pacific War. According to Hartley, the two countries shared basic orientations, policies, and interests.

> The American and British people are drawn together by the community of ideas and feelings that come from a common origin, a common language, common institutions, and a great similarity of race, legal, and moral standards and political thought.

More than tradition was involved, however. Now the two were the only remaining champions of democracy and freedom in a world beset by dictatorship and aggression.

> When free civilization is pushed to the fringe of Europe, it is only natural that our feeling of kinship with the British democracies should increase.

[19] Arnold A. Offner, *American Appeasement, 1933–1938* (Cambridge, Mass.: Harvard University Press, 1969), p. 189.

This being the case, it was only natural for the two to cooperate together in international affairs.

> There is no question in such circumstances that the United States and the British Empire can protect their common interests far more effectively in concert than either can alone.[20]

Since Britain was already deeply involved in Europe and Asia, such a view in effect called for a more assertive American policy.

The idea of Anglo-American cooperation was the intellectual foundation of a new Asian policy that began to emerge in the United States after 1938. As Hartley noted, such an idea implied that the United States should identify its goals and interests with those of Britain, and try to envisage foreign policy not unilaterally but always as part of the two nations' joint strategy. Obviously, in such a context the Asian crisis took on new meaning. Instead of merely being concerned with injuries to American interests in China, for instance, the United States would have to consider Anglo-American interests. It would have to view its and Britain's policies not in isolation but as part of a common response. Thus there grew in frequency exchanges of information and of views between London and Washington throughout 1938 and beyond.

The Brussels Conference, which met in late 1937 to discuss the Chinese question, was the nadir of American power and prestige in East Asia. Despite Roosevelt's assurances that the United States and Britain might jointly stop Japan, he was unwilling to countenance any effective measures to do so. Without America's firm commitment to take action, Britain also drew back from a firm stand. But the fiasco at Brussels if anything reinforced the need for cooperation. For instance, in December President Roosevelt sent Captain R. E. Ingersoll, director of the war plans division of the United States navy, on a confidential mission to London to hold secret staff talks. Just then two British subjects were attacked by Japanese in Shanghai, leading Sir Alexander Cadogan, the British under secretary of state, to exclaim,

> The time had come to tell the Americans we must do *something* (e.g. announce naval preparations) and ask whether they will take 'parallel' action.[21]

The United States refused to commit itself beyond promising that it would announce that the Pacific fleet was being prepared for action. Still, here was a clear case of joint policy formation, and moreover Ingersoll was able to

---

[20] Livingston Hartley, *Is America Afraid?* (Englewood Cliffs: Prentice-Hall, 1937), pp. 239–41, 250.

[21] Sir Alexander Cadogan, *The Diaries of Sir Alexander Cadogan* (New York: Putnam, 1972), p. 33.

discuss an exchange of codes and intelligence information in the event of an emergency. From this time on, collaboration on Asian matters became almost routinized. Although Anthony Eden, the foremost exponent of Anglo-American cooperation, resigned from the Foreign Office in February 1938, exchanges of information and ideas were sufficiently substantial by that time so that Oliver Harvey was able to write of an "invisible cooperation" between London and Washington in East Asia.[22]

The most important implication of the emerging cooperation between the United States and Britain was that it made for greater involvement of the former in Asia, as the latter had to concentrate its resources to areas closer home. Should war come, and should the two countries decide to carry out a joint strategy, it was obvious that the United States would have to take up primary responsibility. Britain simply could not do so, and no other power was in sight that would effectively safeguard the Anglo-American interests in East Asia and the Pacific. Such considerations, while not always clearly articulated, were undoubtedly a basic factor in the visible stiffening of American attitude toward Japan after 1938. In December Secretary of State Cordell Hull denounced Japan's enunciation of a new order in East Asia and denied that country's right to challenge the status quo by its own fiat. Simultaneously, China was granted a loan of twenty-five million dollars to construct a road from Burma to Chungking, a road that was to become a symbol of China's contact with the outside world. In July 1939 the United States took the drastic step of notifying Japan that it intended to abrogate the commercial treaty between the two countries. Coming before the German invasion of Poland, it was the most explicit demonstration thus far that it would not submit to Japan's new order. The United States must stand firm in China as a show of solidarity with Britain, and to discourage any idea on the part of the Japanese that they could take advantage of the impending conflict in Europe to push the Anglo-American powers around in Asia. Moreover, it was considered vitally important to diminish Japan's value as Germany's potential ally against Britain and ultimately the United States. By terminating the commercial treaty, the latter would be serving notice both to Japan and to Germany that they could not lightheartedly combine to challenge the interests of the Anglo-American powers.

The outbreak of war in Europe in September only confirmed the need to prevent Japanese hegemony in Asia. There was, to be sure, no formal undertaking on the part of the United States to come to the aid of Britain in Asia, or even in Europe for that matter. America's initial reaction was limited to the revision of neutrality laws and the application of the "cash and carry" principle to sales of arms, enabling Britain to obtain arms in the United States. But the importance of Asia increased because it was essential to

---

[22] *The Diplomatic Diaries of Oliver Harvey* (New York: St. Martin's Press, 1970), pp. 64–65.

prevent a German-Japanese assault on the British empire. The Pacific and the Indian Oceans were excluded from the "war areas" defined by the new neutrality act from which American ships were excluded. Such a measure enabled China to acquire goods brought over by these ships, at least theoretically. The obvious intent was to stiffen China's will and resistance to Japan, and to make it difficult for the latter to launch an attack southward.

The upshot of all these developments in 1938 and 1939 was that the United States was once again asserting its role, power, and prestige as an Asia-Pacific nation. It would not sit by idly while Japan created a new order in that part of the world. This reversal from the trends prior to 1937, which had seen a gradual erosion of American influence in Asia and the western Pacific, was essentially a product of an idea of cooperation with Britain. As Dean Acheson said in 1939, the United States must play not only a "prophylactic" but also a "therapeutic" role in international affairs.[23] In other words, instead of being satisfied with safeguarding national security and interests closer home, the country must once again interest itself in preserving the structure of world peace that was being threatened with destruction. The United States must resume its role as a world power. In the Asia-Pacific region, it must act as an active opponent of Japanese expansion. The gap between the self-perception as a friend of China, which had never totally disappeared, and actual capabilities in terms of power must somehow be bridged. The stage was thus being set for an ultimate confrontation in East Asia and the western Pacific.

[23] Mark L. Chadwin, *Hawks of World War II* (Chapel Hill: University of North Carolina Press, 1968), p. 59.

CHAPTER
THREE

The
Emergence
of
the
Yalta
System

THE PACIFIC WAR: ITS STRUCTURE AND VISION

Germany's spring offensive in 1940, swiftly conquering the Low Countries and France, set the final stage for Japanese-American confrontation in the Asia-Pacific region. The outcome of that struggle shaped the course of international politics for decades to come, and the Cold War in Asia was a direct off-spring, in fact a continuation, of the search for order in this area. The Pacific War bears scrutiny in such a context.

Anglo-American Globalism

The German blitzkrieg had the effect of bringing about an Anglo-American entente which was virtually an alliance. This was not what Hitler had calculated. He wanted to strike quickly and decisively in Europe so that Britain would fall before the United States came into the conflict. He talked about "Europe for the Europeans and America for the Americans." Germany, he declared, "has never had any territorial or political designs on the American continent, and has none at present." [1] This type of geopolitical argument, seeing the world as being divided into spheres of influence, had some American advocates. They insisted that European affairs were none of America's business, and that the United States should concentrate on its own defenses and on hemispheric solidarity. They would not interfere with the war so long as Germany refrained from challenging American power and interests in the Western Hemisphere. It was dangerous in the extreme to bestir oneself for the sake of Britain and to come to the aid of the latter against Germany. Such steps would inevitably involve the United States in war, a war that could only damage America's essential interests.

This kind of reasoning had already been rejected by the Roosevelt administration, and after the spring of 1940 it had more and more public support for its policy of Anglo-American cooperation. For those who believed in the identity, or at least approximation, of American and British ideals and objectives, it was simply illogical to separate the two countries and think only of American interests. Whatever happened in Europe affected the United States because it affected the Anglo-American entente. There was in fact no such thing any more as purely American policies and strategies; they were part of the Anglo-American framework of policy and strategy. From such a point of view, then, if one was for America one had to be for Anglo-American cooperation because the two nations were inseparable. Whereas the America First Committee, organized in September, preached what its name revealed, its opponents, having by then crystallized themselves into the Committee to Defend America by Aiding the Allies, countered that there was no such thing as "America first." It had to be "Anglo-America first," for America had no separate existence apart from the framework of joint existence with Britain.

Official policy in Washington was derived from the same idea. As President Roosevelt declared in Charlottesville just before the fall of France in June, "We will extend to the opponents of force the material resources of this nation." The "destroyer deal" of September showed how far he was willing to go in this direction. He began to think of "lending and leasing" arms to Britain, which would enable the beleaguered country to obtain much needed ships and weapons without having to worry about paying for them right away. The idea culminated in the Lend-Lease program, passed by Congress in March 1941, but President Roosevelt revealed his commitment to the defense of Britain most explicitly in his fireside chat of December 29, 1940, when he declared America's intention to see to it that Britain survived

[1] Saul Friedländer, *Prelude to Downfall* (New York: Knopf, 1967), p. 95.

the assault of the Nazis. The destinies of the two countries seemed inexorably intertwined, and if America was to survive it was its duty to give all aid to Great Britain.[2]

The definitive policy of Washington to identify itself with the fate of England implied America's decision to remain an Asia-Pacific power. Anglo-American cooperation, as we have seen, was conceived in global terms; the two countries were to coordinate their policies and strategies not just in Europe but elsewhere. This view had dawned upon statesmen and opinion leaders on both sides of the Atlantic as early as 1937, but the German spring offensive impelled them to formulate the theme more clearly than ever before. Henceforth it was imperative for the United States to assume a larger share of the burden of joint defense in Asia and the Pacific as Britain had to struggle for survival at home and to maintain its Middle Eastern empire. After 1940 the bulk of the British fleet, armed forces, and resources were concentrated in the areas west of India, and troops from Australia and New Zealand had to be shipped to the Middle East to reinforce the dwindling supply of English soldiers.

Psychologically and intellectually, it was not necessarily very easy for Americans to cooperate with the British in Asia. In Europe they could justify their common goals, but in Asia what did they have in common? British interests there were essentially Imperial interests, and to work together with Britain meant joining forces with the British Empire. Could America, whose self-image had an idealistic, "Open Door" component, work together with the foremost Western empire in Asia? Did America's support of freedom and democracy in Europe really obligate the country to help preserve the Imperial status quo? These were questions that were to trouble many Americans during the Second World War, and they provided ammunition to the America First group and other anti-interventionists in 1940 and 1941. What facilitated the acceptance of Anglo-American cooperation in Asia for most Americans was the image of the enemy. Both Britain and the United States were irrevocably committed to resisting German aggression. This was one thing that held the two countries together. In Asia, however, Japan was pictured as being closely associated, if not totally identical, with Germany. In such an equation, it followed that since Britain and the United States were united in their opposition to Germany, and since the latter was closely tied to Japan, the two should jointly confront the Japanese menace. Unless they did so, Japanese power would increase to the detriment of Britain, which in turn would encourage Nazi Germany to further acts of aggression. In order to save Britain, which stood for the balance of power and for certain ideals in Europe, it was necessary to be firm toward Japan, which was subverting the status quo in Asia with its power and ideology.

[2] See Warren Kimball, *The Most Unsordid Act: Lend-Lease, 1939–1941* (Baltimore: Johns Hopkins. 1969).

Perhaps the most explicit enunciation of this concept was made by Ambassador Joseph C. Grew in Tokyo in his dispatch to Secretary Hull, dated September 12, 1940. In it he clearly spelled out what he took to be the guiding principles of American foreign policy. First,

> Britain and America are the leaders of a large world-wide group of English-speaking peoples which stand for a 'way of life' which today is being threatened appallingly by Italy, Germany, and Japan.

Here in a nutshell was the convergence of the European and Asian crises. Grew turned into official language what Livingston Hartley had written in 1937: that the Anglo-American powers stood not only for a particular structure of world politics but also for certain conceptions of life, order, and civilization that pervaded the entire world. Germany and Italy were openly challenging them in Europe, and Japan in Asia. There was little difference between these opponents of the Anglo-American world order.

> Japan is today one of the predatory powers; having submerged all ethical and moral sense she has become unashamedly and frankly opportunist, at every turn seeking to profit through the weakness of others.

Second,

> America's security has depended in a measure upon the British fleet, which has been in turn and could only have been supported by the British Empire.

This was a conventional argument in terms of power. But it was specifically related to Grew's perception of the United States as a Pacific power:

> If the support of the British Empire in this her hour of travail is conceived to be in our interest, and most emphatically do I so conceive it, we must strive by every means to preserve the status quo in the Pacific, at least until the war in Europe has been won or lost.

He did not rule out the use of force, since the "status quo in the Pacific" obviously could not otherwise be maintained. The ambassador concluded,

> Until there is in Japan a complete regeneration of thought, a show of force, coupled with the determination that it will be used if necessary, alone can effectively contribute to that end.[3]

Grew's was a plea for more explicit support of British interests in Asia.

[3] *Peace and War: United States Foreign Policy 1931–1941* (Washington, D.C.: Government Printing Office, 1943), pp. 571–72.

The appointments to the cabinet of two prominent Republicans, Henry L. Stimson as secretary of war and Frank Knox as secretary of the navy, both taking place in 1940, strengthened this type of thinking. They were known for their strongly pro-British views, and if anything they went farther than Grew in advocating the use of force, even at the risk of war, to help Britain. While few were prepared to go that far, American officials and military strategists were considering it very probable that if the United States should become involved in war, one of its primary tasks would be to undertake the defense of Anglo-American interests in the Pacific. Joint strategy with the British, which had been begun when Captain Ingersoll was dispatched to London in 1938, was stepped up in 1940, as the United States Army sent two officers to England to discuss future plans with their British counterparts. The British sought to impress on their visitors the crucial importance of America's taking the initiative in, and shouldering the major burden of, defending the British Empire in Asia. President Roosevelt's decision to keep the United States fleet in the Pacific, after its annual exercises in the spring, gave an enormous moral boost to the British. Such action revealed most clearly that when the United States talked of supporting Britain, it did not simply mean the British Isles in Europe but also the Empire in the East.[4]

Preparations for War

Ironically, however, in late 1940 and early 1941 the United States was not really ready to carry its Pacific strategy to its logical consequences. To make effective the nation's resolute stand against Japan in the Pacific, it would have to be prepared ultimately to go to war against Japan. But the best judgment of the military in Washington was that the nation was not ready to go that far. American power was inadequate to engage in fighting both in the Pacific and the Atlantic. Plan Dog, or Plan D, an extension of the war plan Rainbow 5, which was officially adopted by Knox and Stimson in November 1940, gave top priority to the Atlantic. In the event of actual United States involvement in war, the strategic planners preferred to concentrate on that ocean first, remaining in the defensive in the Pacific.

The ambiguity in American policy, being simultaneously belligerent toward Japan and unwilling to go to war in the Pacific, remained in 1941, but it did not alter the essential nature of the Japanese-American crisis: the struggle over the Southwestern Pacific. During the first half of 1941 the official United States position was even more clearly articulated than earlier. The Anglo-American alliance was consummated in all but name when the

[4] Maurice Matloff and Edwin M. Snell, *Strategic Planning for Coalition Warfare, 1941-1942* (Washington, D.C.: Office of the Chief of Military History, 1953), pp. 10, 17–18, 22–23.

Lend-Lease Act passed both houses of Congress in March by large majorities. While it did not single out Britain as a recipient of United States aid, it was obviously intended for that country, a resolute response to Churchill's call for Anglo-American cooperation. The passage of Lend-Lease was a triumph not so much of internationalism as of the idea of Anglo-American solidarity. Simultaneously with it joint strategic conferences were held by military leaders of the two countries. In such conversations the American participants became more aware than ever before of the global nature of the nation's commitments; if the United States were to assist Britain, it must be prepared to protect the latter's imperial interests in such areas as the Suez Canal, India, Singapore, Australia, and New Zealand. The basic strategic concept which emerged in the spring of 1941 was "ABC-1." This was in accordance with the assumptions of Plan D, visualizing a United States defensive in the Pacific and an Anglo-American offensive in the Atlantic. The United States was to concentrate first of all on destroying German power in the north Atlantic.

The debate on the Lend-Lease bill in Congress was concerned almost totally with the British war against Germany.[5] Little thought was given to Japan in connection with the giving of aid to Great Britain. But this reflected the underlying, and often unspoken, assumption that the United States would take care of Asia and the Pacific while Britain fought against Germany in Europe and the Middle East. For instance, Secretary of War Stimson stated, in support of Lend-Lease,

> We are really seeking to purchase her [British] aid in our defense. . . . We are buying the protection which is accorded us by the continuance of the British sea power in the North Atlantic while our own main fleet is busy protecting us in the Pacific.[6]

Furthermore, it was thought that war with Japan was less likely, at least less imminent, than that with Germany. Men like Stimson were convinced that war with Japan could be prevented by a firm policy toward it, by demonstrating to Japan that its ties with Germany would only bring disaster. While not all shared Stimson's belligerent confidence, American policy makers were in agreement that the United States, not Britain, stood in the way of further Japanese advances in Asia and the Pacific.

Whether and in what way confrontation would come between Japan and the United States hinged on decisions made by Tokyo and Washington in the middle of 1941. In April Japan signed a neutrality treaty with the Soviet Union, thereby giving final proof that Japan's next thrust would be southward rather than northward. This was precisely what the Germans

---

[5] Kimball, *The Most Unsordid Act*, pp. 217 ff.
[6] Ibid., p. 167.

hoped to accomplish by means of the Japanese alliance. Although Hitler was preparing for an attack on the Soviet Union, the main objective of the alliance was, as he said,

> to bring Japan into active operations in the Far East as soon as possible. This will tie down strong English forces and the focal point of the interests of the United States will be diverted to the Pacific.[7]

More specifically, Germany wanted Japan to capture Singapore, which would have the effect of reducing the defenses of the British empire in Asia, while increasing Japanese power relative to that of the United States. Such an outcome, it was hoped, would preoccupy America and make that country that much more cautious before intervening in Europe. The Japanese, however, were still undecided. They were all interested in southern expansion, but were not agreed on means and timing. Their indecisiveness reflected the growing conviction that Japan could not simply attack Singapore and other British and European possessions in the Asia-Pacific region without incurring a risk of war with the United States.

The question, then, was whether such a risk was worth taking, or whether it outweighed any advantages that would result from southern expansion. Before the German invasion of the Soviet Union, there was no resolution of the issue, and Japanese policy toward the United States could best be characterized as temporizing. On one hand, the diplomats negotiated with Washington, trying to have the latter consent to resumption of normal trade relations. If trade could be restored, much of the rationale for southern expansion would be dissipated. The army supported negotiations for a different reason; it hoped that the United States would recognize Japanese hegemony over China. Neither of these hopes was realized, and the futile negotiations in Washington only strengthened the conviction that the two countries were on a collision course. But at this time this conviction was sufficient to restrain Japan; because it was felt that the United States would obstruct the path of Japanese expansion, the nation had to be extremely cautious before undertaking it. At this point, then, Stimson's bluff was working. The United States was able to restrain Japan by means short of war. The future of Southeast Asia hung in balance. Neither Japan nor the United States was prepared to step into the vacuum in Asia and the Pacific that was being created as a result of the war in Europe.

The Japanese Offensive Begins

The Nazi invasion of Russia, launched on June 22, finally led to the final phase of Japan's search for a new Asian-Pacific order. There was a chance

[7] Friedländer, *Prelude*, p. 199.

that history might have taken a different course, and that Japan might have sought a new order, not in Southeast Asia, but in North Asia. Germany put enormous pressure on Japan to join it in the war against the Soviet Union, arguing that once the latter collapsed, Germany and Japan could speedily defeat Britain. The United States, according to this reasoning, would be isolated and powerless, incapable of intervening in the war either in Europe or in Asia. Japan's leaders, too, were tempted to follow the German lead and violate the neutrality pact, only two months old, with Russia, in order to attack the latter from the east. In the end, however, the Japanese made the crucial decision to carry into practice their southern expansionism. They had not felt ready for such a thrust before then. Now that Germany and the Soviet Union were at war, obliterating one foundation of Japan's Axis diplomacy, the Japanese leaders might have been induced to reappraise the whole orientation of their strategy. For reasons which are still not entirely clear even today, this did not happen. Instead, they persuaded themselves that Germany's attack on Russia provided just the right opportunity to launch an invasion of Indochina. The struggle for control of Southeast Asia had begun.

Japanese policy, as it was formulated in July, was first of all to establish control over Indochina, and then prepare for an offensive against Singapore, the Dutch East Indies, and other island possessions of the European powers. Furthermore, by then it had become axiomatic that those moves would, at some stage, invite retaliation by the United States. Consequently, serious considerations began to be given to preparedness against America. This entailed planning for attack on the Philippines and on Hawaii. The last point became part of Japanese offensive strategy just around this time, as the navy, through Admiral Yamamoto Isoroku, demonstrated the theoretical feasibility of an aerial attack on the United States fleet anchoring at Pearl Harbor.

As if dictated by a well-rehearsed scenario, the United States responded to Japan's southern advance precisely as Japanese and Americans had expected. When Tokyo announced that it was sending Japanese troops to the southern portion of French Indochina, Washington countered by freezing Japanese assets in the United States and embargoing the export of crude oil to Japan. Since the Japanese navy was dependent on the continued supply of fuel oil, and since this had to come either from the United States or the European colonies of Southeast Asia, the implications of all these steps were unmistakable. Japan had a choice of either continuing the southern advance or desisting from establishing a new regime in the Southwestern Pacific. The choice was Japan's, but it was bound up with Japanese-American relations, since only the United States stood in the way of Japan's new Asia-Pacific order. America's oil embargo would be ineffective if the Dutch and British colonies should provide Japan with oil; they would be expected to resist

Japanese pressure, but in so doing they would count on support by the United States.

In the United States the feeling persisted that by thus taking explicit measures to make known its determination to oppose Japan, the latter could in fact be stopped without a war. Available evidence all points to the policy of preventing Japanese hegemony in Southeast Asia by means short of war. This coupling of drastic firmness and hesitation to contemplate war was a product of the military's desire to postpone a two-ocean war and the State Department's conviction that a premature showdown with Japan should and could be avoided. The Atlantic Conference, the meeting of Winston Churchill and Franklin D. Roosevelt in Placentia Bay, off the coast of Newfoundland, taking place in August, confirmed this approach. The conference symbolized Anglo-American cooperation that had emerged as a substitute for broader international cooperation, as a bastion of order and peace in the world threatened by those nations that sought a different definition of international relations. It was significant that the two leaders and their aides spent as much time discussing Asian and Pacific matters as they did on the actual war in the Atlantic. They tried to formulate a joint strategy to cope with the impending thrust southward by Japan.

Prime Minister Churchill, reflecting the view that Britain could not defend its rights and interests in this region while it was preoccupied in Europe and the Middle East, and anxious to have the United States become involved in the war, tried to commit Roosevelt to an unequivocal position in the Pacific. He sought the President's approval of a policy which would automatically bring America into war in the event of Japan's further aggression. According to a memorandum prepared by Alexander Cadogan and presented to Sumner Welles, the British government wanted the United States government to present an ultimatum to Japan, saying,

> Any further encroachment by Japan in the Southwestern Pacific would produce a situation in which the United States Government would be compelled to take countermeasures even though these might lead to war between the United States and Japan.

The acceptance of this formula by Roosevelt pleased Churchill, who cabled his foreign secretary, Anthony Eden,

> I think this is entirely good, and that we should associate ourselves therewith and endeavor to get the Dutch to join in full agreement. [Moreover,] the Dominions should be told about it and made to see that it is a very great advance toward the gripping of Japanese aggression by united forces.[8]

[8] Winston S. Churchill, *The Grand Alliance* (London: Cassell, 1950), pp. 439–40.

Churchill's optimism was a little premature, as Roosevelt's State Department advisers did not want to precipitate a crisis just at this juncture. Joseph Ballantine of the State Department modified the proposed phraseology of the American note to Japan to read:

> If the Japanese Government takes any further steps in pursuance of a policy or program of military domination by force or threat of force of neighboring areas of the Pacific, including the mainland of Asia, the Government of the United States will be forced to take immediately any and all steps of whatever character it may deem necessary in its own security.

This was further watered down when Roosevelt read his note to Ambassador Nomura Kichisaburō. It concluded by saying

> the Government of the United States will be compelled to take immediately any and all steps which it may deem necessary toward safeguarding the legitimate rights and interests of the United States and American nationals and toward insuring the safety and security of the United States.[9]

Nevertheless, it is clear that the Southwestern Pacific was becoming the key to America's policy toward Japan. There was as yet no unequivocal decision as to whether Japan's further advance southward, presumably directed at the British and Dutch colonies and dominions, would automatically result in United States intervention. This, however, was more a tactical than a policy question. There was broad agreement among the top policy makers that the United States would defend the status quo in the Southwestern Pacific against Japanese encroachment, whatever the timing and the means of doing so. Actually, the War Department, which insisted until the end that a showdown with Japan be postponed as much as possible, took a crucial and symbolic step in late July of establishing a new Far Eastern command under General Douglas MacArthur. Upon learning of his appointment, MacArthur issued a press statement saying,

> This action of the American government . . . can only mean that it intends to maintain, at any cost and effort, its full rights in the Far East. It is quite evident that its determination is immutable and that its will is indomitable.[10]

Here was a reversal of the existing war plan which had envisaged a defensive strategy in the western Pacific, with no further troop commitment in the Philippines. The July decision reflected the army's faith in air power. The development of B-17 army bombers seemed to make it possible for the United

---

[9] Theodore A. Wilson, *The First Summit: Roosevelt and Churchill* (Boston: Houghton Mifflin, 1969), pp. 243–44.

[10] Dorris Clayton James, *The Years of MacArthur* (Boston: Houghton Mifflin, 1970), p. 591.

States to defend the Philippines and the surrounding European colonies against Japanese naval forces. The aircraft were scheduled to be shipped to the Philippines in December and afterwards, making the islands impregnable by the spring of 1942. General Lewis H. Brereton busied himself negotiating with French Indochinese as well as Australian authorities for establishing airfields for the B-17's. According to D. Clayton James,

> The aircraft which Brereton had when the fighting started were in quantity and quality the most formidable of any American overseas department.[11]

Toward the end of November, the Far Eastern command was told to defend the entire archipelago, not just the Manila and Subic Bay areas. MacArthur was instructed to cooperate with the British and Dutch forces in defense of the Malay barrier in the event of war with Japan.[12] On November 27, Marshall and Stark sent a memorandum to President Roosevelt, reporting that 21,000 troops were to sail from the United States for the Philippines by December 8. It was important, they said, "that this troop reinforcement reached the Philippines before hostilities commence." [13]

Even as these steps were taken to strengthen the defenses of the Philippines in conjunction with those of the European colonies and dominions, the Japanese leaders were approaching their final decision to attack these territories. After August it did not enter their thought to separate the United States from Britain and the Netherlands and attack only the latter's possessions. By then it was axiomatic that war, should it come, would involve all these countries. In fact the United States loomed as the major antagonist, the chief obstacle to Japan's new order in Asia and the Pacific.

On the other hand, it seems plausible to argue that if Japan had desisted from further southern advance, there would have been no immediate American involvement in the Asia-Pacific region. Japan would have continued its endless war on the Asia mainland, while the United States would have built up the defenses of the Philippines and improved strategic coordination with British and Dutch authorities in the Southwestern Pacific. There would have emerged a regime of Japanese-American condominium. The United States would not have entered the Asian war to aid China by force. According to Marshall's memorandum of November 3,

> It is desirable that large Japanese forces be kept involved in China. However, from the larger viewpoint, prospective Chinese defeat would not warrant involvement of the United States, at this time, in war with Japan. . . . Most effective aid to China, as well as to the defense of Singapore and the

[11] Ibid., p. 611.
[12] Ibid., pp. 595–96.
[13] Matloff and Snell, *Strategic Planning*, p. 79.

Netherlands East Indies, is now being built up by reinforcement of the Philippines.[14]

This position had the support of Roosevelt, although a few of his advisers, notably Stimson, were anxious to have the country get into the war as quickly as possible, not so much against Japan as against Germany.

This being the case, the crucial factor was Japan's decision to challenge the status quo in Southeast Asia and the Southwestern Pacific. It is true that the final decision by Tokyo for war against the United States and Britain was made on November 27, in response to the "Hull note" of the 26th, which not only warned against southern expansion but also demanded that Japan withdraw from China as well. Even so, nothing drastic would have immediately happened if Japan had ignored the note and at the same time refrained from further acts of aggression in Southeast Asia and the Southwestern Pacific. However, by the end of November 1941 Japan's army, navy, and civilian leaders had come to accept the view that either Japan was going to establish a new order in the region, or the United States would surely aim at driving Japan out as a first-rate power. Japan's status as the major Asian-Pacific power seemed to be at stake, just as the United States was reasserting its role as a Pacific power. It was symbolic that on December 6, just as Japanese ships and aircraft were receiving final orders for attack, President Roosevelt was telling the British ambassador that the United States would "regard it as a hostile act if the Japanese invade Thailand, Malaya, Burma, or the East Indies," and that if Japanese transports were seen crossing the Gulf of Siam, the British forces "should obviously attack them." In other words, the United States, acting together with Great Britain, fully expected hostilities with Japan once the latter undertook forceful expansion southward.

The Japanese Vision
of a New Asia-Pacific Order

So war came between Japan and the United States. It was a war for redefinition of international order in the Asia-Pacific region. The regional international system, long sustained by the unequal treaties as well as the Anglo-Japanese alliance, the Washington Conference, and other agreements, had broken down in the 1930s because of Japanese aggression, itself aiming at establishing a new order. The war in Europe had brought about instability in the Southwestern Pacific, and Japan threatened to step into it. The United States, by its decision not to tolerate this, was itself assuming a role as a stabilizer in that part of the world. Japan and the United States were the only two powers that could define a new status quo by force. The history of

[14] Ibid., p. 74.

international relations in the Asia-Pacific region since the Opium War had culminated in the Pacific War, or the Great East Asian War as the Japanese called it. Whichever name one adopted, it graphically expressed the nature of the struggle. Both Japan and the United States had expanded as Asia-Pacific powers, and now they confronted each other in a region where Britain and other European powers had historically predominated. Neither Japan nor the United States could tolerate the predominance of the other, and "cooperation" and compromise between the two had been ruled out. War was the only result.

Japanese strategy and diplomacy during the Pacific War makes it abundantly clear that such a perception, the idea of a new Asia-Pacific order, had become decisive. The attack on Pearl Harbor was part of an overall assault upon the status quo in Southeast Asia and the Southwestern Pacific. As the December 8 declaration by the Japanese government put it, Japan was firmly determined to create a new order in alliance with Germany, Italy, Manchukuo, and China (through the Nanking regime of Wang Ching-wei). The nation had been "forced to start action in the southern areas," but this was not directed against the native populations.

> It is only intended for the purpose of ejecting the oppressive rule of Britain and the United States, thereby to restore Asia to its natural state and to cooperate together for mutual welfare and happiness.[15]

In accordance with such a concept, the Japanese army and navy launched simultaneous attacks on Hawaii, the Philippines, Singapore, Hong Kong, Borneo, Burma, and other areas of the region. By March 1942 Japanese forces had captured Hong Kong, Manila, Singapore, Batavia, and Rangoon. The immediate objective was to establish control over the Asia mainland all the way to Burma, the Dutch East Indies, the Philippines, and such islands in the Southwestern Pacific as Guam, Wake, the Marshalls, the Bismarcks, and the Solomons. These were to be the components of Japan's new Great East Asian Coprosperity empire.

Certain characteristics stand out in this scheme. First of all, the new Japanese empire was definitely southern-oriented, although it extended northward to the Siberian-Manchurian border. But the northern limits of the empire had been set earlier, and there was no attempt to become further involved in Northeast Asia. This was implicit in the policy to honor the neutrality pact with the Soviet Union. Indeed, one vital part of Japan's wartime strategy was to do all possible to prevent Soviet entry into the war. Moreover, it was hoped that somehow the Soviet Union could be utilized in such a way as to consolidate Japanese gains in the south. For instance, much thought was given to mediating between Germany and Russia so that they

---

[15] *Nihon gaikō nenpyō narabi shuyō bunsho* (Tokyo: Foreign Ministry, 1955), II, 573.

would stop their war and enable the Axis powers to concentrate on the Anglo-American powers. As this proved progressively more difficult, Japan began seeking Soviet mediation in the war. Here again, Japanese leaders were willing to offer such inducements as the giving up of oil concessions in North Sakhalin and even the retrocession of South Sakhalin, in order to maintain peaceful relations with Russia. In the spring of 1945, when Japan was desperately trying to end the war without sacrificing its gains in Southeast Asia, the Tokyo government intimated readiness to discuss Soviet-Japanese economic cooperation in the area.[16] It is clear that the vision of southern empire had become a rigid dogma for Japan during the Pacific War.

It was to Southeast Asia and the Southwestern Pacific, then, that Japanese policy and strategy paid particular attention as an essential part of the emerging regional system. In Japanese conception, the new order embraced such divergent lands as Burma, Thailand, Malaya, and Indochina on the Asian continent, the component parts of the Dutch East Indies, the Philippines, and the islands in the south and central Pacific. In addition, the part of China under the Nanking government's control (mostly coastal areas) was also included. Japan's pan-Asianism, anti-Westernism, and geo-political, strategic needs were the factors that seemed to offer coherence in this wide region. Ideologically, the Japanese justified the establishment of a new order as an act of liberation, to free the colonial peoples of Asia and the Pacific from centuries of Western domination. Economically and strategically, the Great East Asian Coprosperity Sphere was to be closely integrated, each section contributing to the welfare of the whole and thus creating an economically self-sufficient zone, comparable to the German empire. Japan would supply capital and technology, and the yen would become the common currency, while the other components would develop agriculture, heavy industry, and light industry. To oversee all these activities, a Ministry of East Asian Affairs was established in Tokyo in November 1942, separate from the Foreign Ministry.

Japan's Asia-Pacific empire was a study in contradictions. The establishment and maintenance of the new order depended on such factors, all aspects of the war, as Japanese military control over the whole region, prevention of American counteroffensive, cooperation of the native populations, economic self-sufficiency, and some sense of unity of the entire area. None of these conditions was met. Military hegemony was obviously in conflict with intra-regional cooperation, neither of which was successfully carried out. Militarily, Japan's own land and sea power was inadequate to control the vastly extended empire, and there was always the question of priorities. It was extremely difficult to allocate ships and troops most

---

[16] Ashida Hitoshi, *Dainiji sekai taisen gaikōshi* (Tokyo: Jiji tsūshin, 1959), p. 614.

efficiently, when they had to cover the vast spaces between Burma in the west to the Pacific islands in the east. China still tied down the bulk of the Japanese army, but it had to be diverted for use in the Southwestern Pacific, and the fierce battles in New Guinea, the Solomons, and elsewhere throughout 1942 and 1943 made it impossible for Japan to launch a massive assault on the Chinese stronghold in Chungking. Even more serious, the far-flung empire exceeded the capabilities of Japanese shipping to keep strategic and economic machines running. The Japanese naval strategy was to draw out the remnants of the United States fleet and destroy them once and for all, so that the security of the empire would be maintained. The battle of Midway frustrated this prospect, and the increasing use of submarines and aircraft by the United States constantly harassed Japanese sea lanes. Japan's air power, too, began to decline after 1942, as the nation lost crucial aircraft carriers and airfields in the Pacific. Losses of airfields and trained pilots immobilized the Combined Fleet, and the American counter-offensive, striking at different points one after another, exhausted Japanese capabilities.

Nor was there much intra-regional integrity or cooperation. Despite the symbolism of a Great East Asian Coprosperity Sphere, Japan's new empire in fact lacked cohesion except that which was provided by its arms. On December 14, 1941, barely a week after Pearl Harbor, the Foreign Ministry in Tokyo proposed that Japan divide Great East Asia into three zones. The first would include such areas as Hong Kong, Singapore, Borneo, and New Guinea, all of which would be turned into Japanese occupied territories. The second group of states, including Malaya, Sumatra, Java, and Celebes, would be given limited autonomy. Finally, Manchukuo, China, the Philippines, Thailand, and Burma would be granted independence but would be asked to agree to the stationing of Japanese forces within their borders.[17] As such a scheme indicated, what was contemplated was an empire of force, belying any pretension that the new order was a harbinger of freedom for Asia. Even so, part if not the whole of the new order might have been functionally operative if there had been some degree of consistency in Japanese policy in the Asia-Pacific region. In reality, Japanese policy was a series of expediencies. For instance, in Indochina Japan dealt with the French authorities, tenuously under Vichy command, instead of encouraging the native independence movement or putting the country more directly under Japanese control. Until March 1945, when this last step was taken, Japan in effect cooperated with France in the government of Indochina. In the Dutch East Indies, the Japanese armed forces replaced the colonial regime of the Netherlands, the army controlling Sumatra, and the navy Celebes and Borneo. The expulsion of the Dutch resulted in the emergence of Indonesian

[17] Ibid., p. 456.

administrators, educators, and politicians, who would declare independence right after the Japanese surrender in 1945. In the Philippines, Japan worked through a native government, whose status was ambiguous since the United States had not given the islands independence. They had to establish some working arrangements both for the Filipinos and for the Japanese army of occupation.

On the continent of Asia, China of course remained the major object of Japanese policy. Here the basic strategy was to consolidate the base of the Wang Ching-wei regime in Nanking and win over various warlords and factions hostile to Chiang Kai-shek. A final assault on the latter was planned for 1943, but it had to be postponed because manpower and materiel had to be diverted to the Pacific theater. In the areas under Nanking's control, the Chinese government under Wang Ching-wei administered the land, but there were many areas, beyond the coastal cities, where the Japanese army was the only organized power. Only in Burma was there a native regime willing to cooperate with the Japanese army. Long before the latter invaded Burma in December 1941, it had assisted the Burmese independence movement, and the Tokyo government declared its intention of making the country independent. In June 1943 a new Burmese constitution was promulgated, the Japanese military occupation ended, and Burma declared war against the United States and Great Britain.

Because it was war against the United States and Britain that had entrenched Japan in the Asia-Pacific region, it was inevitable that the Japanese chapter in the area evolved in wartime conditions. There was little time to develop a coherent system of Asia-Pacific international relations. The Japanese subordinated all considerations to the one objective of winning the war, but in so doing they undermined their own stronghold; they failed to develop an integral policy toward the wide region.

That Japan was determined to prevent Britain and the United States to enter the area can be seen in the effort, often last-minute, to grant independence or autonomy to many of these countries. The basic rationale was to deny the rich resources and the goodwill of the Asian-Pacific peoples to the Anglo-Saxon powers, so that if Japan could not long hold on to the region by force, it would at least use diplomatic means to ensure their allegiance. The Philippines provided a good example. The islands had been promised independence by the United States, to take effect in 1946. The Japanese invading army, whose basic aim was the expulsion of American forces, quickly approached Filipino leaders and tried to persuade them to request President Roosevelt to halt hostilities. This was tantamount to asking American surrender in return for independence in the framework of the Great East Asian Coprosperity Sphere. The Filipinos had not brought on the war. As they saw it, it was a matter involving the two empires. Even so, some of their leaders preferred United States to Japanese rule and left with

General MacArthur for Australia. But the majority of the islanders remained. Some continued guerilla resistance, but most accepted the Japanese regime. From Japan's point of view, this was as satisfactory an arrangement as could be obtained. The United States had been expelled from the islands, there was established a collaborationist government in Manila and the provinces, and the islands remained relatively stable during the war. Prime Minister Tōjō Hideki visited the Philippines in 1943 and announced Japan's intention of granting independence. Such an act, said the local Japanese commander, should "promote . . . trust in Japan and defeat reliance upon America." [18] Toward the end of the war, as American forces advanced across the Pacific from island to island, Japanese authorities in the Philippines forced the collaborationist government to declare war against the United States. It had little effect, and MacArthur announced his return on October 20, 1944.

The Philippines were the only major American colony in the Asia-Pacific region. Despite the suffering during the war, on the whole they were spared the kinds of turmoil, uncertainty, and ravage into which the British, French, and Dutch colonies were thrown after 1940. The Filipinos had, since 1900, developed their own system of political organization, and their status within the American empire had been fairly clearly defined. Thus there was no point in inviting internal rift by actively cooperating with Japan against the United States, or by turning the country into a vast battlefield. The native leaders knew what they wanted, and had the ability to carry out their programs. They had education and organization. Such was not the case with the colonial populations of the European colonies, where there had been no comparable indigenous infra-structure to replace the colonial superstructure once the latter was demolished. In the Philippines the task of nation-building had begun forty years earlier, but elsewhere the colonial leaders had not prepared the local populations for the emergency. Under the circumstances, stability became bound up with exigencies of the war. Local social and political conditions depended on the fortunes of war between the empires. Japanese promises of independence had a greater appeal to these peoples than to the Filipinos; at the same time, once Japanese power ebbed and rule finished, a long period of uncertainty was inevitable.

The United States Role
in the Wartime Asia-Pacific Region

America's determination not to be ousted from the Philippines, and not to see the British Empire and Commonwealth succumb to Japanese hegemony,

---

[18] Theodore Friend, *Between Two Empires: The Ordeal of the Philippines, 1929–1946* (New Haven: Yale University Press, 1965), p. 233.

provided one new factor on which the shape of the Asia-Pacific region depended. It was that determination, epitomized by the decision to strengthen the defenses of the Philippines, that had brought about the head-on collision with Japan, intent on establishing its new order in the region. It was natural, then, that the major area of confrontation between Japan and the United States should be the Southwestern Pacific. To be sure, the allied strategy called for defeat of Germany first. President Roosevelt and Prime Minister Churchill were in entire agreement that their countries could best cooperate with one another and with the Soviet Union in Europe and the Middle East, regions where their combined strengths might yet succeed in checking German assaults. Coalition warfare dictated that the United States be guided by considerations for allied unity and cooperation, and it was in such areas as North Africa and Iran that saw the effective pooling of resources, strategies, and manpower of the United Nations.

Coalition warfare proved much harder to achieve in Asia and the Pacific. But this fact all the more dramatized the role of the United States and its strategy in shaping the destiny of these areas. Because Britain was preoccupied with Europe and the Middle East, the task of preventing Japanese domination of the Pacific fell almost automatically to the United States. But this was a challenge the latter met decisively and even enthusiastically. Unlike Europe, North Africa, or the Middle East, where American power and diplomacy entered gingerly and sometimes reluctantly, the Pacific was a region where the United States could act more or less unilaterally, unencumbered by considerations of other governments' sensitivities.

One of the first decisions the supreme command in Washington made after the Pearl Harbor attack was not to give up the Southwestern Pacific. The several ships still en route to the Philippines were ordered not to turn back but to proceed to Brisbane. In mid-December a United States army command was created in Australia under General George H. Bret, and an American base was established in Port Darwin, in northern Australia. Combat ground troops were to be sent to that country, thus making it the key strategic center for America's counteroffensive in the western Pacific. It is estimated that of the 132,000 army troops that embarked from the United States for overseas assignments before March 1942 as many as 90,000 were bound for the Pacific Ocean, of whom 57,000 went to Australia.[19] This was by far the most sizable bulk of United States reinforcements anywhere in the world at that time. As if to underscore America's leading, almost exclusive, role in the Pacific theater of the war, the United States and the British governments agreed, in March 1942, to place strategy in the ocean under American control. This in turn was divided into the Southwest Pacific area

[19] Charles Bateson, *The War with Japan* (East Lansing: Michigan University Press, 1968), p. 150.

under the command of General MacArthur, and the Pacific Ocean area under Admiral Chester Nimitz.

In retrospect the infusion of United States forces in Australia turned out to be the crucial factor in checking the Japanese advance. Having fortified the defenses of Australia, the next step was to prevent the enemy's attempt to isolate it. The success of this strategy hinged on control of Papua, the Australian territory of the island of New Guinea. Here the critical battle of the Coral Sea in May 1942 resulted in a failure of Japan to capture Port Moresby, on the southern coast of Papua. Subsequent Japanese attempts to assault Port Moresby overland also failed, and by the beginning of 1943 the Allied position in New Guinea was secured. In the meantime, to the east of New Guinea, in the Solomon Island group, fierce battles were waged between Japanese and American forces. These islands were useful to Japan as air bases, and once United States invading forces seized them, not only Japan's ground troops but its precious aircraft and pilots were lost or immobilized. Guadalcanal in 1942, Bougainville in 1943, and Rabaul in 1944—these battles in the Solomons were a struggle for airfields, and for Japan to lose them was tantamount to giving up its grip on the Southwestern Pacific.

These American victories facilitated a counter-offensive across the Central Pacific from the Gilberts north to the Marshalls and then due west to the Marianas, closer and closer to the Japan mainland. The atoll of Tarawa (in the Gilbert island group) was taken at the end of 1943, opening the way for the building of fighter and bomber bases to carry out the next counter-offensive, that against the Marshalls. The campaign for these islands opened the year 1944, followed by assaults on the Caroline and Mariana islands. The taking of Saipan, in the latter group, was of immense strategic value, since the new B-29 bombers could fly from the island airfield to Japan and back without refueling. Although in late 1944 decisions were made to advance further west and take the Bonins and the Ryukyus (Okinawa) with a view to constructing air and naval bases closer to Japan, the Saipan airfield proved to be of fundamental importance. Air raids by B-29's from their base in Saipan were devastating and did more than anything else to destroy the morale as well as military capabilities of the Japanese empire. By the spring of 1945 American victory was clearly in sight.

On the continent of Asia America's military role was not so clearly defined, nor were its achievements so spectacular. The Pacific theater of war was placed under the unequivocal command of the United States, whereas Britain was assigned responsibility over the Middle East and the Indian Ocean. Such a division of control left the grey areas in the middle, including Burma, Indochina, and China. Since neither the United States nor Britain was capable of asserting leadership in this region, it was inevitable that a tripartite regime, a joint command by these two plus China, should be established. The relationship among the three was never explicitly spelled out, and this theater of war was almost always relegated to a position of secondary importance in coalition strategy. The unexpectedly early collapse of Burma and Singapore necessitated the concentration of United States air combat forces in India, rather than in areas closer to China, thus making all the more difficult the task of coordinating strategy among the various powers involved. Still, it was considered crucial to "keep China in war," a phrase used on innumerable occasions in official American documents, in order to tie down Japanese forces and prevent their use elsewhere in Asia.

In this task the allied powers proved to be successful, despite their limited resources. But this was not a result of large-scale fighting or efficient and massive campaigns against Japan. The most that could be said was that the Japanese forces were immobilized in China, Indochina, and Burma, and were brought to a military stalemate for most of the duration of the war. Anything beyond this would have necessitated a more active participation in the theater by either the United States or China. The grand strategy for global warfare, however, did not allow for a massive infusion of American troops in this area, and the only way the United States could help China was through the shipment of lend-lease goods. Thus the Chinese forces had to continue to bear the brunt of the Asian war, and it became a cardinal aspect of United States strategy to encourage the more efficient training and organization of the Chinese army. The dispatch of General Joseph Stilwell in early 1942 was intimately connected with these two objectives; he would supervise the administration of the lend-lease program in China, and try to increase the combat capabilities of Chiang Kai-shek's troops. Despite Stilwell's frustrations and the bitter enmity which developed between him and the Chinese leader, the fact remains that here was one of America's top generals involving himself in coalition warfare in East Asia. His presence in China was a symbol of the determination of the United States to play a role in the war in Asia as well as the Pacific Ocean. Although there were much more limited supplies and manpower which the United States could provide, and far more complicated problems of joint command, than in the Pacific, it was considered axiomatic that Japan must be defeated not only in the ocean but also on land.

Finally, the United States envisaged an even more limited military role in Northeastern Asia—the Kurile islands, Sakhalin, eastern Siberia, Manchuria, and Korea. It is true that some of the islands in the western Aleutians—such as Attu and Kiska—were invaded by Japanese forces, necessitating diversion of United States resources away from the Southwestern Pacific. But ultimately it was considered crucial to count on participation by the Soviet Union in the war against Japan. Should Russia enter the Pacific War, it could be expected to launch a counter-offensive against Japan's elite forces in Manchuria and to attack the northernmost possessions of the Japanese empire. Once Russia joined the allies against Japan, it could offer its airfields in Siberia as launching sites for American bombers. Such an expectation resulted in United States passivity in Northeastern Asia until 1945. It was enough that the Soviet Union consented, at the Teheran Conference of 1943, eventually to enter war against Japan. Since America and Russia were cooperating to a limited degree in Europe and the Middle East, it seemed plausible to count on such collaboration in the Asia-Pacific region once the tide of war turned in the west. It is interesting to note that the United States dealt directly with the Soviet Union to consider joint Pacific strategy; China and Britain were not involved until 1945.

IN SEARCH OF THE POSTWAR WORLD

Thus, there were gradations of America's military involvement in the Asia-Pacific region. But one underlying fact stood out: the United States was doing all it could to prevent Japanese hegemony. Where it could not act alone to do so, America would cooperate with others. But there was no thought of reaching a settlement with Japan before the latter's complete surrender. No stability or order could be accepted that retained even a modicum of Japanese imperialism.

The New Order in the Asia-Pacific Region:
Lack of a Precedent

What, then, was to be the nature of the international order in the Asia-Pacific region that was to replace the Japanese-imposed system? What roles were the United States, Britain, and their allies to play after the Japanese defeat? What was to be the place of the Soviet Union in postwar Asia? What was the future of the colonial areas, of Korea and of Taiwan?

These were fundamental questions, answers to which would determine the shape of Asia and the Pacific for years to come. But there could be no easy or predictable answers since precedent was totally lacking. The United States had never been more than a secondary Asian power, and even in the Pacific its military strength had been significant only as a counterbalance to that of the Japanese empire. The anticipated defeat of Japan meant the removal from the scene of the one nation that had provided a stable pattern of big-power politics for several decades. Britain and Russia had, from time to time, acted as Japan's partners in the system. But their future roles were by no means clearly perceived. The Soviet Union had been eclipsed as an Asia-Pacific power, but it could be expected to reenter the arena and seek to define a new order of its own. Finally, China had never been more than a victim of imperialist encroachment, but the end of the Sino-Japanese War could be counted on to enhance its position and prestige. It was not very easy to envisage an Asian international system with China as a key component, unless one went back to the pre-Opium War days, but this, of course, was out of the question. Under the circumstances, each power, potential and actual, in Asia and the Pacific had to contribute its own perception of the new order after the war which would not only serve its self-interests but also help stabilize international relations instead of plunging the region into chaos and uncertainty.

Here was the beginning of the search for a new equilibrium in the Asia-Pacific region which was to be carried over into the postwar period and which, it may even be argued, has persisted to this day. The search was not simply in terms of defeating the Japanese enemy and restoring some kind of status quo. From the beginning there was a strong idealistic component as the United States and its allies sought to counter Japan's pan-Asianist doctrine with their own vision of Asian freedom. The United Nations fighting in the Pacific all signed the Atlantic Charter, enunciating their opposition to territorial changes without the express wishes of the peoples concerned, and their support of the principles of self-determination and economic internationalism. Because of the leading role of the United States in that theater of war, these ideals were an important ingredient of wartime perceptions about the future of Asia. At the same time, vision was not always matched by power, nor were military victories always followed by the implementation of the principles of the Atlantic Charter. Since the United Nations and the Axis powers were fighting essentially at two levels—power and ideology—it is not surprising that much depended on the vicissitudes of the war, or that there were often gaps between the Asia-Pacific order which emerged *de facto* from the actual battles and that which adherents to principle visualized.

In such a context, it is possible to view the Pacific War and the origins of the Cold War in Asia as a drama in which participants struggled to establish a new international order where idealistic visions would be provided with a structure of power—in other words, where requirements of power politics would be congruent with certain principles. To see the intricate interactions between vision and power, it is necessary to examine various parts of the Asia-Pacific region. First of all, American strategists fully expected the nation to retain their position of supremacy in the Pacific. There was no thought that American power, having been vastly extended to the western limits of the ocean, could or should be retrenched after the war. The islands which American forces occupied would not be given up but would continue to be used militarily by the United States. Airfields that were constructed on these islands would be of tremendous value, and it would not suffice merely to retain those such as Guam and Wake which had been American possessions. The Marshalls, the Marianas, the Carolines, and others from which the Japanese enemy had been ejected were to be held as a guarantor of the new status quo in the western Pacific. At the same time, as a signatory of the Atlantic Charter, the United States was in principle opposed to territorial aggrandizement which could not be reconciled with the ideal vision of freedom in the liberated Pacific. Under the circumstances, it was considered best to establish some sort of trusteeship over these islands. Such an arrangement could not be formalized until a new international organization was established that would provide for trusteeships, and this was one reason why the United States was seriously interested in the formation of the United Nations Organization.

Much more difficult and bothersome was the question of the future of the European colonial areas in Southeast Asia. The United States had already decided to grant independence to the Philippines by 1946, and the coming of war had not changed this policy, although MacArthur's declaration, "I shall return," revealed a determination to reestablish America's position in the islands before they gained independence. It was unthinkable to let Japan be the liberator of the Filipinos. Moreover, even after independence it was expected that the Philippines would remain closely tied to the United States, especially in terms of its security and military needs. What was visualized, then, was first to drive the Japanese out and then to proceed toward Philippine independence, to be coupled with some arrangements for retension of American strength so as to prevent instability and resurgence of Japanese imperial ambitions.

Matters were more complicated elsewhere—the Dutch East Indies, Indochina, Malaya, Burma, and other parts of the British empire. Although, as stressed earlier, it was in order to defend these areas against Japanese invasion that the United States had taken measures that led to the Pacific War, there was no expectation that the status quo antebellum could be restored after Japan's defeat. For one thing, the war in Europe had resulted in a loosening grip of the colonial powers upon these lands, a fact which was utilized to the utmost both by Japan and by those indigenous groups that were struggling for independence. Japan's appeal to their sentiment, utilizing pan-Asianist and anti-Western language, was well recognized by Washington. Moreover, the Atlantic Charter reiterated the principle of self-determination of peoples. Under the circumstances, it seemed strategically and morally urgent for the United States to define its attitude toward the colonial areas. Their future appeared dependent to a great extent on the policies of the United States because the latter was bound to emerge as the most powerful nation in the Pacific.

A State Department memorandum written within a month after Pearl Harbor reveals this type of thinking. Drafted by Maxwell Hamilton of the Far Eastern division, it stated,

> In connection with the war effort of the United States and the other United Nations, it is very important that the loyalty and wholehearted support of the

native peoples of Far Eastern areas be enlisted. Early Japanese successes will inevitably discourage certain elements among these peoples and will create an atmosphere in which dissident elements can and probably will emerge and increase in strength. Japanese propaganda can be counted upon to emphasize heavily the exploitation by Western powers of Far Eastern peoples.

Accordingly, Hamilton wrote it was imperative for the United States and its allies to

> create a situation which would serve to cut the ground from under such propaganda.

Specifically, he would suggest that Britain accord dominion status to India and Burma and provide for "gradually increased native participation in government" in such other colonial areas as Malaya, North Borneo, and New Guinea (Papua), and that the Netherlands government do the same for the Dutch East Indies. Hamilton would grant that the colonial powers would need to retain military and naval bases in their possessions, and in fact he would urge them to do so; but this consideration, indeed, should enable the former to grant greater liberties to the latter. Finally, the memorandum noted,

> In the present emergency war situation, British and Dutch problems are to some extent our problems, and vice versa. There therefore appears ample warrant for this Government to offer and indeed to urge upon the Governments with which we are united in a war effort adoption of any program which may contribute materially to the success of the war effort.[20]

It is curious that Hamilton's memorandum did not mention Indochina. By a strange coincidence it was French Indochina to which Washington's officials paid greater attention during the war than to the other areas of Southeast Asia. Despite the awareness of the problem, the United States government failed to evolve a clearcut policy or develop a coherent vision for this part of the world after the war. Only with respect to Indochina did President Roosevelt and his top advisers show some interest. By 1943 they had come to conceive of a trusteeship for the peninsula, in which the United States would participate. Admittedly still vague, the idea implied continued American presence in Southeast Asia. Whether France was to be permitted to return or not, it would no longer be in a position to control the destiny of the Indochinese people. It would have to work with or through the United States and other constituent elements of the proposed trusteeship. Not even this much definition of the future was developed in other parts of Southeast Asia and the Southwestern Pacific.

[20] Hamilton memo, Jan. 6, 1942, State Department archives, 740.0011PW/2030½.

The gap between perceived need and actual policy merits explanation. For concern with the future of the colonial area was very intense during the war, and it was a vital aspect of popular notions about the war against the Japanese empire. Japan was trying to create a Great East Asian Coprosperity Sphere, and it was up to the United States to propose an alternative system. For instance, E. Stanley Jones, a noted churchman, wrote to President Roosevelt in June 1942 and urged him to enunciate a Pacific charter to complement the Atlantic Charter. It was an explicitly anti-imperialist proposition. Jones argued that

> many of the people of the East think that we are fighting to maintain the status quo in the Pacific. If so, then we are simply bolstering up decaying imperialism.

To combat that impression, it was imperative for the United States to declare its stand for "the liquidation of imperialism." Moreover, the nation should take a lead in establishing a new order in the Asia-Pacific region on the basis of such principles as equality of access to raw materials, equality of opportunity for immigration, and a

> more equitable distribution of opportunity for settlement of surplus populations in the less occupied portions of the world.[21]

Such a vision represented one extreme; it would entail a whole reordering of the colonial structures in Asia and the Pacific and integrate the region into a new world order of freedom and economic interdependence. Few went that far at this time, but various organs, including liberal magazines, were intent upon defining the Pacific War as one between imperialism and freedom. Thus already in March 1942 the *New Republic* was speaking of "A New Order for Asia," which would be a substitute both for European and Japanese imperialism. The author called for a

> plan for a democratic new order in Asia, based on India and China, but including also all the other Asiatic peoples.[22]

Another article in the following month insisted that the United States should declare that

> the native peoples of the Orient and the Southwest Pacific will be given complete freedom as rapidly as possible.[23]

Pearl Buck echoed such a sentiment when she wrote,

[21] Jones to Roosevelt, June 1942, Franklin D. Roosevelt Papers (Hyde Park, New York).
[22] *New Republic*, March 9, 1942, p. 320.
[23] Ibid., April 27, 1942, p. 556.

Only a firm stand on the principle of human equality for all peoples will give us the final victory necessary for a real peace in this world. If we do not make that stand now by speaking out clearly and independently to reassure the great peoples of the East, then while we fight this war we are beginning the next one.[24]

Despite such urgings the United States government failed to interest itself actively in the question of the future status of the European colonies in Asia. Reasons for this can be debated endlessly, but one key factor seems to have been Roosevelt's reluctance to consider political questions apart from immediate military contingencies. This becomes clear when one looks at his handling of the European war. He was intensively interested in political questions in such countries as French North Africa, Italy, and Germany. This was because United States forces were involved in these areas, and Roosevelt considered diplomatic-political questions in terms of the presence and safety of American power. The "politics of war" was essentially the politics of areas occupied by American forces. As the President said to Secretary of State Hull in October 1944, "I dislike making detailed plans for a country we do not yet occupy." It seemed useless and unnecessarily cumbersome to bother with problems that were not directly related to the actions and movements of the United States armed forces in cooperation with those of the allies. Roosevelt and his advisors did not doubt that the United States would have a voice in the postwar settlement in Asia and the Pacific, but the degree of its influence would depend on the extent of its military involvement. Until American forces occupied a territory, it was idle to talk of its future. And even then, the question of administering occupied lands would have to be dealt with on an ad hoc basis. As was stated in a decision reached by the Joint Chiefs of Staff and the State Department in September 1944,

> the scope and the structure of military administration of any area [recovered from Japan] is to be left largely to the discretion of the local commander because of the need of fitting in military administration with the local military situation.

Moreover,

> the personnel of the military administration depends primarily upon the composition of the forces engaged in conducting the actual military operation.[25]

Such pragmatism militated against larger, idealistic considerations for the future of Southeast Asia and the Southwestern Pacific. It was of

[24] Ibid., June 1, 1942, p. 762.
[25] Arthur L. Funk, *Charles De Gaulle: The Crucial Years* (Norman, Oklahoma: University of Oklahoma Press, 1959), p. 303. JCS to Stilwell, Sept. 15, 1944, Roosevelt Papers.

fundamental importance that American forces were not seeing action throughout most of the Dutch East Indies or Malaya. There were units of the United States army and air force in Burma and India, but they were outnumbered by those of China and Britain. Under the circumstances, it is not surprising that no blue-print after Japan's defeat was developed for this region. All that existed was some sentiment that the United States would play a vastly more extended role here after the war. Its occupation of the smaller islands and its return to the Philippines guaranteed that it would no longer be a secondary Asian-Pacific power. The outline was there, but the specific content remained unclear. To put it another way, the vision of a free Asia, derived from the Atlantic Charter, was not matched by a specific structure of power which the United States would help define after the war.

Plans for Japan Proper
and Its Possessions

American policy was somewhat more clear toward the territories that had formed an integral part of the Japanese empire: Taiwan, Sakhalin, the Kuriles, and Korea. There was no difficulty in coming to the decision that Taiwan and its adjacent islands should be restored to China. They had been ceded to Japan in 1895, and few American officials, if any, supposed that they would remain under Japanese control. There was the possibility that a trusteeship might be established over the island, but unlike Indochina where such a scheme was considered, China had a legitimate claim to Taiwan. It had been a province of China since the seventeenth century, and the Chinese had regarded it the first victim of Japanese imperialism. Under the circumstances, the United States could readily visualize a situation in which Japanese rule would be expelled and Chinese suzerainty restored on the island. The occupation of Taiwan by United States forces was never considered.

Similar reasoning was behind the readiness with which the United States viewed the retrocession, in due time, of South Sakhalin and the Kurile islands to the Soviet Union. The former had been given up to Japan after Russia's defeat in the Russo-Japanese War, and the latter had been assigned to Japanese rule in the Russian-Japanese treaty of 1875. Considering Soviet entry into war in the Pacific only a matter of time, the United States government assumed that Russia would get back these territories in the event of allied victory. It was, to be sure, not up to the United States to dispose of these lands; the Soviet Union would have occupied them regardless of American intentions. The United States was more interested in the use of Siberian airfields for American heavy bombers to launch attacks on Japan. The frustrating delay in implementing an accord in principle on this point revealed clearly that the Soviets would not look with favor on any attempt on the part of the United States to have a say in the disposition of Northeast Asian lands. But the fact remains that the Roosevelt administration did little or nothing to resist the considerable extension of Soviet power in this area that was expected to result from the war. The very decision to seek Soviet entry into the Pacific war, rather than honoring Soviet neutrality in accordance with the 1941 Soviet-Japanese treaty implied acceptance of a new situation which would see the Soviet Union replacing Japan as the predominant power in that region.

Korea was not so simple a case. It could not be casually assigned to China or the Soviet Union, as it had been more or less independent before its annexation by Japan. At the same time, both its continental neighbors showed a great deal of interest in the strategic and political significance of the peninsula. They would be interested in ejecting Japanese power from Korea after the war, but the resulting power vacuum must somehow be filled. The Korean people themselves had been subjugated to increasingly stringent Japanese control, and it had not been easy to organize a resistance movement. But their leaders had long agitated abroad, and with the coming of war in the Pacific several of them sprang to action, each claiming to represent "Free Korea." There were active organizations in the United States, headed by such men as Singman Rhee and Kim Ku. Others agitated for Korean freedom in Chungking, Hawaii, and the Maritime Provinces.

In the United States there was general agreement, in and out of government, that ultimately Korea should be made an independent country. But the circumstances in which independence would be achieved remained vague. As Stanley K. Hornbeck, adviser on political relations in the State Department, wrote in April 1942,

> A commitment now that the Korean people shall be made free would be one thing, but a pledge that Korea shall be made an independent state might become a source of most embarrassing involvement.

This was because it was extremely difficult to predict Korea's domestic and international conditions at the end of the war. Hornbeck tended to agree with the opinion of the Council on Foreign Relation's study group that "Korea was not capable of self-government at the present time." Independence implied the existence of a recognizable government, but the various factions claiming to speak for the Korean people did not seem capable of uniting among themselves.[26] Moreover, it was far from certain what the Chinese and the Soviet governments wanted, and it seemed premature for the United States to take the initiative on the Korean question before their views became

[26] Hornbeck memo, April 11, 1942, State Department archives, 895.01/96 2/3.

more affirmative. In a perceptive report from Chungking in May 1942, Ambassador Clarence E. Gauss pointed out that

> the Chinese feel that the Korean issue is one of primary concern to the Chinese Government and that, while they welcome our interest in a solution of the problem, they desire to retain the initiative and are somewhat fearful that our well-intentioned efforts might as readily lead to confusion as to solution.

As for Russia, Gauss insisted that since Soviet entry into the war was very likely

> recognition of a Korean government which did not have the support of Russia at the conclusion of the war might readily lead to embarrassment; that general agreement on the Korean government to be recognized would be preferable to action now with a view to presenting the Russians with a 'fait accompli' which might not actually prove to be a solution.[27]

Such caution remained with the principal American policy makers, and they never specified what type of independent government they visualized for Korea after the war. At the Cairo Conference the vague expression, "in due course," was used to indicate the readiness of the United States to see Korea becoming independent. This was a vague formula which at best satisfied the demands and interests of the major governments involved, but was a grave disappointment to Korean leaders. In the context of United States involvement in East Asia, however, even such a mild expression is revealing. It indicates a desire and determination on its part to play a role in postwar Asia. What role it would be remained a question, but the active interest the United States took in the Korean question was in great contrast to its passivity before the war. No matter what was going to happen in the peninsula after the war, there was recognition that the United States would be there as one of the concerned powers. In fact President Roosevelt toyed with the idea of a trusteeship for Korea as early as May 1943, an idea that remained a general State Department policy for the duration of the war.[28] It was always assumed that the United States would be one of the powers entrusted with such a regime, the others presumably being China, Britain, and the Soviet Union. After 1944 the four powers kept in touch with one another regarding military operations involving the use of Korean underground activities, and it was somehow expected that through encouraging such activities and with the blessings of the United Nations the Korean people could be prepared "for the tasks ahead," as a memorandum of the Far Eastern division put it.[29]

Vague and indefinite as most of these ideas were, they show a

[27] Gauss to Hull, May 16, 1942, ibid., 895.01/130.
[28] Gabriel Kolko, *The Politics of War, 1943–1945* (New York: Random House, 1968), pp. 601–3.
[29] Far Eastern division memo, July 31, 1944, State Department archives, 895.01/7-2144.

fundamental assumption that the Pacific War was changing the realities of power relationships in the Asia-Pacific region and that the United States was to play a far more active role in the area's postwar affairs than ever before. In the areas where American military forces were already or likely to be engaged, it was visualized that they would be dispelling Japanese power. At the same time, ideals and principles would play a prominent role, and the nature of postwar American influence would be as much ideological and political as military and economic. The United States would at once exhibit military might and espouse ideals as it transformed itself as the predominant power in the western Pacific.

By far the best indication that the United States was determined to be such a power was its policy toward Japan proper. From the beginning it was recognized that the United States would not only have to defeat Japanese ambitions but also to cripple permanently Japan's militarism and imperialism. At the bottom was a view of Japan and Japanese-American relations that was current during the war. An excellent example of this is a series of essays written by the staff of the Far Eastern division of the State Department soon after Pearl Harbor. As they were the officials most knowledgeable about and concerned with Japanese affairs, their memoranda are of considerable interest. One of the papers, entitled "What the United States Has Done for Japan," referred to "the American efforts to promote understanding and to secure a peaceful Pacific" since the mid-nineteenth century and castigated Japan for its failure to respond in kind.

> Japan has perverted her knowledge of things western to fit the pattern of an extravagant and cruel imperialism. The materials, the inventions, the ideas, the sympathetic suggestions for the creation of a peaceful Pacific—all these have gone to Japan from America. With them in her possession, she has professed peace and treacherously planned for and waged war.

This was because Japan was ruled by an insidious form of dictatorship. As John P. Emmerson wrote in one of the memoranda,

> Backed by the powerful prestige of the Emperor, and responsible neither to the people nor to the people's representatives, the rulers of Japan determine her destiny. Only a decisive defeat can wrest control from these conquest-mad military dictators. It is our responsibility to administer this decisive defeat! [30]

Given such views, it readily followed that the United States would assume main responsibility for crushing Japanese militarism and encouraging the emergence of alternative leaders. What the latter objective entailed became clear only on the eve of Japan's surrender, but thinking along the

[30] Far Eastern division memos, Jan.–Feb. 1942, ibid., 740.0011PW/2037.

above lines continued among the specialists in the State Department. As Emmerson wrote,

> There are those in Japan who do not subscribe to the philosophy of life which has in recent years led their nation down a path of aggression and destruction of the rights of peoples. The future hope of Japan will rest with new leaders and with a changed philosophy to arise when peace again prevails upon the Pacific.[31]

Much time was spent subsequently to define these "new leaders," and by 1944 there was agreement that they included those political, educational, and economic leaders who had been prominent in the 1920s but eclipsed during the period of militarist ascendency in the 1930s. The decision whether to abolish the Emperor system was never reached, although it was assumed that the person of the Emperor was less important than the uses the militarists were making of him. Given the prevalent image about the past relationship between the two countries, there was the expectation that the new postwar leaders in Japan would be pro-American so that they would not subvert America's desires for a peaceful Pacific.[32] Here again, it is obvious that an expanded role of the United States after the war was visualized. Although it was not clear whether Japan was to be allowed to remain a viable power, it would certainly be no match for the United States, and for all practical purposes it would cease to have sufficient power and wealth to stand in the way of the postwar international order.

New Status for China

Finally, American conceptions of postwar Asia included a view of China as a power. The mere fact that China was now a member of the coalition fighting against Japan ensured its status as an ally of the United States, entitled to consultation and cooperation with the latter. This immediately enhanced China's prestige, and the United Nations' pledge to continue the war until victory was achieved implied that China would recover lands which had been lost to the Japanese empire. The Cairo declaration of 1943, stating that Japan would be made to restore to China all the territories it had obtained at the expense of the latter, was tantamount to visualizing a new order in Asia after the war in which China would play an important role. The Cairo Conference itself, attended by President Roosevelt and Generalissimo Chiang Kai-shek, was a dramatic episode in this respect; the meeting was a symbol of the American recognition that the United States would work closely together with China during and after the war.

[31] Emmerson memo, Jan. 26, 1942, ibid., 740.0011PW/2037 3/8.
[32] Kolko, *Politics of War*, p. 544.

Yet the idea of China as a great power was much easier articulated than carried out. In practice the idea had at least three aspects: the military strengthening of China itself, Chinese participation in the administration of occupied areas, and China's voice in Southeast Asia. Of these three the first was destined to plague wartime Sino-American relations. It took up so much time and attention of the leaders of the two countries that the other questions tended to be slighted. This was unfortunate, for it was if anything in these questions that the United States and China could have achieved some degree of successful cooperation in restructuring Asian international relations. From the American point of view, however, it was idle to talk of China as a great power unless the Chiang Kai-shek regime exerted its efforts to modernize and increase the fighting potential of the Chinese armed forces. There was growing dissatisfaction that the Chungking government, having more or less by a windfall secured great-power status for China, seemed complacent and uninterested in playing a larger military role in the struggle against Japan. As Ambassador Gauss reported to Washington in December 1943, the Chinese seemed to feel

> that China has done her full part in resisting the Japs for more than six years and that America should now undertake the full burden of the conflict.

While such an attitude was understandable in view of the fact that the United States had let China fight alone throughout the 1930s, Gauss believed that

> there is . . . a great deal that China can and should do but is not doing . . . to help herself and thus further the war effort by giving whole-hearted assistance to the American air force and other American operations in this theater.

Unless Chiang Kai-shek undertook some positive action, not only would the war be that much prolonged, but China itself would suffer in the end.[33]

This sort of misunderstanding between American and Chinese officials in Chungking, which culminated in the estrangement and open clash between Chiang Kai-shek and General Stilwell, was never resolved. Basically this was because men like Gauss and Stilwell were thinking of China as a potential power in a military sense, capable of doing more to defeat Japan and contributing to stability in postwar Asia. Such an attitude had important implications. United States officials, especially those stationed in wartime China, assumed that military strengthening was possible only when there was a unified command over all available forces in China, under a vigorous leadership that embodied the country's determination to crush the aggressor. Moreover, a militarily strengthened China would be one that actively

[33] Gauss to Hull, Dec. 9, 1943, Roosevelt papers.

cooperated with American forces. Conversely, those groups in China that reciprocated American desires for military collaboration and shared similar views of China's needs were the ones with which the United States could and should work.

By 1944 more and more American officials, civilian and military, were coming to the view that to strengthen China by aiding Chiang Kai-shek was a hopeless proposition. On the contrary, it appeared to contribute to weakening China by demoralizing other groups in Free China and by encouraging Chiang's dictatorial tendencies. One of the clearest expositions along these lines was written by John P. Davies, Jr., second secretary of the United States embassy in Chungking, at the end of the year 1943. By then it seemed to him to have become entirely evident that Chiang's position was insecure and unstable.

> His reluctance to expend military strength against Japan, his anxious preoccupation with securing domestic supremacy, his suspicion of everyone around him and his increasing emotional instability betray a subconscious realization of this.

Such being the case, Davies argued, it did not serve the purpose of building up "a strong and independent China" to continue to commit the United States "unalterably to Chiang." The alternative, he concluded, was to be prepared "to support a strong new coalition offering cooperation mutually more beneficial to China and the United States." [34]

In this way the idea of China as a power had the effect of involving the United States in considerations of Chinese domestic politics. As is well known, President Roosevelt was not as willing as Gauss, Stilwell, or Davies to weaken Chiang's authority within China. Just once, in September 1944, Roosevelt warned Chiang against further delay in modernizing his armed forces and fighting efficiently against Japanese troops. The only way to preserve a strong China, the President told the Generalissimo, was to seize the initiative and press the offensive against the enemy, "while at once placing General Stilwell in unrestricted command of all your forces." Only then could the United States "maintain and increase" its aid to China.[35] This came close to being an ultimatum, but when Chiang Kai-shek responded in kind, demanding the recall of Stilwell, Roosevelt backed down. He was extremely reluctant to alienate Chiang in the middle of war and decided to mollify him by replacing Stilwell with General Albert Wedemeyer. The decision was essentially a pragmatic one, Roosevelt reasoning that it would be detrimental to the war efforts of the United States and China if their leaders openly clashed or if the former gave the impression of encouraging

[34] Davies to Hopkins, Dec. 31, 1943, ibid.
[35] Roosevelt to Chiang, Sept. 16, 1944, ibid.

anti-governmental movements in China. Roosevelt's support of Chiang was much like his earlier preference for Henri Giraud in French North Africa or for Pietro Badoglio in Italy. They had had de facto authority over sizable territories in these countries, and they had seemed the best rallying point for carrying out the war efficiently against the enemy. The question of how democratic or representative these men were had not been considered so crucial in wartime conditions. It was enough that Chiang would be gently pressed, as had been Giraud and Badoglio, to reorganize his government and armed forces so that they would better reflect the popular will. With this purpose in mind, President Roosevelt sent General Patrick J. Hurley as his special emissary and later ambassador to Chungking. He was to coordinate American efforts to help bring about a more unified government and military command in China under Chiang Kai-shek. As Roosevelt told Hurley in a cryptic message in November,

> a working arrangement between the Generalissimo and the North China forces will greatly expedite the objective of throwing the Japanese out of China. . . . I cannot tell you more at this time but he [Chiang] will have to take my word for it.[36]

Despite the tumultuous chapter in wartime Sino-American relations involving these principal characters, one should not lose sight of the image of postwar China that was held by practically every American official: an independent country rid of foreign aggressors, with which the United States would work closely. To put it another way, the United States was not to be the predominant power on the continent of Asia, as Japan had been, but was to retain its influence through China. Hence the need for a militarily viable and pro-American oriented China to emerge after the war. Otherwise, it seemed that there would be continued instability and chaos on the Asian mainland, and the war would not have solved the question of what international order was to be constructed. While American officials disagreed, often vehemently, among themselves concerning the policy of continued support of Chiang Kai-shek, they shared a vision of postwar China that would somehow be linked to the United States and enable the latter to play a role as one of the key Asian powers. It was this consideration that induced the Roosevelt administration to favor bilateral talks between the two countries even before the end of the war on the matter of the administration of territories reconquered from the enemy. The United States government was reluctant to discuss such matters with Britain, but the State Department considered it

> expedient politically to enter into such an agreement [regarding occupation policy] to satisfy the Chinese in the matter of "face."

[36] Roosevelt to Hurley, Nov. 17, 1944, ibid.

In September 1944 Chiang Kai-shek was informed of this readiness on the part of the United States.[37] Nevertheless, as suggested earlier, there was no thorough-going discussion between the two governments concerning the future of Southeast Asia, and there developed no clear vision of what roles the United States would like to see assigned to China and to itself in this region after the war.

Sino-Soviet Relations

One question that assumed greater and greater importance in American approaches to policy in China was that of Sino-Soviet relations. As noted earlier, officials in Washington took it for granted that the anticipated Soviet entry into the Pacific War would result in Russia's regaining Sakhalin and the Kuriles, thus becoming the foremost power in Northeast Asia. But the question of what this implied for the relationship between China and the Soviet Union was not really faced until 1943 when, at the Teheran Conference, Stalin intimated that the Soviet Union would insist on obtaining certain rights and concessions in Manchuria as a price for entering the war against Japan. Since the United States had already foreseen postwar Soviet power in Northeast Asia, such demands did not seem objectionable, and there was general agreement that Russia should be induced to join the allies in their war against Japanese forces in Manchuria and elsewhere in that region. The resulting preponderance of Soviet power was to be anticipated, and not to be objected to by the United States. On the other hand, the vision of Soviet predominance in Northeast Asia had to be accommodated to the idea of China as a power, another part of the American perception of postwar Asia. Obviously, too powerful a Russia would be a threat to a China just recovering from ravages of war and civil strife. But if China were to emerge as a viable independent entity, it would have to obtain some sort of understanding with the Soviet Union which would inevitably be playing a more extended role in Asia after the war. A really strong China, however, would resent the expansion of Soviet influence and interests in Northeast Asia, especially in Manchuria.

An added complication was the presence of the Chinese Communists in North China, more or less sandwiched between the Soviet Union in the north and the Chungking regime in the south. They were growing in strength and prestige inside China and were less and less willing to remain subordinate to Chiang Kai-shek's authority. China could not be a unified military power so long as their rivalry continued, but more seriously, the Communists were in a strategic position because of their proximity, geographically and historically, to the Soviet Union. From the American point of view, therefore, it was

[37] Joint Chiefs of Staff to Stilwell, Sept. 15, 1944, ibid.

essential to come to grips with the Chinese Communist question in order to form a coherent image of future Sino-Soviet-American relations in Asia. Unfortunately, there was no agreement among American officials on this issue, and they were unprepared for the rapid turn of events inside China at the end of the war.

On one hand there were those who believed that the Soviet Union would look favorably upon a unified China under Chiang Kai-shek. From such a perspective there was no serious problem arising out of the presence of Communist Chinese in North China. They were Chinese first and only incidentally Communist. They would somehow merge with the Nationalists and cooperate with the latter to build a strong and centralized government. The resulting new China would then stand face-to-face with the Soviet Union, and the two would share responsibilities for stability and peace in postwar Asia with one another and with the United States. This, in rough outline, was the thinking of men such as General Patrick J. Hurley. As he telegraphed President Roosevelt soon after his arrival in Chungking, via Moscow, in September 1944,

> the so-called Communist troops in China are not considered real Communists by [Soviet Foreign Minister V. M. Molotov]; Russia's attitude toward China is friendly and . . . Russia is not attempting to use the Communist troops to prevent military unification in China. Russia desires closer and more harmonious relations with China.

Obviously, an image of Soviet policy and intentions was at the core of these ideas. Hurley was convinced that it was possible to

> cooperate with China in bringing about closer relations and harmony with Russia and Britain for the support of the Chinese objectives.[38]

He was far more suspicious of British designs in Southeast Asia than of Soviet ambitions in Northeast Asia, and believed that somehow Russia would welcome the emergence of a strong China on the basis of collaboration among Nationalists, Communists, and other groups.

Diametrically opposed were views of men like John P. Davies and John S. Service, foreign service officers of long residence in China. Their declining enthusiasm for Chiang Kai-shek and growing admiration for the Communists in Yenan are well known. What needs emphasis at this point is their critical image of the Soviet Union. Unlike Hurley they viewed Russia as an ambitious, expansive Asian power, eager to take advantage of any and all opportunities to extend its influence in East Asia. It seemed axiomatic to them that the Soviet Union would gladly support the Chinese Communists in

---

[38] Hurley to Roosevelt, Sept. 23, 1944, ibid.

their struggle against Chungking, not necessarily because the former were Communists but because this would give Russia a further means for penetrating North China. The basic question, according to such an interpretation, was not whether Russia would encourage close ties with the Chinese Communists but rather what could be done about it. Starting from the assumption that the preponderance of Soviet power in China was undesirable from the point of view both of China and of the United States, Davies and others called for an effort by America to cultivate the Communists to stimulate their nationalism and latent pro-American senti-ment. But this could be done only if the United States stopped dealing with the Chiang regime as the sole representative of China but looked to more liberal factions as the leaders of the new China. Otherwise the Communists and other dissident groups would further be alienated from Chungking and America and be driven closer to Russia. Already at the end of 1943 Davies was coming to such a conclusion. As he wrote to Harry Hopkins, the United States must

> avoid finding [itself] at the close of the war backing a coalition of Chiang's Kuomintang and the degenerate puppets against a democratic coalition commanding Russian sympathy.[39]

A year later Davies reiterated the same position:

> We must make a determined effort to capture politically the Chinese Communists rather than allow them to go by default wholly to the Russians.[40]

In the end President Roosevelt adopted a policy which came closer to Hurley's recommendations than to those of foreign service officers. The President authorized Hurley to undertake the task of bringing Nationalists and Communists together to organize a coalition government, but he decided not to aid the Communists directly with arms and advisers, instead continuing to regard Chiang Kai-shek as the only recognized government of wartime China. Reasons for this decision can only be speculated, but it seems clear that considerations of Soviet-Chinese-American relations were quite fundamental. Roosevelt knew that the Soviet Union would be a formidable Asian power after the war as a result of its anticipated declaration of war against Japan. He also knew that Chiang was afraid of the Russians. But the vision of China as an independent country with friendly ties to the United States could only be realized if there were some sort of stability in Chinese-Russian relations. Given Hurley's reports from Moscow that the

---

[39] Davies to Hopkins, Dec. 31, 1943, ibid.
[40] Akira Iriye, *Across the Pacific: An Inner History of American-East Asian Relations* (New York: Harcourt, Brace & Jovanovich, 1967), p. 247.

Russians professed their support of Chungking, it must have seemed to Roosevelt that the Soviet leaders would at least tolerate a unified China under Chiang Kai-shek. To accept the alternative of seeking to align America more closely with the Communists incurred the risk of United States involvement in domestic Chinese affairs, and it was not altogether clear to Roosevelt that the outcome would necessarily be advantageous to the United States. He wanted a friendly China, but not one that caused massive American intervention that left the United States face-to-face with the Soviet Union on the Asian continent.

Thus one comes back to wartime American perceptions of the nation's position and role in the emerging international politics in that part of the world. The above sketch indicates that as far as the United States was concerned it was expected to replace Japan as the predominant military power in the western Pacific, but that on the continent of Asia some sort of condominium was visualized on the basis of the vastly extended power of the Soviet Union and the limited involvement of the United States, with a rehabilitated and stronger China standing in between. Such a scheme left out the whole colonial regions, where it was not at all clear what sort of equilibrium would emerge after the war.

On the whole the other powers fighting on the side of the United States—China, Britain, and the Soviet Union—accepted most of these assumptions about the role of America in the Asia-Pacific region after the war. The factions in China, for instance, were in agreement that the United States would be a far more influential Asian power after the war than before 1940. The fact that both the Nationalists and the Communists turned to the United States for support against the other indicated their assumption that America was likely to remain a critical factor in Chinese domestic politics. Each side knew that once the United States committed itself unequivocally to one side, it was assured of success in the struggle for power inside China. For the same reason the two factions accepted mediation efforts by Hurley in order not to alienate the United States. While his talks with Chiang and Mao failed to bear fruit, it was important for them to retain the goodwill of the United States. In other words, both sides accepted an image of America as a powerful factor in Chinese politics, not only during the war but long after the war was over. Mao Tse-tung told John S. Service,

You are here as China's greatest ally. The fact of your presence is tremendous.[41]

Chiang Kai-shek could not have agreed more. They visualized the continued role of the United States as an Asian power, and each sought to turn this fact to his own advantage.

[41] *Foreign Relations of the United States 1945*, VII, 277 (Washington, D.C.: Government Printing Office, 1969).

Outside China proper, the Chinese were agreed that the European domination in Southeast Asia must either be ended or drastically checked. From the beginning of the Pacific War, the Chinese government and press harped on the theme that China must champion the cause of the oppressed peoples of Asia. As Sun Fo, the son of Sun Yat-sen and a prominent Nationalist official, declared in June 1942, China must destroy not only Japanese imperialism but also other types of imperialism if the nation were to promote lasting peace. Korea, Vietnam, Burma, and India must all become independent.[42] Chiang Kai-shek corresponded with Gandhi and sought to obtain America's support for putting pressure on the British government to grant freedom to the Indians. He was convinced that China had a say in the future of India and of other colonial areas. He more than once approached President Roosevelt with a view to conferring with one another concerning the postwar status of the European colonies in Asia. The Chinese government was also interested in the Korean question and sought to work closely with Koreans in Chungking who might prove to be the leaders of Korea after its liberation from Japanese imperialism. All these initiatives were summed up in a 1943 publication of the Foreign Policy Association in Chungking entitled *Kuo-min wai-chiao* (People's diplomacy). In it the assertion was made that after the war China would emerge as "the stabilizing force in the Pacific" and would have responsibilities toward the oppressed peoples of Asia. If another war was to be prevented, the authors pointed out, then the postwar world must recognize the interests and rights of smaller countries and remove racial prejudices.[43] Here was an image of China as the champion of Asian freedom, whose influence would be opposed to that of the European colonial powers. It is important to recall that such an image was shared by practically all Chinese, and that Chiang Kai-shek was as strongly anti-imperialist as his political opponents.

He had good reason to be even more nationalistic in Northeast Asia. His government repeatedly asserted Chinese sovereignty over Manchuria, and the return to China of Manchuria, Taiwan, and the Pescadores was considered the absolute minimum the country would insist upon at the end of the war. From Chiang's point of view it was essential to regain sovereignty over Manchuria in order to solidify Nationalist control over North China and to build a strong bulwark against Soviet power. For the same reason, the Nationalists were eager to promote the cause of nationalistic Korean groups which would closely cooperate with the Chinese government in the event of Korean liberation from Japanese control. Aware that some Korean nationalists were active in the Soviet Union as well as the United States, Chiang wanted to make sure that the peninsula did not fall to Soviet domination as a result of the return of pro-Soviet Korean nationalists.

[42] Sun Fo, *Chung-kuo yü chan-ho de shih-chieh* (Chungking, 1944), p. 57.
[43] *Kuo-min wai-chiao*, May 15, 1943, pp. 4–5.

The position of the Chinese Communists regarding Northeast Asia was a complicated one due to the history of their association with the Soviet Union. Mao Tse-tung, whose leadership depended on his emphasis on the uniqueness of the Chinese Communist experience, rather than his being a loyal follower of Soviet and Comintern decisions, envisioned a China that would be free of all foreign control. To the extent that he recognized future foreign influences, he had the United States rather than the Soviet Union in mind as the country that might play a vital role in postwar China. However, some of his comrades were more oriented toward the Soviet Union and viewed it as a model for the Chinese Communist movement. They would welcome close ties with their counterpart in Russia and postwar Korea. Even Mao could not ignore the potential advantages of such ties if the struggle against the Kuomintang were to continue. For these reasons there was an element of ambiguity in the Communists' perception of postwar Northeast Asia. Nevertheless, the basic ideology of anti-imperialism was as much part of Nationalist as of Communist thinking. No matter what happened internally, therefore, China as a nation was certain to emerge as a powerful spokesman for national independence and sovereignty throughout Asia.

The Future of European Powers in Asia

The European colonial powers, on their part, were not inclined to take the initiative to redraw the map of Asia after the war. They recognized that the situation in Southeast Asia had altered drastically as a result of the war and Japanese domination, and until the tide of war turned in Europe in the winter of 1943–44 it was at any event unrealistic to give much thought to the future of the region. But Great Britain, to which the colonial governments looked for leadership, did not hesitate to assert its voice in the conduct of the Pacific War as regards its Southeast Asian theater. The coalition warfare, in which Britain was allied with China and the United States, was disadvantageous for the British insofar as they would have to reckon with the strongly anti-colonial orientation of the two. But fortunately for them, American military operations did not extend themselves in any massive way to the European colonial areas, and even before the recall of Stilwell at the end of 1944 the China-Burma-India theater was subdivided between China and Southeast Asia, the latter being placed under undisputed authority of the British command.

From the point of view of the British, French, and Dutch authorities after 1944, when they were able to turn their greater attention to Asian colonial matters, it was essential to recover the colonies and reestablish control over them. They would discuss varying reforms of colonial administrations to accommodate the nationalistic sentiment that had been aroused by the war, but they would not succumb to demands for immediate independence or autonomy. Britain's Southeast Asia Command, under Lord Louis Mountbatten, began to include representatives of France after the latter's liberation. Dutch officers also joined the organization, causing General Wedemeyer to wire Marshall,

> British-Dutch-French are integrating intensified effort to insure recovery of political and economic prewar position in Far East.

Officials of the three governments also set up a liaison office in Kunming with a view to coordinating their policies with respect to China. The European governments acted together on so many occasions that they gave the impression of opposing the efforts by China and the United States to prosecute the war against Japan with vigor. General Hurley, like Wedemeyer, was impressed with what he took to be their imperialist collusion and accused the British, French, and Dutch governments of using

> Chinese and American forces and American Lend Lease equipment for reconquest of their colonial empires [and engaging in] propaganda to justify imperialism as opposed to democracy.[44]

From the British point of view, however, there was no real contradiction or conflict between their policy and that of the United States. Thanks to the recent partial opening of wartime British documents, it is possible to follow the outlines of official perceptions in London. Basically, there was the view that the war would turn the Pacific Ocean into the American sphere of influence, thus creating some sort of an imperial equipoise between it and the European colonies in the rest of Asia. When, toward the end of 1944, the State Department broached the subject of trusteeships to be established for the Japanese mandated islands, Churchill said,

> There must be no question of our being hustled or seduced into declarations affecting British sovereignty in any of the Dominions or Colonies. Pray remember my declaration against liquidating the British Empire. If the Americans want to take Japanese islands which they have conquered, let them do so with our blessing and any form of words that may be agreeable to them. But "hands off the British Empire" is our maxim and it must not be weakened or smirched to please sob-stuff merchants at home or foreigners of any hue.[45]

As is revealed here, the British welcomed the extension of American

[44] Wedemeyer to Marshall, Nov. 15, 1944, Roosevelt Papers; Hurley to Roosevelt, Jan. 2, 1945, ibid.
[45] Churchill to Eden, Dec. 31, 1944, Prime Ministers' Papers, PREM 4, 31/4, Public Record Office (London).

control over the Japanese islands in the Pacific, visualizing a long reign of stability as a consequence, thus precluding the threat of the resurgence of Japanese aggression aimed at the Commonwealth. Cooperation with the United States, then, was to be a major aspect of the postwar order to be established on the ruins of the Japanese empire. When the War Cabinet established a Far Eastern committee in November 1944 to consider peace aims in the Asia-Pacific region, its chairman stressed "the vital necessity to bring about the greatest possible degree of cooperation with the United States." [46] In practice this meant giving America a virtual free-hand to the disposition of the Japanese mandated islands. The Far Eastern committee readily agreed to the view, as a member expressed it in January 1945,

> that, whatever the form of administration and defense, the United States should in fact be primarily responsible for the Japanese mandated islands.[47]

In return for such a policy, it was hoped that the United States would look tolerantly at Britain's imperial policies. As Foreign Secretary Eden wrote to Churchill,

> There is not the slightest question of liquidating the British Empire. On the contrary, we are anxious to persuade the Americans not to go in for half-baked international regimes in any ex-enemy colonies they may take over, nor to advocate them for others, but to accept colonial responsibilities on the same terms as ourselves.[48]

It was much more difficult to visualize Anglo-American cooperation in China. Britain had long been one of the leading powers on the China mainland, with rights and prerogatives going back to the 1840s. Unlike its empire in other parts of Asia, however, British officials were not very sanguine about the prospect of reestablishing their former position in China. They were aware that the United States and possibly the Soviet Union would replace Japan as the preeminent outsiders in postwar China, and that America, in particular, would have vastly expanded its interests and influence, due both to its military involvement in China and its idealistic policy of supporting that country's aspirations as an independent, strong power after the war. Given these developments, British leaders considered it axiomatic that there would be very close ties between China and America, and that the latter would do its best to expand further its interests after victory over Japan. As Eric Teichman, one of the China specialists in the Foreign Office, wrote, in 1943,

---

[46] Far Eastern committee minutes, Nov. 15, 1944, Cabinet Papers, CAB 96/5, ibid.
[47] Far Eastern committee minutes, Jan. 17, 1945, CAB 96/5, ibid.
[48] Eden to Churchill, Jan. 8, 1945, PREM 4, 31/4, ibid.

Comparing China's foreign policy in 1943 with her attitude of ten years earlier, nothing is more striking than her dependence on America and her acceptance of American leadership in her affairs. . . . China looks primarily to America, not Britain, to defeat Japan; to furnish her with the sinews and materials of war; and to build up the Great New China after the war is over. . . . [We] have . . . abdicated from the position of leadership which we have occupied in China for the past hundred years. China is by agreement regarded as in the American theatre of war, a decision the consequences of which seem to become more far-reaching every day. . . . [In] the diplomatic sphere, where ten years ago we naturally took the lead, we now wait anxiously to see what the American Government may do.[49]

As is well known, Churchill and his advisors refused to endorse the American vision of China as a great power, but this was because they interpreted "great power" to mean a world power, having a potential say in affairs outside Asia. When Roosevelt, Hull, and other Americans pictured China as one of the great powers to emerge after the war, they did not have anything specific in mind concerning its role in other parts of the globe. Rather, they thereby sought to bolster China's, and especially Chiang Kai-shek's morale, to keep the country in war and to rid it of Japanese forces and influence. They would support a reunified, strong, and independent China as part of the postwar Asian order, but this did not mean that China would necessarily involve itself in affairs of Europe or the Middle East. The British thought it did, and that was why they reacted to the American idea so vehemently. As Churchill said in March 1943,

It is quite untrue to say that China is a world power equal to Britain, the United States or Russia.

A month later, he was more specific:

The idea that China is going to have a say in the affairs of Europe "other than ceremonial," or that China should be rated for European purposes above France or Poland or whatever takes the place of Austria-Hungary, or above even smaller but ancient, historic and glorious states like Holland, Belgium, Greece and Yugoslavia—has only to be stated to be dismissed.[50]

Not even American officials, however, were contemplating such an eventuality, and what was at issue was not so much China's role in Europe but the extent of American and British interests after the war. Here the spectacle of Chinese-American intimacy, although blown out of proportion

---

[49] Memo by Prideau-Brune, Nov. 30, Far Eastern committee, CAB 96/5, ibid.

[50] Churchill to Cadogan, Mar. 22, 1943, PREM 4, 100/8, ibid.; Churchill memo, Apr. 1943, PREM 4, 100/8, ibid.

by some in Chungking and Washington for propaganda purposes, was a genuine challenge. Britain was clearly on the defensive, and if it was unwilling to join the chorus of praise for China's greatness, it had at least to provide for ways to restore some of the lost economic opportunities. The best tactic under the circumstances was to stress willingness to cooperate with America to restore peace, stability, and prosperity in China in which all could share. As J. C. Sterndale Bennett, the Foreign Office representative in the Far Eastern committee, reported,

> the Foreign Office were much concerned at the way in which the Americans were establishing a monopolistic position for themselves in China. . . . [We] ought to consider how best to protect our interest without entering into rivalry with the Americans, and if possible in cooperation with them.[51]

Given British dependence on the lend-lease, as well as American suspicions of British imperialism in Asia, however, it was not very easy to determine in what ways such "cooperation" could be achieved in postwar China. Ambassador Horace Seymour in Chungking admitted as much when he telegraphed London in January 1945:

> Americans in their task of getting some sort of order into Chinese chaos will want to keep everything under their own control and will not welcome British participation, at any rate, at present stage, except perhaps in production and similar fields. Attitude is likely to be that our help must be so small that it would not be worth the additional complications.[52]

The result was that at the beginning of 1945 there was no comprehensive program for reestablishing British interests in China after the war. Officials had a vision of Anglo-American cooperation in China, but they admitted that it might not be feasible in the immediate future. For all practical purposes, then, their perception of postwar international order in Asia included an image of China that would be primarily under American control and in which Britain would be ejected from the once leading position of power. Admittedly such an interpretation is highly speculative, but if it is basically valid, then it may be noted that there was no overall conflict between the American and British perceptions of China after the war, at least insofar as that country's relations with the powers were concerned.

Russian Aspirations in the Far East

The same observation may be made about Soviet attitudes, although here one has to be even more tentative in drawing conclusions from the limited

---

[51] Far Eastern committee minutes, Dec. 21, 1944, CAB 96/5, ibid.

[52] Seymour to Foreign Office, Jan. 17, 1945, in Far Eastern committee memo of Mar. 5, 1945, CAB 96/5, ibid.

amount of available sources. Soviet historians usually describe Russian policy during the Pacific War in ideological terms. V. B. Vorontsov, for instance, has written that the victories of the Red Army in Europe enhanced Russian prestige among the colonial peoples of Asia and raised their hopes for independence, whereas the United States, although ostensibly supporting self-determination and national liberation, was in fact hoping to replace the European powers in Asia and the Pacific. America's espousal of trusteeship arrangements was calculated to achieve this objective; they would substitute the old colonialism with a new order in Asia and the Pacific under the control of the United States. The Soviet Union, on the contrary, accepted the idea of trusteeships as a transitory device to help the colonial peoples obtain ultimate independence. As of the beginning of 1945, however, the direction of American policy was not yet definite, part of its leaders, including President Roosevelt, accepting the inevitable participation of the Soviet Union in the postwar Asia-Pacific order and the rest determined to establish American hegemony to suppress the Russian-supported national liberation movements.[53]

As for Soviet policy toward China, a recent book by O. B. Borisov and B. T. Kolaskov points out that conditions in China were deteriorating by the winter of 1944–45, and that the anti-Japanese front was crumbling. It was only through arms sent by the Soviet Union that the Chinese were able to maintain their opposition to Japan. The latter held on to its position on the Asia mainland, especially in Manchuria, because its ambitions for establishing a new order would never be fulfilled without destroying Russia, given its support of anti-Japanese partisans, and for this reason it was preparing for an ultimate war with the Soviet Union. Under the circumstances, the anti-imperialistic, revolutionary forces in China needed the support of world progressive forces, of which Russia was the leader. The Soviet role in China was thus in contrast to that envisioned by some in the United States who were seeking to entrench American power in postwar China through their aid to and encouragement of Chiang Kai-shek.[54]

These generalizations indicate an idealized image of what, from the Soviet perspective, should have happened, an *ex post facto* vision of what historians would like to have seen happen. While they are useful as a guide to the ideological component of Soviet policy, they do not give enough detailed information concerning the specific content of policy. All one can attempt, in the absence of sufficient data and studies, is to draw rough outlines on the basis of documents on wartime agreements and conferences. First of all, in Northeast Asia it seems reasonably clear that Stalin wanted the retrocession of South Sakhalin and the Kuriles from Japan, and he wanted to regain the

---

[53] V. B. Vorontsov, *Tikhookeanskaia politika SShA, 1941–1950* (Moscow: Nauka, 1967).

[54] O. B. Borisov and B. T. Koloskov, *Sovetsko-kitaiskie otnosheniia, 1945–1970* (Moscow: Mysl', 1971).

rights Russia had enjoyed in Manchuria before the Russo-Japanese War. These, plus the organization of Korean partisans in Moscow, were obviously intended for postwar Soviet extension of power in that part of the world. Stalin was determined not to share such power with other countries. As was the case in Eastern Europe, he did not look with favor upon a scheme to internationalize control over areas adjacent to the Soviet Union. While the Chinese, for instance, suggested the establishment of a mandate system for the Kuriles, Stalin insisted on their outright retrocession. He was also extremely reluctant to have Russian air bases in eastern Siberia used by American bombers for raiding Japan. While he agreed to their use in principle, negotiations dragged on for months, and in the end no American installation was permitted in the Maritime Provinces. The underlying cause was the fear that American forces, once established on Soviet soil, would be difficult to remove, and the whole region of Northeast Asia would be affected as a result. Russia wanted sole and not shared control over the area. Such a fear in part explains why Stalin delayed Soviet entry into war against Japan. A premature declaration of war against the latter might justify the United States as an ally in name as well as in fact to insist on joint strategy and use of the Siberian airfields. So long as Russia was not technically in the Pacific War, American requests could be denied on legal grounds.

Toward China Soviet policy seems to have been likewise calculated to maximize Russian power in Northeast Asia. There was no thought of establishing Soviet hegemony over China. Rather, the assumption was that China would continue to be unstable and disunified after victory over Japan, and therefore that it was unlikely to pose a serious threat to Soviet interests. Stalin and his advisers were willing to continue to deal with Chiang Kai-shek as the government of China, knowing fully well that the latter was incapable of strengthening Kuomintang authority over the country. But little seemed to be gained by an open avowal of support for the Chinese Communists. Stalin did not altogether trust Mao and his followers. Molotov was not intentionally being deceptive when he told Hurley in 1944 that the Chinese Communists were not really Communists. From the Russian perspective, they indeed seemed a strange gang of ragged agrarian reformers. Until and unless the Chinese Communists came under control of Moscow-trained and oriented leaders, it was unwise to commit the Soviet Union exclusively to their support. Their campaigns against the Nationalists would not be discouraged, but the Soviet Union would do little to promote their cause. In the meantime, Russia would acquire certain harbors and railways in Manchuria, and make sure that these rights would be safeguarded no matter what happened in China domestically.

Thus the Soviet Union viewed China as something less than a full-fledged power. In fact, Russian leaders may have assumed that postwar China would fall within the American sphere of influence. Certainly, if

China was not likely to emerge unified and strengthened immediately after the war, and if an outside power was to exert its influence, the United States must have appeared to be the most likely candidate. In this sense, there was no real gap among the Russian, American, and British perceptions of postwar China. The main contrast was in the willingness of some Americans to have an idealized image of a strong China, whereas the Russians, like the British, did not consider China one of the great powers to be predominant in postwar world affairs.

The Yalta Conference

By the beginning of 1945, then, there had been a vast transformation both in the structure of international relations in the Asia-Pacific region and in the role of the United States. Japanese imperialistic expansion and contraction had not only shaken the foundation of the European colonial empires in the Southwestern Pacific and East Asia, but had also provided an opportunity for reassertion of power by China and the Soviet Union. As Japan, the one country that had defined the international order of the area for over a decade, was about to be defeated and its far-flung dominion demolished, a new Asian-Pacific system of international relations was in the process of creation. By far the most striking aspect of the emerging order was the vast extension of American power westward across the Pacific. The United States was now the predominant power in the western Pacific, and it had established close ties with various groups in China. Its influence was felt among Koreans, Vietnamese, and others struggling for sovereignty. And yet most of these developments were the consequences of the war against Japan, and military expediencies had dictated America's responses to them. How far the United States was going to involve itself in Asian affairs, and what roles it was to play in the whole region, were questions that had not been systematically dealt with. What sort of structure for postwar peace and stability would emerge, then, depended on the as yet undefined policies and attitudes of the United States as much as on those of Russia, China, Britain, and other countries.

The Yalta Conference, convened in February 1945, can be characterized as the occasion when such defining was attempted.[55] It was here that the heads of the three greatest powers—Churchill, Roosevelt, and Stalin—met and came to a number of crucial decisions which were to determine the shape of the postwar world for years to come and which, in fact, laid a foundation for what later developed as the Cold War. These decisions covered practically every region of the globe, and therefore it is important to view the Yalta

[55] For the best treatment of the Yalta Conference, see Diane Shaver Clemens, *Yalta* (New York: Oxford University Press, 1971).

agreements on Asia as related to those on Europe, the Middle East, and other matters. The agreements signified the readiness of the three powers to come to some basic understanding on the nature of their interrelationships after the war and on the way each would play a role in postwar world politics.

These agreements can be summarized briefly. In Europe the three powers accepted new boundary lines between Poland and Russia. Eastern Poland was awarded to the Soviet Union, but Poland was to be given compensation at the expense of Germany. The three powers were to divide up Germany into zones of occupation and consult further on amounts of reparation payments the latter would be required to pay. In the Middle East the three governments agreed to revise the Montreux Convention of 1936 that had restricted wartime navigation through the Straits, so that the Russian wishes for some extension of rights and interests in Turkey could be accommodated. In Asia and the Pacific the conference established the trusteeship system for the mandate territories held by the enemy, thereby assuring America's control over the Pacific islands seized from Japan. The Soviet Union on its part was formally guaranteed the retrocession of the Kurile Islands and South Sakhalin in the event of its entry into the Pacific War. It would also receive a lease of Port Arthur, while the port of Dairen would be internationalized. A joint Sino-Soviet management would be established for the railways in Manchuria, and in Outer Mongolia the United States and Britain would recognize its autonomy, separating it from China proper. However, these agreements concerning Manchuria and Outer Mongolia would require concurrence of the Chinese government, and, according to the language of the Yalta agreement,

> The President will take measures in order to obtain this concurrence on advice from Marshal Stalin.

Moreover, the Soviet Union would negotiate with the Chungking regime for a new pact of friendship and alliance to formalize Russian assistance to Chiang Kai-shek. The final agreements signed at the Yalta Conference did not mention Korea, but Roosevelt and Stalin came to a meeting of minds regarding a possible trusteeship for Korea, to be sustained by the United States, the Soviet Union, and China.

The Yalta agreements more or less corresponded to the realities of power politics toward the end of the war, to the perceptions of these realities by the three leading nations, and to their visions of a new world order which would provide a framework for postwar international relations and accommodate their respective interests and desires. Thus in Europe it was clear that liberated France, tied to Great Britain, would be restored as a viable power, while these two plus the United States and the Soviet Union would establish a condominium over Germany. Greece and Italy would be under British influence, but Eastern Europe and the Balkans would fall under Soviet domination. In the meantime, the United States would be involved militarily in France, Italy, and Germany as an extension of wartime operations, but President Roosevelt expressed his intention of withdrawing American forces from Europe within two years. In other words, the United States would, for the time being, play a role as a European power in certain areas, but not in Eastern or Southeastern Europe where Soviet supremacy was recognized. In the Middle East the Yalta conversations revealed some understanding that Russia had certain rights and interests in Turkey and northern Iran, the rest being considered a British sphere of influence and power. American interests were growing throughout the Middle East, but they were not of a military or political nature as yet. In all these instances the Yalta accord awarded to each of the Big Three either what it already controlled or was on the point of controlling, and sought to restructure international relations on the basis of the emerging power realities. Churchill expressed his confidence in the new balance of power when he remarked, "Poor Neville Chamberlain believed he could trust Hitler. He was wrong. But I don't think I'm wrong about Stalin." [56]

In the Asia-Pacific region, likewise, the Yalta Conference explicitly or implicitly defined the dispositions and limits of the respective spheres of influence of the Big Three. The United States would remain the dominant power in the Pacific and exercise the greatest control over Japan after the war, while the Soviet Union would reestablish its predominant position in Northeastern Asia. Together the two countries would expand their power and influence in China, although the latter would maintain its status as an independent power, much as Turkey would in the Middle East. This was a rather ambiguous situation, certainly a far cry from the view expressed by some American officials earlier that China was to become one of the great powers after the war. The Yalta agreements on China suggest that, as far as the framework of postwar politics was concerned, the United States was looking to the Soviet Union as a stabilizing force, as a partner in the new equilibrium, rather than to a balance of power among America, Russia, China, and Britain on the mainland of Asia. This does not mean that the *idea* of China as a sovereign nation was no longer important. It will be seen that such an idea was to play a critical role in the development of American-Soviet relations after Yalta. But China as a *power* was no longer as relevant to American policy as bilateral cooperation between the United States and the Soviet Union, both in the war against Japan and in building a durable structure of peace after the latter's defeat. President Roosevelt's willingness to agree to Soviet demands on Manchuria and Outer Mongolia was symbolic; it meant that he preferred to deal with Russia as a major partner, even if it

---

[56] *The Diaries of Sir Alexander Cadogan* (New York: Putnam, 1972) p. 716.

involved sacrificing part of Chinese sovereignty. He seems to have believed that American-Russian understanding was absolutely essential if China was to be a viable entity in postwar Asia.

As for Great Britain, nothing was done to alter its status in the colonial regions. Roosevelt and Stalin generally agreed during Yalta that the European powers should make their exit from Southeast Asia sooner or later, but no formal initiative was taken by them in this direction. The trusteeship principle, adopted at the conference, specifically excluded the existing mandates and colonies from its application, thereby ensuring the continued presence, at least theoretically, of European colonialism in Asia. In other words, the Yalta Conference was in accordance with British desires to retain its predominant status in Southeast Asia, conceding the Pacific to the United States and Northeast Asia to the Soviet Union. Nevertheless, it was painfully evident to British officials that their nation's position and influence in the Asia-Pacific region would not compare with those of the other two powers. Churchill was adamant about problems closer to home, such as the participation of France in the occupation of Germany, the suppression of rebels in Greece, and the maintenance of superior rights in the Middle East. He was willing and eager to see Britain fully participate in postwar politics, in particular vis-à-vis the Soviet Union, in Europe and the Middle East. In Asia and the Pacific, however, the future was far from certain. The best that could be hoped for under the circumstances was the possibility that the American hegemony in the Pacific would adequately safeguard Imperial security and that the United States would find it possible to "cooperate" with Britain in China. In the meantime, preparations would be made so as to claim at least Southeast Asia as Britain's sphere of influence. At least that would serve to help Britain maintain the status of a great power in the area. As Churchill told the War Cabinet after Yalta, it was only through the "strong sense of unity and common purpose" linking together different parts of the Empire that "we could maintain the influence of the British Commonwealth as a world power." [57]

Thus was created the Yalta system of international relations. Necessarily vague as any international system is, it nevertheless was a landmark in the history of world politics in general and of Asian-Pacific relations in particular. It formally put an end to one era of international relations and ushered in another. In the Asia-Pacific region, it replaced the long period of Anglo-Japanese domination, which had been followed by Japan's determination to establish a new order, with a situation in which the United States and the Soviet Union divided the region into two spheres of predominance, with certain grey areas in between, of which China was the most conspicuous. It would recover lands it had lost to Japan, but it would compromise its

[57] War cabinet confidential annex, Apr. 3, 1945, CAB 65/52, Public Record Office.

sovereignty in Manchuria. Japan would be totally crushed and come under United States control, while Korea would be detached from Japan and placed under some sort of trusteeship. In the meantime, Great Britain, a junior partner in Big-Three politics, would try to regain and retain a position of predominance in Southeast Asia. It remained to be seen how viable such a system would be, and whether it would bring about a period of peace and stability in the Asia-Pacific region.

CHAPTER
FOUR

The
Decline
of
the
Yalta
System

TWO TYPES OF COOPERATION

The Yalta system of international relations entailed essentially a United States-Soviet definition of world politics. It expressed the two strongest powers' interest in reaching an understanding on the framework of international relations after the war. Both the Soviet Union and the United States perceived themselves as global powers, and they recognized the desirability of outlining the limits of each other's spheres of influence outside the national boundaries. The assumption was that the two countries would find it possible to live with the emerging global status quo which would provide the basis for postwar peace. At the same time, their respective national interests—such as considerations of domestic stability, national security, and economic well-being—seemed well served by the new arrangements. The Yalta system granted each power overseas bases to ensure national security, and it codified the existing influences of the two countries in Europe and Asia based on actual armed strengths. In other words, both calculations of national interests as traditionally defined and geo-political considerations of world-wide power balances were factors that sustained the American and Soviet governments as they accepted the Yalta agreements.

Security and Power

These were also principles that persuaded American officials to accept the framework of United States-Soviet understanding in the emerging world order. They approved of it in part because it seemed to safeguard the national interest—which was in the process of broadening and redefining, but which was still couched in terms of the nation's basic security and economic needs. For instance, Secretary of War Henry L. Stimson wrote that the Yalta agreements

> so long as they are interpreted consistently with our traditional policy toward China, should not cause us any concern from a security point of view, assuming always we keep clear our control over the Pacific islands. By our traditional policy toward China I refer, of course, to the Open Door and the recognition of Chinese sovereignty over Manchuria.[1]

Here was a clear enunciation of the national interests as they were being perceived at the end of the war, and as they were related to the Yalta system. As Stimson noted, United States security now embraced the Pacific islands, including those captured from Japan. The entire ocean, in fact, was now turning into an American zone of defense. The Yalta conversations had accepted this *fait accompli*. At the same time, toward China Stimson was content with the age-old policy of economic expansion which had traditionally been couched in terms of Chinese sovereignty and the principle of equal commercial opportunity. This was an economically-oriented policy, and the Yalta agreement concerning China seemed conducive to creating a favorable environment for promoting such a goal. After all Japan, which had kept China under its economic control and denied its rich market and resources to other countries, would be ejected from the continent, and the United States would be provided with a real opportunity for undertaking the modernization and development of the postwar Chinese economy. Although the principle of equal opportunity was a little compromised by the special privileges accorded the Soviet Union in Manchuria, the Yalta agreement had specifically said that China would "retain full sovereignty in Manchuria." Such a declaration might be worth little, but it was entirely consistent with

[1] Stimson to Truman, July 16, 1945, *Foreign Relations 1945*, VII, 943.

the traditional American approach to China. The United States would now, as it had in the past, assert certain key principles of the Open Door in China, but their practical implications would be primarily economic. There was little in the Yalta accord that was disturbing from the traditional perspective of United States interests in East Asia.

Considerations of more or less immediate conventional national interests, however, were not the sole determinant of policy. There was also concern with power politics in the world arena. American approaches to the Asia-Pacific region not only reflected specific national needs but had meaning as part of a global strategy as the United States sought to cope with the aftermath of the war. The Yalta agreement could be seen as a reflection of the worldwide balance of power among the Soviet Union, the United States, and Great Britain. In the Asia-Pacific region the former two would be the main stabilizing forces. To the global strategists the power realities of an international situation defined the basic structure for peace and understanding among nations, and it was desirable to seek to accommodate the requirements of the national interest to this overall framework. As George F. Kennan wrote in September 1944 in discussing Soviet foreign policy, the issue

> is not a question of boundaries or of constitutions or of formal independence of areas under Soviet control. It is a question of real power relationships, more often than not carefully masked or concealed.[2]

From such a perspective, it made sense to come to grips with the realities of Soviet power and deal with it in terms of the power of the United States. The Yalta Conference was an occasion for doing so, and the resulting agreements would be worthwhile to the extent that they corresponded to such realities. The Yalta system, insofar as it defined the limits of power for the three strongest nations, was a viable foundation for developing postwar relations among them.

It is only in this sense, in the context of globalistic considerations, that there can be said to have been some degree of "cooperation" between the United States and the Soviet Union. What the Yalta agreements signified was cooperation in a power-political sense. The Big Two, plus Britain as occasion called for, would "cooperate" in that they would have a basic understanding of each other's relative strengths and weaknesses in specific areas of the world, and would oppose attempts at radically altering the existing power realities. This was expedient cooperation derived from considerations of power. Since power is by definition amoral, American-Russian "cooperation" as developed through the Yalta system was also devoid of ideological or moralistic content. It was purely a military and Realpolitik-like concept. It did not mean that the two nations would cooperate in an

[2] George F. Kennan, *Memoirs 1925–1950* (Boston: Little, Brown, 1967), p. 228.

idealistic sense, for instance by sharing certain political ideals, entertaining moralistic visions of the new world order, or pursuing similar economic goals.

The Role of Ideals

Nevertheless, it was extremely tempting to think that cooperation with the Soviet Union entailed not merely military collaboration against the common enemy and global agreements on the basis of power relations, but also, and even fundamentally, some sort of genuine understanding between the two countries. Walter Lippmann, for instance, argued in his *U.S. War Aims* (1944) that lasting peace after the war could be achieved only on the basis of regional systems of security, of which the "Atlantic Orbit" under American-British control and the "Soviet Orbit" would be predominant and would balance themselves against one another. This was pure power politics. But then Lippmann proceeded to talk of America's mission to spread democracy throughout the world and the need to persuade the Russians to practice freedom and democracy within its "orbit." In this way there would be universal adherence to these principles, and the two powers would be establishing a moral basis for the peace. This was not power politics. It was more ideological and more universalistic than the global-strategic stress on power. This type of image of American-Russian relations may be termed "internationalist." In contrast to the Realpolitik concern with the structure of world politics, it represented an idealistic vision of American-Soviet relations, characterized by the assumption that there was a great deal more than simply military power and political expediencies that tied the two nations, indeed any combination of nations, together.

Idealistic vision, of course, had always constituted one strand of American perceptions of international affairs. We have seen how the United States had related itself to other nations in terms both of the structure of international politics and of an idealized image of what the country stood for in the world. Lippmann was heir to this tradition. He wanted to find moral meaning in the war, and to view the wartime alliance not simply as a military undertaking but as an ideological and idealistic commitment. Since it was much easier to perceive such a relationship between the United States and Great Britain than between the former and the Soviet Union, it is not surprising that he was fascinated by the possibilities of genuine understanding and cooperation between America and Russia. From such a perspective, he could argue that there would be no viable peace until these two countries came to the meeting of minds, not merely on power-oriented questions, but fundamentally on the issue of how the great powers were going to conduct themselves after the war in areas under their predominant influence—in short, until there was a shared vision, an internationalist perception, of the postwar world to serve as an ideological underpinning for the new balance of power.

The Yalta Conference could easily abet optimism in this direction. The final communiqué expressed the Big Three's resolve to maintain "continuing and growing cooperation and understanding among our three countries and among all peace-loving nations" so that "the highest aspirations of humanity [may] be realized—a secure and lasting peace." This was internationalist language *par excellence.* It seemed that the wartime alliance would be transformed into postwar "cooperation and understanding" among the great powers. In fact, of course, the secret agreements at Yalta dealt mostly with conventional questions of power, security, and spheres of influence. Big-Three "cooperation" was achieved, but not in an idealistic sense but primarily in geo-political terms. By attributing to the Yalta system much idealistic meaning that did not exist there, the initially enthusiastic supporters of American-Soviet "cooperation" were soon to turn bitterly against it.

This proclivity to assume the existence of an idealistic basis of the Yalta system was to contribute to conceptual ambiguity when the relationship between the two powers deteriorated. Here was a fundamental root of the Cold War ideology in the United States, as will be seen. At this point it should be sufficient to note that the government in the United States also tended to identify (and thereby confuse) the geopolitical and idealistic aspects of the Yalta agreements, and to view United States-Soviet "cooperation" idealistically. Because the two had accepted some specific arrangements at Yalta, they believed that an era of real understanding and cooperation between the two had arrived. That is why they were prone to be dismayed by the Soviet government's ruthless tactics in Eastern Europe, especially Poland, to impose pro-Russian regimes against democratic principles. The Yalta Conference had adopted a "declaration on liberated Europe," calling for establishment of representative governments in areas liberated from Germany, an expression of America's internationalist concerns. Although neither Stalin nor Roosevelt seriously thought such a goal was practical, the American people made much of the declaration, especially since the secret clauses of the Yalta accord were unknown to them. Officials, too, from time to time stressed the internationalist as opposed to geo-political aspect of the Yalta agreements, and they professed to be disappointed when Stalin did not carry out free elections and practice parliamentary procedures in Eastern Europe. President Roosevelt himself told Stalin a month before his death that the continuation in office of the Soviet-supported Lublin government in Poland was a violation of the Yalta accord, saying,

> I must make it quite plain to you that any such solution which would result in a thinly disguised continuance of the present Warsaw regime would be unacceptable and would cause the people of the United States to regard the Yalta agreement as having failed.[3]

[3] Cited by John Lewis Gaddis, *The United States and the Origins of the Cold War* (New York: Columbia University Press, 1972), p. 172.

Obviously, he was giving the Yalta system a different meaning from Stalin's view. There was an internationalist ingredient that was lacking in the Soviet understanding of the Yalta agreements. Roosevelt was never totally captivated by a vision of true cooperation with Russia, and he was willing to stress the positive achievements of the Yalta Conference, relating to the three powers' spheres of influence. But ambiguities remained, and they were to produce not only the rhetoric of the Cold War but also conceptual confusion in the rhetoric itself.

Given such a wide range of assumptions about the achievements of the Yalta Conference, it is not surprising that East Asia should have been as critical an area as Eastern Europe in the implementation of the new accord. If anything, the picture in East Asia was far more complex, since Eastern Europe had been assigned to the Soviet Union as its sphere of influence, whereas the Yalta system envisioned an independent though militarily still weak China. In terms of the structure of Asian politics, China was not to fall either under Soviet or American control but was to exist as an entity sandwiched between the two strongest powers' extended dominions. China's sovereignty had been compromised by the granting of rights and privileges to Russia as well as the presence of American armed forces, but it was expected to emerge from the war as lying outside the Big Two's immediate spheres of predominance. This was an imprecise formulation, leaving open the possibility either that one of the Big Two might try to extend its power to China, or that the latter itself might come to challenge their roles in Asia.

Even more difficult to foresee was the nature of American-Russian "cooperation" in the internationalist sense. To those who viewed the Yalta system in an idealistic way, as ensuring real cooperation between the two, it seemed axiomatic that they would cooperate in China as well as elsewhere in Asia, as they shared the vision of a new peaceful East Asia. This would entail Soviet encouragement of Chinese unification and sovereignty, aims which the United States government had promoted. America and Russia, in other words, would pursue similar objectives and principles in China as they worked together to consolidate the new order in that part of the world. China would thus be providing a specific content in which the Big Two would try to achieve the "cooperation and understanding" they talked about at Yalta. That country would thus become the symbol of American-Russian cooperation in Asia. From such a perspective, events in China and in Sino-Soviet relations were apt to be viewed in terms of their relevance to the vision of understanding between the United States and the Soviet Union. If things did not go as expected in China, then the whole edifice of Yalta internationalism would be at stake.

A good example of official thinking along these lines was a memorandum by John Carter Vincent, chief of the division of Chinese affairs of the State Department, written for Ambassador Hurley on April 2, 1945.

Vincent's view of American-Russian-Chinese relations was quite clear:

> We want Chinese military unity now for more effective prosecution of the war against Japan; and we want China united territorially and politically in the post-war period so that she can in cooperation with us and the Russians make her contribution toward security and well-being in the Far East. The Russians can understand this; and they can understand that obverse: disunity in China will surely lead to dissension and threaten conflict among the Pacific Powers.

The last sentences revealed Vincent's image of what had been agreed to at Yalta: a unified China as part of the new structure of peace being erected by the Soviet Union and the United States. The first half of this passage, on the other hand, was an expression of an idealistic hope that "cooperation" among the three countries could be achieved in such a way as to establish and promote peace in postwar Asia. Power and idealistic assumptions were neatly combined to present a coherent picture of American policies toward both Russia and China. Chinese unification, in this analysis, was a test-case and a symbol of American-Soviet understanding, both in a realpolitik sense and in terms of internationalist "cooperation." More specifically, according to Vincent, the United States should put pressure on Chiang Kai-shek, and Russia on the Chinese Communists, so that the contending factions in China would come together politically instead of attempting to defeat the other by force of arms. Vincent was convinced that

> Chiang will yield only to firm and consistent pressure—but he will yield.

As for the Communists, his view was equally unequivocal:

> It is useless to bring Chiang around to 'coalition' if you can't count on the Communists and you can't count on the Communists unless you can count on Russia.

Thus one came back to where one started: American-Russian cooperation. Vincent firmly believed, in his words, that

> In spite of the reports on Rumania and Poland . . . we can reach an understanding with Russia in regard to China on which we can rely.

Then, like an afterthought, he concluded the memorandum by introducing the ingredient of national-interest considerations. As he said,

> It is essential that we make clear our interests, that our interests be real—not theoretical or sentimental, and that Russia be convinced of our determination to support our interests fully but not in a manner antagonistic to Russia.

Vincent did not specify what these interests entailed, but obviously there was a harmony and unity among the geo-political, idealistic, and national-interest components of United States policy in China.[4]

Allied Cooperation for the Pacific War

The period between the death of President Roosevelt (April 12) and the Japanese surrender (August 14) was to test the validity of such a perception. In Europe this was a period of increasing mutual suspicion between America and Russia, and the vision of their "cooperation" throughout the world was becoming blurred. Nevertheless, it provided much of the conceptual framework of American policy at the end of the Pacific War, the more so since Soviet entry into the war against Japan continued to be seen as a necessity by most American officials. From Stalin's point of view, now that the war in Europe was about over, there was every reason to look favorably upon participation in the Pacific War. A week before Roosevelt's death, the Soviet government notified Japan that it had no intention of renewing the neutrality treaty between the two countries, due to expire in 1946. The obvious implication was that Russia would regard itself freed from the terms of the agreement and enter war as soon as practicable—three months after the German surrender, according to what Stalin had told Roosevelt at Yalta. Soviet aircraft and ground troops were shifted to the East and readied for action.

If there was one country that was taking the apparent friction between the Soviet Union and the United States in the spring and early summer of 1945 with the utmost seriousness, it may have been Japan. The defeat of Germany coincided with the firebombing of major Japanese cities, the March 10 raid on Tokyo alone destroying 15.8 square miles and 267,171 buildings, killing 83,793 people, injuring an additional 40,918, and leaving 1,008,005 homeless. Simultaneously with the bombing raids, bloody battles were fought on the Ryukyu islands, and their fall in June brought United States forces physically close to Japan proper. It was in response to such disasters that the Japanese Emperor began expressing his desire for peace and the Tokyo government decided to seek Soviet mediation. The rationale for such an attempt was the Japanese government's perception of the intricate relations among the United States, the Soviet Union, and Great Britain. Rift seemed to be developing between Russia on one hand and the Anglo-American powers on the other. Given the major thrust of Japanese wartime policy, it is not surprising that the officials should have tried to take advantage of such a rift by befriending the Soviet Union. If indeed there was friction between America and Russia, it made sense to approach the latter and, by offering it

[4] Vincent to Hurley, April 2, 1945, *Foreign Relations 1945*, VII, 323–25.

inducements, to obtain its good offices to bring the war to an end on something other than unconditionally dictated terms. The Japanese were so eager to mollify the Russians and so confident of preserving the latter's technical neutrality in the Pacific War that they were willing to offer to give up its rights in Manchuria as well as Sakhalin. As the Supreme War Council's May 14 decision put it,

> We should persuade the Soviet Union that, in view of the inevitable conflict between Russia and America in the future, it would be to its advantage to preserve Japan's strong international position, and that it would be desirable for Japan, Russia, and China to cooperate against Britain and the United States.

To indicate Japan's earnestness in seeking Soviet mediation, it would be willing to restore South Sakhalin, the railways in northern Manchuria, the leases of Dairen and Port Arthur, and other rights to the Soviet Union. In the worst case, Japan would be prepared to cede the northern half of the Kurile islands, although it would still wish to retain Korea under its control. In other words, Japan would give up the rights it had acquired after the Russo-Japanese War, the rights the United States had just promised the Soviet Union at the Yalta Conference.

Russia was thus in a position of being wooed simultaneously by Japan and the United States, both of which were offering it almost identical prizes. Soviet policy for the time being was to play with time, not willing to break off relations with Japan prematurely. But the latter was fighting a losing battle, diplomatically as well as militarily, not the least because its assumption about the inevitability of American-Russian conflict was too simplistic. It ignored the fact that the Yalta system had assigned Japan to the sphere of American preponderance, and Japan would not have much leverage after the war to play the victorious powers off against one another. Stalin had already been promised Sakhalin, the Kuriles, and various rights in South Manchuria by the United States, and because these were the limits of Soviet ambitions, there was little point in breaking up the wartime coalition, now concretized in the Yalta system, by accepting the Japanese offer of an alliance in an as yet only dimly perceived future conflict. Soviet global strategy as well as its immediate national interests in the Asia-Pacific region were much better served by the preservation rather than by destruction of the Yalta system.

In the United States, too, there was little inclination after the death of President Roosevelt to give up the framework of the Yalta understanding. For most officials, there was the immediate objective of obtaining Soviet entry into the Pacific War. Since it was expected to take place sooner or later, they believed that the Yalta agreements would provide the continuing basis for military collaboration against Japan. Actually, Soviet participation in the war would have the effect of strengthening the ties between the two countries. American officials were aware of Japanese overtures to the Soviet Union, as well as of the desires of some in Tokyo for an early peace. But they believed Russia was destined to come into the war and help shorten its duration. Even those who were becoming more and more skeptical about the feasibility of "cooperation" with Russia in Eastern Europe had little cause for worry as far as the Pacific Ocean was concerned. Soviet entry into war would merely confirm the Yalta arrangements and confer Russia what was essentially its possessions and rights.

Most American officials, of course, did not know that the secret Manhattan Project, developing atomic weapons, was nearing completion and that the first atomic bombs were being readied for use against Japan. They continued to draft memoranda on the war and postwar policies without this knowledge, and they assumed that the Soviet war against Japan would have vital military significance. Even those who were privy to the atomic secrets, however, viewed them primarily in the context of the war against Japan. They accepted as a matter of fact that any weapon would be used to hasten the end of the war, whether the weapon be the atomic bomb or Soviet troops. These two were not considered mutually exclusive except by a few officials who felt that the successful development of atomic bombs would obliterate the need to rely on Soviet military aid. But the matter was primarily a military-strategic one, and the atomic weapons did not initially present themselves as anything other than a means of bringing about Japanese surrender as speedily as possible. Since the Pacific Ocean, including Japan proper, had already been recognized as an American sphere of power, all that the bombs or Soviet troops did was to shorten the duration of the Pacific War; they did not alter the nature of America's postwar position in the Pacific. It may also be pointed out that regardless of when Japan surrendered—before or after the dropping of the atom bombs—the United States would have emerged as the predominant Pacific power. It can be argued, as some writers have, that the use of the terrible weapons would have been unnecessary if the Japanese had been given specific assurances that the Emperor system would be preserved. Joseph C. Grew, John P. Davies, and several other officials of the State Department were convinced in the spring of 1945 that Japan had been so badly beaten that it would consent to end the war on that basis. An earlier defeat would not only have spared the Japanese the atomic holocaust, but it might have served to preserve Japan as a viable military entity. But it would not have altered the basic fact that the country would fall under the control and influence of the United States. In the larger framework of American-Soviet relations, Japan's surrender either shortly before or shortly after the dropping of atomic bombs would not have affected the Yalta system.

At any event, at the Potsdam Conference, held in July, the United

States, now represented by President Harry S. Truman, reaffirmed its interest in seeking Soviet participation in the war. He also intimated to Stalin that a new type of bomb would be used against Japan. The two leaders reiterated their policy that Korea should be detached and placed under a trusteeship, although American officials told their Soviet counterpart that the invasion of the peninsula by United States forces was unlikely until after the landing of the home islands. The Potsdam Declaration of July 26 with which the Soviet Union associated itself on August 8, the day of its entry into the war against Japan, called on the Japanese government to surrender unconditionally or risk total destruction by new weapons. Although the Japanese Emperor and cabinet were receptive, the latter decided to seek clarification of terms through the Soviet Union, still holding on to the lingering hope that it could be separated from the Anglo-American enemies. In the meantime, Prime Minister Suzuki Kantarō announced that his government was going to "ignore" the Potsdam Declaration, which in Japanese parlance meant he was going to continue to study it while seeking clarification. This was a grave mistake in the use of language, and the United Nations launched their final assault on Japan, bringing about its formal surrender on August 14.

Domestic Politics in China

This sequence of events was essentially as foreseen in the scenario of the Yalta Conference. Paralleling these developments, however, was the far more intricate question of China. The spring and summer of 1945 saw the beginning of the erosion of the kind of synthesis Vincent's April 2 memorandum had postulated concerning the future of American policy on the continent of Asia. There continued the policy of maintaining the Yalta status quo as far as American-Soviet relations in China were concerned. In other words, American officials maintained the stand that China as an independent entity, placed between the two great powers, was a vital part of the new structure of international relations in East Asia. This meant that the United States should oppose a possible violation of the system by the Soviet Union, going beyond the limits delineated at the Yalta Conference. As a memorandum by the State Department's division of Eastern European affairs put it in May,

> While we should in no case try to prevent the attainment of legitimate Soviet interests in China, we should in our own interest exert every effort to prevent Soviet influence from becoming predominant in China.[5]

In the same vein President Truman telegraphed Chiang Kai-shek in July,

[5] Durbrow memo, May 10, 1945, ibid., 865.

I asked that you carry out the Yalta agreement but I had not asked that you make any concession in excess of that agreement.[6]

The United States was officially committed to, and willing to accept, the Yalta definition of the Asia-Pacific status quo, but it would not want China to be submerged into the Soviet orbit.

In thinking about the application of the Yalta understanding to China, American officials were compelled to pay closer and closer attention to Chinese domestic politics, in particular the growing strength and belligerency of the Communists. A unified and more or less independent China was essential if Soviet power were to be confined to the limits prescribed by the Yalta system, and, conversely, the continuing civil strife and chaos in China could conceivably bring about Soviet predominance on the Asian continent, either by supporting the Chinese Communists or by taking advantage of disorder in China to obtain further rights and concessions. Thus a crucial question for United States policy in China shortly before Japan's surrender was in what specific ways such an eventuality could be avoided. More specifically, the United States government had to consider alternative approaches to the Nationalists, Communists, and other groups in China. It is important to recognize that virtually all American officials were in agreement on the objective of sustaining the Yalta status quo. But they failed to reach consensus on the means of attaining this goal, as these means related to policy toward the various factions within China. One's policy recommendation hinged on one's assessment of their receptivity to pressure, overt or covert, by the United States. Disagreement on these points marked the beginning of the China controversy that was to form one aspect of the ideology of the Cold War in Asia.

Roughly speaking, there were three types of policy proposals put forth by American officials in the spring and summer of 1945. One, best represented by John P. Davies, assumed that "the Chinese Communist regime is here to stay," as he wrote in April, but that "Mao Tse-tung is not necessarily a Tito simply because he is a Communist." In other words, the Chinese Communists were not puppets of the Soviet Union. They were nationalistic, they resented the Kremlin's "shabby treatment" of them, and they had great misgivings about the Soviet invasion of Manchuria and North China. They were unlikely to turn to Russia for exclusive help unless they were forced to do so by circumstances both inside and outside of China. Given the American policy of confining Soviet expansion to certain limits, the only sensible alternative open to the United States was to encourage the nationalistic and anti-Soviet tendencies within the Chinese Communist movement. This could be done by adopting a "possible American policy of

[6] Truman to Hurley, July 23, 1945, ibid., p. 950.

cooperation with and assistance to the Chinese Communists." In Davies' opinion such cooperation and assistance did not mean abandonment of Chiang Kai-shek's regime but simply a realistic policy of being ready for any eventuality in Chinese domestic strife and, more important, drawing the Communists away from actual and potential Soviet influence. This being the case, the United States need not contemplate massive military involvement but rather economic aid to Yenan and much closer cultural relations between Americans and Chinese Communists.[7] Such a policy recommendation was tantamount to establishing a pro-American, anti-Kuomintang regime in North China as a buffer against the extension of Soviet power in Asia. Davies, however, admitted that even if friendly Communists were to cooperate with the United States in North China, they might be "liquidated" if the Soviet army should enter the area, as had been demonstrated in Eastern Europe. Davies did not say how such an outcome might be prevented, except to suggest that the sooner Japanese troops were removed from the region, presumably through cooperation between American and Communist forces, the better it would be since the Soviet Union would then be deprived of an excuse for penetrating southward from Manchuria. Despite this ambiguity, Davies' exposition was unique in that it explicitly suggested the possibility of cooperation between the United States and the Chinese Communists against the expansion of Soviet power.

The basic weakness in this recommendation was that it would tend to divide China rather than unifying it as had been assumed by the Yalta Conference. Davies' perception of China was one that was divided between two camps, each vying for supremacy. Starting from the premise that two such bitter opponents were not likely to come together in the near future, he argued that the United States had no choice but to deal with them both, but that cooperation with the Communists was more urgent because of the possibility of the latter's turning to Russia as a last resort, an eventuality that must by all means be avoided. Here was a subtle modification of the Yalta system insofar as Davies considered China as divided and yet standing on the whole against Soviet encroachment through American-Communist coopera-tion. In fact such a view was going beyond the limits visualized for the position of the United States in China. It may be concluded, therefore, that Davies' scheme entailed an extension of American power and influence in China through close ties with the Communists. Nevertheless, the basic thrust of his recommendation was to maintain the overall balance between Soviet and American spheres of predominance in East Asia.

Another group of officials were not so sanguine about the possibility of detaching the Chinese Communists from the Soviet Union and inducing them to come closer to the American orbit. According to Elbridge Durbrow,

[7] Davies memo, April 15, 1945, ibid., pp. 334–38.

chief of the division of Eastern European affairs of the State Department, the Communists were already tied to the Soviet Union which, in his words,

> through its encouragement of the Chinese Communists in central China . . . has maintained an effective apparatus in that country for future eventualities.

Dismissing the view of Davies and others that the Communists in Yenan were more nationalistic than Soviet-oriented, Durbrow argued that "the structure of the Communist Government (in Yenan) is a replica of that of the Soviet Government." Therefore, should the latter decide to extend Russian power to China,

> they will, if they wish to use it, have at their disposal an effective machine to build upon and expand their influence in a somewhat similar manner to the methods they have used in central and eastern Europe.

Under the circumstances, if the Yalta system of Asian stability were to be maintained, the United States must do what it could to assist the non-Communist forces in China. But since the Soviet Union and the Chinese Communists were likely to have a great appeal to those Chinese who were dissatisfied with the Chungking regime, the United States

> should bend every effort to bring about a liberalization of the Chungking Government, assist them in drawing up a positive program which would have a direct appeal to a large section of the population and assist them financially and materially to carry out effectively such a program.

In sharp contrast to Davies, Durbrow perceived America's role as a supporter of "liberal non-Communist elements" who could turn to the Communist side unless they were given material and moral assistance of the United States. And yet both these views assumed that the United States must prevent the extension of Soviet power beyond the limits of the Yalta accord, and that in that process America would be further drawn into Chinese politics. The United States, wrote Durbrow, should

> start China on the path which should lead eventually to the creation of a truly liberal regime rather than the establishment of another 'proletarian' dictatorship.[8]

Whether one agreed with Davies or with Durbrow, one would have to accept as inevitable a more extensive role for the United States on the continent of Asia than had initially been foreseen when the Yalta system was defined.

[8] Durbrow memo, May 10, 1945, ibid., p. 865.

A third approach to an interpretation of Chinese-Russian-American relations was exemplified by Ambassador Patrick J. Hurley. He differed from the above two viewpoints in that he was confident of Russia's support for Chinese unification under Kuomintang leadership, and that he felt the United States should continue to deal with the Chiang Kai-shek regime as the sole representative of China. In this sense he embodied the spirit of the Yalta system, never doubting that the Soviet Union would abide by the terms of the agreements, in particular those that prescribed the limits of Soviet power and supported the idea of an independent China. He was convinced that the Soviet Union and the United States could cooperate in China to help it establish "a free, united, democratic government." Hurley saw Stalin, Molotov, and others in Moscow in April, and felt his beliefs were once again justified when Stalin expressed, as Hurley put it,

> his complete support for the unification of the armed forces of China with full recognition of the National Government under the leadership of Chiang Kai-shek.

From his point of view, the United States need not fear Soviet collusion with or encouragement of the Chinese Communists. The latter were an important factor in Chinese domestic politics, but not a semi-independent movement as alleged by other American observers. They would and should be willing to negotiate with the Nationalists for military unification of China, the more so since the Soviet government was dealing only with Chungking. The most sensible approach for the United States, accordingly, was to ignore Communist importunities but encourage all groups in China to come together to build a free and united country.[9] It is interesting to note that Hurley, an outspoken supporter of Chiang Kai-shek, was less willing than Davies or Durbrow to see the United States become involved in Chinese affairs. This was because he did not share their fear of Soviet penetration of China. This again was linked to his conviction that the Chinese Communists did not enjoy Soviet support and therefore would sooner or later come to accept Chiang's leadership. He was a firm believer in the Yalta understanding, which to him had succeeded in bringing about an era of American-Soviet cooperation in East Asia on the basis of their joint support of a "free, united, and democratic China." It is little to be wondered at that given such an internationalist perception of the Yalta system his ideas should have been at variance with the more power-politically inclined notions held by other officials.

Actual United States policy at this time came closest to Hurley's recommendation, without totally accepting his faith in the continued workability of American-Soviet "cooperation." The Truman administration encouraged direct negotiations between Moscow and Chungking to formalize

[9] Kennan to Stettinius, April 17, 1945, ibid., pp. 338–40.

the Yalta agreement on Manchuria and Outer Mongolia, but it did little to give aid or support to dissident factions in China. The Chiang Kai-shek regime was still the only group recognized by the United States. At the same time, there was no firm policy as to the extent to which America would maintain its close relations with the Nationalists, and no thought that the United States would become involved in a massive scale in Chinese politics. In other words, the basic framework of American policy was still the big-power balance formulated at Yalta. Whether its idealistic, internationalist significance would be retained hinged on Soviet "cooperation," namely Russia's attitude toward the Nationalists and the Communists in China. In the summer of 1945, as the war against Japan came to a close, this was a far from clear question.

Communist Influence in North China and Manchuria

The war's end, coming on the heels of the Soviet declaration of war against Japan, severely tested the internationalist aspect of the Yalta system in East Asia. The Soviet Union, to be sure, had no intention of establishing its hegemony over Manchuria or North China, or of giving extensive aid to the Chinese Communists. Precisely on the date of the Japanese surrender, August 14, Moscow and Chungking signed a series of agreements confirming the general outline of the Yalta accord and providing for detailed arrangements for such things as a joint operation of railways in Manchuria, the establishment of a Sino-Russian military commission at the naval base of Port Arthur, the administration of Dairen which was to be made a free port, and a plebiscite in Outer Mongolia. These agreements had political significance insofar as they were negotiated with the Nationalist regime, thus implying that the Soviet Union would find it to its advantage not to jeopardize its relations with Chiang Kai-shek. Elsewhere in the Asia-Pacific region, Soviet armed forces quickly carried out the terms of the Yalta agreement by invading and occupying South Sakhalin and the Kuriles. Soviet troops entered Korea, occupying the peninsula north of the thirty-eighth parallel. This was in accordance with arrangements worked out by the American and Soviet governments whereby they were to divide Korea into two zones of occupation.

All these were more or less according to the scenario foreseen at the time of the Yalta Conference. What had not been foreseen was the rising tension between the United States and the Soviet Union on the Chinese question. Russians as much as Americans were puzzled by their deteriorating mutual relations not only in Eastern Europe but also in East Asia. From the Soviet point of view, they were merely availing themselves of the rights and privileges that had been formally recognized by the United States and now by the Chinese government. They constituted Russia's part of the bargain, and the Soviet Union on its part conceded America's predominant position in the Pacific, Japan, and the southern half of the Korean peninsula. As for China the Soviet understanding of the Yalta accord seems to have been that American influence in China proper would be strong but essentially non-military in nature. It had not been expected that the United States would involve itself on a massive scale in China, thus creating a situation of face-to-face confrontation with Soviet power in the north. Manchuria, in the meantime, would be made an area of special Russian interests, but there would be no extensive Soviet interference in the civil strife in China or overt aid to the Communists. In other words, the Soviet Union had retained an image of China which, while never "free, united, and democratic" in the American sense, would not fall to total domination of either of the two great powers.

Under the circumstances, mutual suspicion was bound to increase once the war came to an end and Soviet and American forces involved themselves in China. Seventy divisions of Russian troops seized key Manchurian cities and railways, accepting the surrender of Japanese armed forces. Most of them were interned, and some sent to Siberia. Ports and harbors were controlled by the Soviet fleet. Thus Russia was now the undisputed power in Manchuria. But Stalin had expressed his intention of withdrawing Soviet forces within three months after Japan's formal surrender—which came on September 2—or at least by the end of the year, and he wanted to make the most of this brief moment of supremacy by confiscating food and removing industrial equipment from Manchuria. These confiscations and removals were no different from what the Russians were doing in Germany and were considered part of Russia's claim to Japanese reparations. They also had the additional significance of destroying the productive capacities of Manchuria, revealing a Soviet interest in keeping the region weak and underdeveloped in view of the history of the strategic value of the region as a base of operation against Russia. Finally, as Chinese Communist soldiers began pushing northward and arriving in Manchuria, they were not turned back by the Soviet army of occupation, although there was no clearcut policy of transmitting Manchuria intact to Communist control. The Soviet Union still assumed that the Nationalists would be the ruling power in China proper. But the Communists were the de facto authority in North China, and it seemed wise for the Soviet Union to keep China in turmoil by encouraging Communist strength in subtle ways. It was hoped that by the time Soviet troops withdrew from Manchuria Communist forces would be in control of at least some cities and ports of the country.

On the whole it may be said that Soviet policy at this time was cautious. It made use of the opportunity provided by the presence of its troops in Manchuria, but not in such a way as to alter radically the Yalta equilibrium. There was, however, one new factor that the Russians had not quite calculated: the arrival of American forces in China and their active support of the Nationalist government in airlifting Chiang Kai-shek's forces to North China or escorting them by ship to Manchuria. As Molotov told Secretary of State James F. Byrnes in Moscow at the end of December,

> the presence of American forces in north China was a new development and one which had not been contemplated when the Soviet Government signed its agreement with China.

There is no doubt that this was an honest expression of Soviet concern with the arrival and activities of American troops in China in a far greater number and in much more extensive ways than had been anticipated. It seemed sensible, therefore, for the Soviet Union to insist on simultaneous withdrawal of Russian and American troops from China. Otherwise, the United States might take advantage of the situation for further establishing its control over China. The continued presence of Russian forces in Manchuria could give a pretext to the United States to retain its troops in China, resulting in a dangerous confrontation between the two. Under the circumstances, the best strategy from the Soviet point of view in order to safeguard the Yalta framework was to call for evacuation of all foreign troops. China would then be on its own, with Russian privileges guaranteed by Yalta remaining intact.

Thus Soviet policy was also closely related to shifts and turns in American policy in China immediately after the war. Most American officials assumed that the Yalta synthesis was still workable, but its implementation was becoming more and more difficult without further involvement of the United States in China. One could continue to place one's faith in American-Russian cooperation in bringing about a unified China. This remained Ambassador Hurley's position until his abrupt resignation in November. He had believed it possible to mediate between the two contending factions in China to help develop a united and independent country, and he had been convinced that these were objectives shared both by the United States and the Soviet Union. But he was faced with a situation where the rift between Nationalists and Communists seemed to be widening and where Soviet forces were in control of Manchuria. These were factors not congenially fitted into Hurley's perception of American-Russian-Chinese relations, and he chose to resign rather than to accommodate his long-cherished beliefs with the new realities.

Given the fact that China was far from being unified and that the Soviet Union was in a predominant position in Manchuria, there seemed to be a great danger that the Yalta equilibrium might be upset irreparably.

Soviet preponderance in Manchuria, of course, had been anticipated at the Yalta Conference, and in fact it had been an integral part of the Yalta system. But the actual sending of Soviet troops to Manchuria had a tremendous psychological impact on the thinking of American officials. All of a sudden they were confronted with a reality in which not only scores of divisions of Soviet troops were seizing Manchuria but were in physical contact with the Chinese Communists in North China. A fear was created that unless checked, Soviet power might extend itself further southward, far beyond the limits conceded to Russia at Yalta. From the Realpolitik viewpoint, it was incumbent upon the United States to maintain a balance by bolstering up the Chiang Kai-shek regime's effort to unify China. This could be done, it was felt, by providing him with military support so as to transport Nationalist forces to all parts of China to accept Japanese surrender and, incidentally, to entrench themselves in those parts of China that had never before been controlled by the Kuomintang.

American Participation in the
Chinese Civil War

This was, however, just the beginning. Some key American officials felt that the involvement of the United States in China, to a far greater extent than had been foreseen, was necessitated in view of the danger, as they saw it, of the erosion of the Yalta system because of Soviet expansion in China. As Everett F. Drumright, chief of the division of Chinese affairs of the State Department, wrote in a November 16 memorandum, the Chinese Communists were intent upon establishing control over Manchuria and North China through Soviet assistance. This meant that the two basic principles of the Yalta system—confinement of Soviet power to specific rights in Manchuria, and a unified China—were already being undermined. In Drumright's words,

> A divided China will obviously further the forces of insecurity, invite foreign intervention, and may eventually bring about conditions which will plunge the world into a third world war.

In other words, the delicate structure of the Yalta compromise would be broken. Under the circumstances, there was no choice left to the United States but to do what it could to prevent such an eventuality from occurring. If the basic structures of Asian peace and order were to survive, the United States should move resolutely and effectively . . . assist the National Government of China to effect restoration of the recovered areas of China, including Manchuria.

The alternative would be to do nothing of the sort and to withdraw all American forces from China. Such a policy, according to Drumright, would result in a divided China, with the northern half under the Communists and closely tied to the Soviet Union.

> The creation of such a Communist state would seem, in effect, to bring about a situation which in many important particulars would be little different from that obtained before the defeat of Japan. Instead of a Japanese-dominated puppet regime we should probably find in its place one dominated by the U.S.S.R.

The outcome could only lead to a clash between the United States and the Soviet Union, thus negating the fundamental premise of the Yalta system.[10]

This was a language of geo-politics, based on the assumption that the prevention of further extension of Soviet power was of crucial importance to world peace and stability after the war. But Drumright's memorandum showed how easy it was to go beyond Yalta and develop an argument for large-scale American involvement in China. Such involvement had not been part of the Yalta system, but now a key American official was arguing that the United States must extend its spheres of operation and its influence beyond those areas—such as the Pacific islands, Japan, and south Korea— that had been assigned to it in the Yalta accord. He was advocating a policy of United States entrenchment on the continent of Asia, a policy, as he wrote, of supporting "a strong, united China with close and friendly attachments to the United States." A disunited China that was friendly to America might be tolerated, but every indication was that such a China would be oriented toward or controlled by the Soviet Union. In a strikingly frank expression of readiness to give up the internationalist advocacy of a "free and democratic" China, Drumright asserted that considerations such as "democracy in China [or] questions as to the relative efficiency of the two contending factions" were of only secondary importance. Rather, the basic guiding principle, according to him, should be "the promotion of the security of the United States." Here was a startling departure from the traditional language of national-interest considerations. Drumright's opposition to Soviet expansionism called for massive United States involvement in China, which in turn was justified in the name of "considerations of our own security interests." Somehow national security seemed bound up with the outcome of the civil strife in China, and it seemed to call forth a policy of supporting the Nationalists. This was the way in which a change in the Yalta system—from one of maintaining a balance

[10] Drumright memo, Nov. 16, 1945, ibid., pp. 629–34.

between the Soviet Union and the United States, with China in the middle, to one of establishing greater American control over China—was justified. Here was a direct challenge not only to the Chinese Communists and the Soviet Union but also to the Yalta equilibrium itself. An image of Soviet expansion to the detriment of the equilibrium was producing a reaction, similarly destined to upset the balance but in favor of the United States. A memorandum written by the State-War-Navy Coordinating Committee on October 22 endorsed the same principle of assertiveness in East Asia. It declared that America's objectives in this area were, one, to

> provide for the security of the United States and its territory and for the maintenance of international peace

and, two, to

> create a political atmosphere conducive to the establishment of mutually beneficial commercial and cultural relations between the United States and its citizens and Far Eastern Areas and their nationals.

The latter objective was internationalist and national-interest oriented in the traditional sense, but the first objective was a bolder assertion of American power, reflecting the vastly extended spheres of United States involvement in the Asia-Pacific region. Both national security and regional stability were considered an essential foundation of American policy in postwar Asia.[11] That such a policy affected not only the Pacific Ocean but China was clearly demonstrated when, on the same date, the Joint Chiefs of Staff adopted a policy paper recommending the establishment of a military advisory group in China. The purpose of such a mission was succinctly stated:

> One of the immediate functions of this group would be to collaborate with the Chinese military and naval authorities in the preparation of a detailed plan outlining the exact nature and extent of U.S. military support to China.

The Joint Chiefs pointed out the importance of establishing the advisory group before the deactivation of the United States forces in the China theater, still engaged in helping Chinese troops disarm Japanese. Here was a blueprint for continued presence of United States armed forces in China. Moreover, the paper insisted that "certain economic and military rights in China should be obtained by the United States" as part of the program. Among such rights were the "unrestricted use of U.S. military and governmental communications facilities and cryptographic systems" to be installed in China, "the right to operate U.S. aircraft, vehicles, ships and craft over and through Chinese territory and waters," "development of Chinese

[11] SWNCC memo, Oct. 22, 1945, ibid., pp. 583–90.

commercial aviation, airways, communications and navigation systems under U.S. supervision," and "agreement to furnish military, economic, and scientific information about China to the United States." [12]

These memoranda clearly reveal that in the United States there was readiness on the part of responsible officials to go beyond the Yalta understanding and entrench American power and interests firmly in China. No wonder that John Carter Vincent, now director of the office of Far Eastern affairs of the State Department, criticized the Joint Chiefs' proposal in the strongest language. He said,

> The size and character of the Group, the statement of concessions desired, and the general tenor of the Joint Chiefs of Staff papers raise a question as to whether we are not moving toward establishment of a relationship with China which has some of the characteristics of a *de facto* protectorate with a semi-colonial Chinese army under our direction.

As a believer in the Yalta system, Vincent was concerned lest the sending of a military advisory group to China should result in destroying the structure of American-Russian understanding in Asia. As he put it,

> we should have in mind possible political and international reactions to determine whether, in seeking to provide for military security in this manner, we have not disturbed our international political relations to a point that might negate the assumed security advantages of our military position in China.

He clearly had in mind the possibility that the planned entrenchment of American power on the Asian mainland might undermine the framework of American-Soviet relations that had so painfully been erected.[13] In his view, the Yalta system had not depended on the continued presence of United States armed forces in China, and certainly it had not anticipated additional reinforcements. Rather, he believed that complete withdrawal of American troops, coupled with evacuation of Soviet forces from Manchuria, had been postulated as a basic prerequisite for the implementation of the Yalta accord. Vincent's unhappiness, paralleling that of Ambassador Hurley even though they were personally at odds, was a telling demonstration of the progressive breakdown of the Yalta system from within.

U.S. "Mediation" in China and the Threat to the Yalta System

In the end the Truman administration rejected the idea of massive involvement in China and sought to sustain the Yalta system primarily through diplomatic and political means. The decision to send General

---

[12] Joint Chiefs of Staff memo, Oct. 22, 1945, ibid., pp. 590–98.
[13] Vincent to Byrnes, Nov. 12, 1945, ibid., pp. 614–17.

George C. Marshall on a mediatory mission to China reflected a policy not to transform the Yalta formulation drastically but to reinforce it. Marshall was to go to China to exert what pressure he could upon both the Nationalists and the Communists so that they would come together peacefully and cooperate in the task of making a "strong, united, and democratic" China. If successful, the mission would contribute to perpetuating the Yalta agreement by reducing chances of disorder in China and by preventing penetration of North China by the Soviet Union through its ties with the Chinese Communists. In time Soviet troops would be withdrawn, and so, too, would be American forces.

This was the ultimate objective. In the immediate future, however, the Marshall mission was not entirely in accordance with the spirit of the Yalta Conference. Available documents concerning the origin of the mission and the drafting of instructions to Marshall clearly indicate that the ideal solution championed by Vincent, in strict adherence to the Yalta agreement, was rejected in favor of limited interventionism. The United States, according to Marshall's instructions, was not prepared to give massive military support to Chiang Kai-shek with a view to unifying China. But military means would be available to Marshall in carrying out his mission. Specifically, as President Truman wrote Marshall,

> the U.S. will continue to furnish military supplies and to assist the Chinese National Government in the further transportation of Chinese troops so that it can reestablish control over the liberated areas of China, including Manchuria.

Moreover, should Marshall be successful in promoting unity in China, the United States would be prepared to "grant a Chinese request for an American military advisory group in China." As can be seen here, the emphasis was on preventing Soviet penetration of China, and therefore on promoting Chinese unification and independence. In view of the fact that Soviet forces and Communist troops were already in contact in Manchuria, such a policy implied giving support to the Chiang Kai-shek regime. But somehow it was felt that the Chinese groups could be persuaded to come together, and that the deployment of massive American power would be unnecessary. This was an ambiguous position, but under the circumstances the only apparently sensible alternative, given the civil strife in China and the continued adherence to the framework of the Yalta accord.

At the end of 1945, then, the American position in Asia was still defined in terms of the Yalta system. But it was becoming clear that the maintenance of the system, insofar as it referred to a balance between the United States and the Soviet Union, might necessitate limited American involvement in China. Such involvement was inherently incompatible with the Yalta idea of an independent China. As long as American intervention was political, there would be little direct challenge to the Yalta system. That is why the Marshall mission was welcomed by exponents of American-Russian understanding. But General Marshall clearly understood that his mission had larger implications. After all, here was a prestigious American general intruding himself upon the Chinese scene and trying to settle a domestic dispute which had been going on for two decades. Behind him stood the armed forces of the United States, a symbol of America's new power and increased role in Asia. As Marshall told Chou En-lai soon after his arrival in Chungking,

> he doubted if China realized the tremendous American land, sea and air power in the Pacific which precipitated the end of the war. . . . [The American people] brought the war to an end by generous expenditures of men, air power and sea power and atomic power, of which they are very conscious. Now having made that expenditure, they are intensely concerned in anything that might start a war again.[14]

In other words, the United States was now a great power in the Asia-Pacific region, and it was concerned with maintaining peace and order in the area. Such preoccupation justified an American role in Chinese domestic affairs. In this way, Marshall was subtly redefining the Yalta framework to accommodate the extending power of the United States. Just as the Soviet Union was extending its power beyond the specific limits of the Yalta accord, but not in such a way as to destroy completely the system itself, so the United States was exerting its influence in China proper. A balance between the two great powers was still maintained, but in the meantime China's own sovereign rights were inevitably being jeopardized.

Chinese groups of all political persuasions were quick to realize that their country was far from emerging as a strong power in Asia after the war. According to their scenario they should have witnessed the rise of China from the ashes of World War II as a key stabilizing power in postwar East Asia. Instead the country was disunited, foreign troops were all over China, and the two outside powers were extending their influence on the continent. The fact that the Communists turned to the Soviet Union and the Nationalists to the United States for varying degrees of support made the situation worse. By seeking external assistance in their task of unifying the country, they were undermining the cause of China's emergence as an independent nation. Unfortunately, the less united the country, the greater would be the danger of further foreign involvement. Since both Nationalists and Communists were agreed on the ultimate objective of creating a strong and united country, theoretically they should have done so without turning to outside sources of support. However, given the types of pressure emanating both from Moscow and Washington as sketched above, it would have taken much more than an ordinary effort to maintain national independence.

[14] Marshall's conversation with Chou, Dec. 23, 1945, ibid., pp. 800–804.

There was no agreement between Nationalists and Communists as to how best to achieve this objective. From Chiang Kai-shek's point of view, domestic unification and peace were the crucial prerequisites for the construction of a new China. There could be no strong China willing to play a major role in international affairs unless the country were unified. The main obstacle in the way of unification, according to him, was Communist obstinacy. It was, therefore, imperative to crush the Communists and bring them to the realization that their armed insurgency was doomed to failure. It is difficult to quarrel with Chiang's contention that

> the existence of autonomous armies such as that of the Communist Army [is] inconsistent with and actually makes impossible political unity in China.[15]

However, the Nationalist armed forces, too, had been little more than regional, "autonomous" units. They had never been in control of Manchuria or North China. By his decision to send his troops to North China and beyond, therefore, Chiang Kai-shek was in effect trying to extend his power base and unify the country by force. The only alternative would have been a division of China, a possibility he refused to contemplate at this time because of his image of China as a unified power.

Because he believed that his regime represented China—and he was technically right—Chiang saw little contradiction between his goal of unification and his eagerness to obtain support from the United States. He welcomed the Truman administration's reiterated statements that the United States continued to recognize only one government in China, that then existing under Chiang Kai-shek. He also believed that his position was recognized by the Soviet government, although his attitude toward the latter was ambiguous. As he told Marshall, "in all matters of broad policy, the Chinese Communists rely upon the Russians." [16] But this was not altogether a bad thing, for the Soviet government could hopefully be counted upon to put pressure on the Communists. There is little evidence that Chiang was genuinely concerned with the presence of Soviet troops in Manchuria, despite the help they were giving to the Communists. In fact he preferred Soviet to Communist forces to be in control of Manchuria, to maintain law and order until the Nationalists were ready to take over the region. Moreover, Chiang was confident that he could deal directly with Stalin and have him restrain the Communists. He obviously felt that Marshal Stalin would not risk jeopardizing the precious gains of the Yalta accord, only recently confirmed by the Sino-Soviet treaty, for the sake of assisting rebel bands. Basically the same reasoning made Chiang ready to seek American support. Since he was engaged in the critical task of unification, it seemed logical to turn for

---

[15] Marshall's conversation with Chiang, Dec. 21, 1945, ibid., pp. 794–99.
[16] Ibid., p. 797.

assistance to the United States, the country which had done more than any other to destroy Japanese imperialism and to promote the idea of China as a power. American forces, moreover, were already in and around China, conveniently situated to render military aid to the Nationalists. In the latter's perception, Chinese unification under them and the extension of American influence as a result of its support of Chiang were not mutually contradictory. The United States, after all, was supporting the only recognized government of China.

Viewed by the Communists, however, Chinese independence and American military involvement were incompatible. They, too, shared the image of China as a unified, independent country, although they were not very sanguine about the prospect of their successfully unifying China by force in the near future. As the *Chieh-fang jih-pao* (Liberation daily) put it, the Communists identified themselves with the Chinese people's fifty-year-old aspiration to develop a unified and democratic country so that China might "regain the international position which it deserves." From their point of view, these goals could only be attained through the efforts of the Chinese people themselves, with the encouragement of friendly democratic nations. Interference by external forces could only complicate the task and delay the achievement of national unity and independence. For this reason they welcomed Marshall's mediatory mission, viewing it as an expression of America's continued interest in reforming Chinese government so as to destroy the Nationalist monoply of power. However, the presence of American troops and the statements by some American officials, intimating vastly increased roles of the United States in Chinese domestic politics, were extremely disturbing to the Communists. They not only gave the impression of America's interference in China, but also implied a changed situation of power relationships in which the United States would be emerging as a formidable factor in postwar East Asia. Whereas the Nationalists welcomed such a development as helpful to their attempt to bring about Chinese unification, the Communists viewed it as fundamentally transforming the picture, both domestically and externally. If the United States should actively intervene to support the Nationalists, not only would the latter be emboldened to hold on to their control of power, but Americans would become identified with the Nationalist regime, which would in fact become little more than a puppet of the United States. China would fall into the American orbit of power and influence, exacerbating international relations in East Asia. Under the circumstances, the Communists would be compelled to turn almost exclusively to the Soviet Union for help. The latter, on its part, would be justified to extend its hold upon Manchuria and North China to cope with the expanding influence of the United States. Such a situation would naturally bode ill for what the Chinese Communists stood for: a unified and independent China not dominated by the Kuomintang.

Such seems to have been the thinking of the Communist leadership at the end of the year 1945. As a Communist spokesman said in December, the Truman proposal for cessation of hostilities in China was fair and constructive; the Chinese and American peoples could yet try to promote friendly relations on the basis of the principle of self-determination. It was regrettable, however, that American troops were still on Chinese soil and that some of them had exceeded their duty which was merely to disarm Japanese soldiers. It was to be hoped that these American forces would be withdrawn as speedily as possible. At the very least, the *Chieh-fang jih-pao* asserted, they should desist from interfering in Chinese domestic politics. Certain American officials and especially army officers in China were acting as if to intensify the civil war by actively aiding the Nationalists but no other groups in the country. The Chinese people would welcome American-Chinese friendship on the basis of certain principles, of which mutual non-intervention and American neutrality in the Chinese civil strife were among the most important. Since American personnel in China seemed to do little but support one faction against others, they must be withdrawn if a lasting foundation for friendly relations between the two countries were to be established.[17]

Thus already within less than half a year after the end of the Pacific War one aspect of the Yalta structure of postwar Asian relations was faced with a serious crisis. The assumption that China would be more or less free of foreign intervention, retain its sovereignty save for the rights it granted Russia, and function as a unified country was proving daily less and less tenable. Although neither the United States nor the Soviet Union intended active intervention in China, the presence of their armed forces, coupled with the civil war in China, had the effect of extending American and Soviet power beyond what had been envisaged at Yalta. This situation also caused deterioration in American-Russian relations, each of which began to accuse the other of violating the Yalta agreement. It remained to be seen whether they would choose to do away with the system, fragile as it was, and set up an alternative structure of Asian international relations, or somehow decide to abide by the broad principle of American-Russian equilibrium as defined at the Yalta Conference.

Postwar Japan, Korea, and Southeast Asia

Confusion and uncertainty in China, both in terms of power relations and of policy conceptualization, were the greatest threats posed to the Yalta equilibrium in Asia. Elsewhere in the Asia-Pacific region, however, the United States and the Soviet Union acted in essential accordance with the

[17] See Iriye, *Across the Pacific*, pp. 260–61.

scenario. Russian forces took over the northern islands, and American forces seized the Pacific islands from Japan, and promptly proceeded to incorporate them into their new security systems. Of these islands the most crucial in terms of long-range strategic and political implications were the southern Kuriles for the Soviet Union and the Ryukyus (Okinawa) for the United States. The former were geographically very close to Hokkaido, and the latter to Kyushu, the northernmost and the southernmost territories of the now-shrunken Japan. Soviet and American retention of these islands was a reminder that Japan would now be defenseless, that its destiny would be in the hands of its new next-door neighbors, the Russians and the Americans.

Of these two the latter played by far the decisive role in the occupation and control of postwar Japan. The United States was turning Okinawa into an occupied land, where Americanization proceeded as if in direct proportion to the retreat of Japanese power. The Ryukyu islands were to all intents and purposes an American territory, although they were not formally made one. Here a military government held sway over the native civilian administration which also was under the direction of American officials. The dollar replaced the yen as the currency. Inhabitants of the islands required a passport to visit Japan proper. On the mainland of Japan, too, the United States enjoyed as absolute a command as any power was exercising over alien territory at this time. Compared with the occupation of Germany, the United States had a much firmer grip on Japan, the general headquarters under General Douglas MacArthur being in a position to dictate terms to the Japanese virtually on his own authority. Unlike Germany, Japan was not divided into zones of occupation but was treated as a whole, and American forces were the preponderant power that carried out the occupation. Moreover, whereas in Germany the occupation authorities established a new regime and Germans became its mere functionaries, retaining important roles only in local government and administration, in Japan the basic framework of government and bureaucracy was kept. Although the country was effectively disarmed and the top military and civilian leaders arrested and purged, the bulk of bureaucrats stayed on their jobs—including officials of the central government, policemen, and public-school teachers. Most important, MacArthur decided to keep the Emperor system. The decision, which he called "the greatest gamble in history," was derived from the view that the occupation of Japan could be carried out much more smoothly by keeping the Emperor as head of the state and using his authority for purposes of the occupation, than by risking confusion and possible resistance to occupation authority as a result of purging the Emperor. Paradoxically, because the Emperor system was kept and chaos avoided, and because the United States did not share power with others in Japan, it was possible to carry out some far-reaching reforms of Japanese society. Already in 1945 steps began to be taken to rewrite school textbooks to eradicate ultra-nationalistic philosophy from the educational system, to draw up draft constitutions to prevent the resurgence of militarism, and to undertake land redistribution.

The content of occupation-imposed reforms varied in accordance with the wishes and ideas of Supreme Commander MacArthur, but there was little doubt of his authority. It was ultimately derived from the Yalta agreement that had assigned the United States the primary task for defeating and occupying Japan. The Soviet Union well understood this, and while it made feeble protests from time to time against America's monopoly of power in Japan, it did little to obstruct MacArthur's policy. Certainly there was nothing like the equivalent of Soviet assertiveness in Germany, where the Russians did more or less as they wanted in their zone of occupation. Considering the fact that the United States and the Soviet Union had never before been joint occupiers of foreign lands, and in view of their divergent social philosophies and systems, it was not surprising that there should have been tension and friction between the two powers in Japan as in Germany. Nevertheless, in these two countries Russia and America still adhered to the Yalta framework, and to that extent there continued basic understanding between them. Just as the United States conceded Soviet authority and control in the latter's zone of occupation in Germany, in Japan the Soviet Union accepted America's preponderant power and acquiesced in policies promulgated by MacArthur's headquarters.

Elsewhere in Asia, the two powers behaved essentially in accordance with the same principle. Korea was a good example. While some sort of trusteeship sponsored by the United States, the Soviet Union, Great Britain, and China had been accepted at the Yalta Conference, it was the first two powers that in fact exercised control. Neither America nor Russia claimed Korea as part of its new sphere of influence, but unlike China neither of them saw the possibility of Korea as an independent entity in the near future. Under the circumstances, the division of the peninsula at the 38th parallel into the American and Soviet zones of occupation was a pragmatic response to the situation at the end of the war. Such a division, while a military expediency, had immediate political implications, as events in Germany were clearly demonstrating. In each zone of occupation the occupying power established law and order, disarmed Japanese troops, and dealt with whatever indigenous organizations it found congenial. This meant that in the northern half of the peninsula Communists and Soviet-trained Koreans gained influence and recognition, whereas in the south General John R. Hodge, the American commander, lagged in setting up a Korean government because he did not like the politically active groups. He treated south Korea from a military point of view, as an occupied land, and to administer the territory he was even willing to turn to the Japanese for assistance. But here again it is clear that American and Soviet authorities viewed these developments essentially as part of the Yalta system. Not surprisingly, toward the end of 1945, the two governments agreed to cooperate in order to set up a provisional Korean government. The United States and the Soviet Union were to consult with the provisional government with a view to establishing a four-power trusteeship "for a period up to five years." In other words, Korea would either be divided between American and Soviet spheres of influence or turned into a trusteeship. In either event, there would not be a likelihood of the whole of Korea falling under Soviet or American control. The Yalta equilibrium would be maintained more or less unimpaired.

Of the other components of the former Japanese empire, Taiwan was a very clear-cut case. There was complete agreement that the island should revert to China, and neither the United States nor the Soviet Union had much to do with the reestablishment of Chinese authority there. The Kuomintang-Communist rift on the China mainland did not immediately affect Taiwan, as it was quickly placed under Nationalist control, its armed forces and civilian personnel replacing Japanese soldiers, police, administrators, and teachers on the island. Japanese banking and commercial facilities were taken over by Chinese. The only source of instability was the latent hostility of the island's inhabitants whose response to the coming of the Nationalists proved to be less than enthusiastic. But the Taiwanese resentment of the way mainland Chinese established themselves in predominant positions in the politics and economy of the island did not find an effective institutional expression in the absence of a strong organization or movement against Japanese rule, as had been the case in Korea. Moreover, since neither American nor Soviet forces were involved, China was able to reestablish control over Taiwan relatively free of complications. In fact this was the only instance of China's regaining lost territory, and Taiwan's recovery had symbolic importance; it demonstrated that the war had ended and seemed to ensure that China was once again becoming a power.

Southeast Asia was an altogether different matter. It had never been clearly fitted into the Yalta scheme. Unlike the situation elsewhere in the Asia-Pacific region, the two greatest powers did not consider the area part of their respective spheres of influence. They had discussed the possibility of setting up some sort of trusteeship for the European colonies that had been invaded by Japanese forces, but the war had come to an end before anything was done. To the extent that the region lay clearly beyond the limits of American or Soviet spheres of preponderance, the future of the area remained ambiguous, dependent upon the interaction between Chinese and European policies at one level, and between the colonial and indigenous populations' divergent wishes at another. There would persist instability and uncertainty, but there would be no duplication of the situation in China where the United States and the Soviet Union were directly confronting each other despite the Yalta accord that had seemed to preclude such an eventuality. If there was any degree of American or Soviet involvement at this time, it was primarily ideological; the two powers were generally sympathetic to the nationalistic movements in Indochina, Indonesia, and elsewhere, although they would not give overt support to them.

The situation was not unsatisfactory from the point of view of Great Britain, the third of the big-power triumvirate whose role in the Asia-Pacific region was noticeably less substantial than that of the other two. Between Yalta and the Japanese surrender officials in London sought to make sure that Southeast Asia would remain within the British and European spheres of influence. It is interesting to note that the War Cabinet's Far Eastern committee, presumably the key organ at the sub-cabinet level for considering peace terms affecting Asia and the Pacific, spent more time discussing the future of Southeast Asia than problems dealing with China or Japan. Of the thirty-four memoranda drafted by the committee between January and July 1945, eighteen of them directly concerned the region. Of particular interest was the future of Thailand and Indochina. The memorandum of April 5, for instance, noted:

> Indo-China is the key to the defense of Burma, Malaya, and also of Siam. . . . The use of facilities and communications in Siam by Britain and Allied forces would . . . assist in the defense of Indo-China and, therefore, in the area as a whole. . . . In general, our paramount military interest in Siam is that . . . we should be able to rely on the cooperation of her Government and armed forces in measures for the defense of Southeast Asia as a whole.

When peace was restored, therefore, according to the memorandum,

> The Siamese Government must be prepared to act on British advice as regards all her defense measures, including the training and equipping of her armed forces and the organization of her air defenses. For this purpose it would probably be necessary to establish a British Military Mission in Siam.[18]

Apart from the security and stability of Southeast Asia, the British government was concerned with procuring sufficient quantities of rice in Thailand to feed the colonial populations, and for this reason, too, it was considered imperative to have some sort of control over the Thai government after the war. For all these reasons, Britian conducted secret negotiations with Thai agents toward the end of the war to facilitate smooth transition from a Japanese-controlled, anti-United Nations regime in Bangkok to one more pliable to British demands.

On the military front, Britain succeeded in having the allies assign Southeast Asia south of the sixteenth parallel to itself for operational

---

[18] Far Eastern committee memo, Apr. 15, 1945, CAB 96/5, Public Record Office. For British policy toward Thailand, see Russell H. Fifield, *Americans in Southeast Asia: the Roots of Commitment* (New York: Thomas Y. Crowell, 1973), Chaps. 2–3.

purposes, and the decision effectively shut out American or Soviet interference with British action. American troops in Indochina were withdrawn soon after the Japanese surrender. Only China expressed unhappiness, having championed the cause of Asian liberation from European colonialism. Chiang Kai-shek was particularly irked by the French attempt, supported by the British, to recover its empire in Indochina. MacArthur's order that all Japanese troops in Indochina north of the sixteenth parallel surrender to Chinese forces did not prevent French troops from entering the area, assisted by British forces. Lacking support of the United States or of the Soviet Union, China was incapable of repelling the British, French, and Dutch efforts to return to their colonies.

At the end of 1945, then, an outline of Asian-Pacific international relations was becoming visible. The United States and the Soviet Union would now be the two predominant powers, defining a status quo essentially in terms of the Yalta system. But their military involvement in China was already creating difficulties, actual as well as conceptual, in accommodating China to the system. It remained to be seen whether the Yalta hypothesis that China would be a viable independent state would be destroyed by the policies of the two powers. Elsewhere the region was being divided up into three areas: America's and Russia's spheres of preponderance, and the third area in Southeast Asia which was witnessing the return of the European colonial regimes. Compared with the situation before 1940, by far the most striking change was the role of the United States. From being a negligible factor in Asian-Pacific relations, it had developed as the predominant Pacific power and a prominent Asian power. From viewing its concerns primarily in narrow national-interest terms or in a vague internationalist language of support for Chinese integrity and the Open Door, Americans had come to perceive of the global implications of their position in Asia. Their internationalism now took the form of an idea of "cooperation" with the Soviet Union, while their national security, too, was being redefined to entrench American power more deeply in the mainland of Asia. President Roosevelt's assertion in October 1944, that

in the current world war there is literally not a single problem, military or political, in which the United States are not interested,

was becoming daily more relevant. The fundamental question after the war, as it had been in 1944, was whether the newly extended power and interests of the United States could accommodate themselves to the equally expanding influence of the Soviet Union, and whether American-Soviet relations could be stabilized through the Yalta mechanism so as to ensure worldwide order and peace.

THE EMERGENCE OF THE COLD WAR

Events in 1946 and 1947 demonstrated that the Yalta system still provided the basic framework of international relations, although it underwent some partial changes of vital significance. Instead of developing as partners in maintaining peace and stability in the world, however, the two nations came to view one another through the lens of hostility and the imagery of conflict. There was still a devotion to the balance of power, but the internationalist connotation of "cooperation" disappeared from the vocabulary of American-Russian relations. Instead, images like confrontation and containment were now used to make sense out of what appeared to be happening. In time ideology came to define reality, and it became extremely difficult to view international affairs in any other way. The Cold War replaced "cooperation and understanding" as a conceptual framework to describe American-Soviet relations.

It is important to distinguish between different strands of American-Russian relations after the war. At one level they were definable in terms of power. They were the two global powers, and they were interested in defining their respective spheres of predominance. The Yalta agreements provided the basic guideline to both of them. At another level, their relationship was ideological, an embodiment of the search for a new world order which characterized the Yalta synthesis. American-Russian relations were seen to be in harmony or in conflict, not so much in power terms but dependent on the degree of their "cooperation." At still another level, these relations were no different from the relationship between any two given nations; they were a reflection of two countries' respective national interests. The United States and the Soviet Union had certain security, economic, and prestige matters that constituted the core of their respective national interests. An analysis of postwar American-Soviet relations in general and Asian-Pacific affairs in particular must take all these levels of their interaction into consideration. Because America and Russia were new arrivals as super powers, it was little accident that a great deal of semantic and conceptual ambiguities character-ized the way their governments and people looked at each shift and turn in their relations after 1945. But it is essential for our purposes to penetrate the surface and discuss the Cold War in Asia in the context of the Yalta system both in its power and ideological aspects.

The Imagery of Conflict

It was not surprising that among the first manifestations of a serious rift between the United States and the Soviet Union were incidents involving the

Middle East. Like China and Southeast Asia, the Middle East had not been assigned to either of the two super-powers in the Yalta scheme. Like Southeast Asia, the Middle East was an area of European colonial domination, with Britain occupying the leading position. Again like China, moreover, there was a possibility of American-Soviet friction if one of them gave the impression of trying to extend its power at the expense of the global balance. Iran was a good case in point. The country had been occupied by British, Soviet, and American troops during the war, but it had been stipulated in 1942 that they would be withdrawn within six months after the conclusion of the war, that is, by March 2, 1946. Actually, only American forces had been withdrawn by then. British and Soviet troops remained, and the latter were setting up separatist regimes in northern Iran, calling forth strong American-British protests. Soviet policy was a violation of wartime agreements, but from Moscow's point of view Iran was much like Manchuria; it was territorially contiguous to the Soviet Union and rich in oil resources, which Russia needed. Moreover, American oil interests were becoming active in Iran, backed up by the State Department. The fact that the British and the United States governments acted together to condemn Soviet action seemed to indicate that America was extending its sphere of interests to the Middle East. Here was a classic case of misunderstanding between the powers that were the mainstay of an international system. In terms of the global balance Iran fell within the British sphere of influence, but British predominance was being chipped away by the two super-powers. They, however, did not desire direct confrontation or a radical transformation of the status quo. In time Soviet troops were withdrawn. But the spirit of American-Soviet cooperation was injured. Their acrimonious debates at the United Nations demonstrated to the entire world how difficult it was to sustain an atmosphere of friendly and peaceful relations between the big powers.

The Turkish crisis of 1946–47 also had similar characteristics. Traditionally, the European powers had been the predominant influence in Turkey, but Russia had developed a strong strategic interest in the Straits, an interest that was recognized by Britain and the United States at Yalta when the three all agreed to future revision of the Montreux Convention (1936) that had restricted wartime shipping through the Straits. Otherwise, the Yalta system envisaged a more or less independent Turkey like China. America's role in Turkey was also similar to that in China before the war—there had been a long tradition of missionary and educational enterprises by Americans, but no real economic or strategic interest. For a while after the war the United States emphasized its function as a great power who might cooperate with the Soviet Union and Great Britain to establish a new *modus operandi* for the Straits area. For instance, in November 1945 the American government proposed the opening of the Straits to all

Black-Sea powers in wartime. The United States was not asking for much for itself—a good example of its internationalist role. The situation changed as the British found it more and more difficult to maintain its superior position throughout the Middle East by means of its own effort, and sought to get the United States involved in the area in order to prevent the possibility of the latter's falling under Soviet domination. It is well to recall that Winston Churchill's famous "iron curtain" speech at Fulton, Missouri, on March 5, 1946, was inspired by his concern with what he took to be Soviet designs on Turkey, and that he specifically called for a "fraternal association of the English-speaking peoples" outside the United Nations to meet the Soviet challenge. Here was a clear-cut summons to a new Realpolitik without the accompanying internationalism of the wartime alliance. The rhetoric was unambiguous; Churchill was putting an end to the internationalist vision of big-power relations. But the substance was equally significant; he was trying to confirm and consolidate the Yalta system as it applied to Soviet-British relations in the Middle East by having the United States join forces with the latter to maintain a balance of power, which seemed to call for an independent and friendly Turkey. The Soviet Union, on its part, was interested in keeping Turkey from falling under British domination. As was happening in China, such attempts by Britain and Russia only resulted in their entrenchment in Turkey by all means short of active military involvement. By the end of 1946, moreover, the United States was beginning to play Britain's role in some parts of the Middle East, in effect extending the American-Soviet Yalta equilibrium to that region of the world.

By then the rhetoric of the Cold War had come to be accepted by key American officials. Even before Churchill's Fulton speech, George F. Kennan had telegraphed from Moscow his view that "cooperation" with the Soviet Union was no longer tenable and that the United States must be prepared to accept a relationship of mutual hostility and suspicion with Russia. In his view, the Soviet Union could not be counted upon as a partner in building a durable peace. Rather, it would remain a self-centered, egoistic power seeking to promote its self-interests wherever it could. According to his own account, Kennan's telegram fell on fertile soil and helped conceptualize and confirm what the officials in Washington were coming to sense. Instead of cooperation, they now began to see mutual antipathy and even conflict between the United States and the Soviet Union. Once this view was accepted, everything that Russia did seemed to fall into place, as an instance of its worldwide expansionism. What emerged was a bipolar image of world politics, in which the two greatest powers represented divergent principles and interests and were pictured as being engaged in a perpetual struggle, if not on the battleground then at least in nonbelligerent manners. Kennan himself did not share this extreme form of global dualism, but it came to affect the way men looked at international events and to provide them with a vocabulary for describing what they thought they saw in the world arena.[19] The language used by President Truman in March 1947 when he recommended immediate aid to Greece and Turkey was a typical example of the Cold War rhetoric.

The rhetorical aspect of American-Soviet relations, however, did not sum up the totality of these relations. While the American people and officials were becoming accustomed to perceiving international affairs in a dualistic way, the American-Soviet balance that had defined the power aspect of the Yalta system did not break down. In fact neither the United States nor the Soviet Union was willing to risk war which could cause, or result from, such a breakdown. What Kennan was suggesting was that the concept of "cooperation" was unrealistic, not that there should be no American-Russian understanding on the basis of the power realities of the situation. He would discard the idealistic but not the Realpolitik aspect of the Yalta synthesis. In practice this meant that the United States should not waste its effort trying to come to an agreement with the Soviet Union on an outstanding international problem, but that it should try to discourage any potential Soviet attempt to violate the Yalta system by being vigilant in areas where American power predominated. In the Middle East, since it lay outside both America's and Russia's immediate zones of preponderance, Kennan would have been content to see a flexible and more or less neutral situation. He was confident that there could be a chance for world stability on the basis of the Yalta equilibrium, envisaging Soviet supremacy in Eastern Europe and American-British preponderance in Western and Southern Europe. The policy of "containment" which he advocated was a geo-political argument based on these considerations, not a new world-view envisaging ideological and idealistic American opposition to the Soviet Union in all parts of the world.

During 1946–47, then, the idealistic, "cooperative" aspect of the Yalta system progressively weakened, but, as Kennan recognized, there was no military conflict between America and Russia because they both refrained from infringing on each other's spheres of predominance as defined at the Yalta Conference. To be sure the United States was fast replacing Great Britain as the key power in parts of the Middle East, an outcome never anticipated at Yalta. But at least initially, American action was seen as designed to support British policy as the latter struggled to maintain the Yalta status quo in the Middle East. To that extent there was no substantial transformation of the balance between the Soviet Union on one hand and the Anglo-American powers on the other.

---

[19] Kennan, *Memoirs 1925–1950*, Chapter 11. See also Gaddis, *The United States and the Origins of the Cold War*, pp. 302–4.

Solidification of Spheres

These developments inevitably had repercussions on the Asia-Pacific region. Reflecting the demise of the spirit of American-Russian cooperation in international affairs, there was a tendency in this region, too, to view events in the framework of the confrontation between the two greatest Asia-Pacific powers. In areas outside of China, however, there was no overt conflict, and no crisis of the Yalta order. South Sakhalin and the Kuriles were formally incorporated into the Soviet Union in 1946, while in north Korea a provisional committee headed by Kim Il Sung was set up with Soviet blessings as a central organ of governmental authority. The Soviet Union refused to agree to economic unification of Korea, and aimed at keeping north Korea under its control through Soviet-oriented Korean Communists and by means of the presence of Soviet troops. All these moves shattered the ideal of a negotiated, cooperative settlement of territorial questions, and the United States protested against Soviet policy repeatedly and in vain. But there was no likelihood that the American government would do more than express its regrets at the breakdown of the cooperative system. No matter how strongly opposed to Soviet action, the United States basically recognized that Russia had been assigned specific spheres of predominance, and it was not going to challenge them by force.

Conversely, the United States insisted on having its say concerning matters that lay within its zones of preponderance, in particular Japan. Sessions of the allied council for Japan, with representatives from the United States, the Soviet Union, the British Commonwealth, and China, were an exercise in futility, and the American and Russian representatives disagreed on almost all questions. But the United States, through General MacArthur, was not deterred from ruling the occupied country with an iron hand. The occupation authorities drafted a new constitution for Japan, persisted in their refusal to try the Emperor as a war criminal, instituted land reform and other programs, and set up their own criteria for purging persons from public office. In south Korea, too, American officials went ahead with various programs to establish a provisional government south of the thirty-eighth parallel. By the end of 1946 the division of Korea into two distinctive administrative units had been completed.

It did not mean, however, that at this time the United States was contemplating an armed conflict with the Soviet Union in Asia or the Pacific. There persisted the assumption that a balance that had been defined at Yalta was worth preserving, and that within America's zones of predominance it was entitled to carry out what it considered appropriate. There was little thought of military confrontation with Russia, and no program for a massive build-up of United States armed forces in this region. The primary goal of occupation authorities in Japan and Korea was still the elimination of Japanese militarism, and the United States took the view that economic rehabilitation of the country was primarily the responsibility of the Japanese, who would first be expected to pay reparations to their former enemies. The recommendation of the Pauley reparations mission that the Japanese be allowed only a minimum standard of living and that everything else be taken away from them for reparations summed up American policy in 1945–46. The United States would not brook Soviet interference with its occupation policy in Japan, but it would be just as vigorous as the latter in eradicating vestiges of Japanese militarism. American forces would remain in Japan to ensure the success of the occupation, and incidentally to safeguard the new sphere of influence of the United States, but they would not challenge Soviet power in areas of *its* predominance. In Okinawa, too, American officials did not consider it an essential base for United States strategy, but a country to be kept under control to frustrate the resurgence of Japanese imperialism. An American military government officer on the island even believed that just one thousand United States troops would suffice for security and defense purposes.[20]

Unfortunately, the situation was vastly more complex in China. As seen above, the sending of the Marshall mission had signaled America's intention to uphold the Yalta system in the face of Soviet presence in Manchuria, its ties with the Chinese Communists, and the civil strife in China. Such a policy had necessitated limited interventionism by the United States and resulted in an extension of American power and influence beyond what had been envisaged earlier in 1945. But there was no thought that the United States and the Soviet Union would collide frontally in China or that they would divide the country up into their respective spheres of influence. Any such eventuality would have destroyed the Yalta system. The key question throughout 1946 was in what way the system could best be preserved. Already by the middle of the year it was becoming evident that Marshall's mediatory efforts had failed and that there would not be an effective cease-fire, let alone a truce or an eventual formation of a coalition government, in China in the near future. Both Nationalist and Communist forces were reluctant to give up their positions of strength or to desist from attacking the opponent wherever practicable. As Marshall and John Leighton Stuart, president of Yenching University who had just been appointed ambassador to China, jointly declared on August 10,

The fighting is daily growing more widespread and threatens to engulf the country and pass beyond the control of those responsible.

[20] John P. Emmerson, *Arms, Yen, and Power* (New York: Dunellen, 1971), pp. 159–60.

They particularly pointed to the difficulty of getting the two sides to agree on the character of local governments to be set up after a cease-fire. Obviously, both Nationalists and Communists wanted to have as much control over them as possible.[21]

The domestic situation was ironically exacerbated by the withdrawal of Russian troops from Manchuria in the spring of 1946, although the Nationalists had long demanded it. The removal of Soviet forces, just when Nationalist armies had come to control some cities and railways in Manchuria, caused intensified fighting between the latter and the Communists who had established sway over the countryside. The major central Manchurian city of Changchun, for instance, was evacuated by Soviet troops in mid-April, attacked and captured by Chinese Communists a few days later, and then a month later retaken by the Nationalists. They were determined to remain in Manchuria against the counsel of some generals who wanted to concentrate on the defense of China proper. Events were to prove the latter correct, that the Kuomintang armies had spread themselves too thin. But the longer the civil hostilities lasted, the more dependent on American support became the Nationalists. Chiang Kai-shek and his advisers were in fact convinced of their ultimate successes because they believed they could count upon aid and assistance from the United States.

American policy was thus faced with a serious dilemma. There was virtual unanimity among officials that the Yalta balance between the United States and the Soviet Union must be preserved. They may or may not have agreed with the operations division of the War Department General Staff that

> The obvious Soviet aim in China is to exclude U.S. influence and replace it with that of Moscow.

But few would have taken exception to its view that

> Our exclusion from China would probably result, within the next generation, in an expansion of Soviet influence over the manpower, raw materials and industrial potential of Manchuria and China. The U.S. and the world might then be faced in the China Sea and southward with a Soviet power analogous to that of the Japanese in 1941, but with the difference that the Soviets could be perhaps overwhelming[ly] strong in Europe and the Middle East as well.[22]

This was a language of power politics that had become accepted as axiomatic by policy makers, civilian as well as military, in Washington. They might

[21] *Foreign Relations of the United States 1946*, X, 1 (Washington, D.C.: Government Printing Office, 1972).
[22] Carter to Marshall, Aug. 14, 1946, ibid., pp. 27–28.

disagree as to whether the Soviet Union consistently pursued a policy of expansion in China or of exclusion of American power and interests from China. But it was evident that America's unilateral withdrawal from China would mean a relative increase of Soviet power and a consequent disequilibrium in East Asia. That was why, as John Carter Vincent told Ambassador Wellington Koo in August

> There was no intention to abandon or 'wash our hands' of the China problem. Our interest in the Far East, and its relation to world peace, overshadowed any immediate feeling we might have concerning the inability of the Chinese to settle their internal problems, and we would therefore continue to have a profound and active interest in developments there.

Significantly, however, Vincent added, "In what special manner that interest would express itself I couldn't say." [23]

The United States was actively interested in maintaining the framework of American-Soviet balance as a touchstone of the postwar international system in East Asia. As Vincent realized, however, its implementation was filled with uncertainties, even more so than in Iran or Turkey, because of the Yalta assumption that China would remain more or less independent and unified. Since the country was neither independent nor unified in 1946, the United States had to decide whether such a China was a prerequisite to the Yalta system or, conversely, whether a clarification of American-Soviet relations in Asia must precede the unification of China. It had been assumed that the two objectives—an American-Soviet balance and a unified and autonomous China—were factors in the same equation, to alter one of which would result in changing the equation itself. In view of the developing situation, however, there grew a serious division of opinion within the United States government concerning the practical application of the Yalta principles. Among those who stressed the importance of maintaining an equilibrium in American-Soviet relations, some, especially the military, called for a greater degree of United States involvement in China to prevent it from falling under Soviet control. Even here, however, opinions were divided. While most assumed that such involvement would take the form of giving aid to the Kuomintang, a minority believed in establishing close ties with the Communists so as to keep them from turning to the Soviet Union for help. Others were persuaded that the American-Soviet balance would be upset by an extension of American power in China, whatever the degree of Soviet aid to the Chinese Communists. It seemed best to disengage gradually from China since the Soviet Union was not likely to turn it into its exclusive sphere of influence. Premature and precipitated American involvement, from such a point of view, would actually bring about a counter-expansion by the Soviet

[23] Vincent memo, Aug. 13, 1946, ibid., pp. 23–25.

Union and defeat the basic objective of upholding the Yalta status quo. Then there were those who stressed China's unification as still the best means of preserving the Yalta system. Only when China was united and became a stabilizing force of some magnitude in East Asia, could there be a real equilibrium in the region. But here again, there were as many views as to what constituted such unity as there were factions in China.

American Debate over China

Official American policy for the time being was to consider Chinese unification the key to postwar stability in Asian international affairs. Through most of 1946 the dual programs of the Marshall mission—to mediate between the factions in China and to give aid to the Kuomintang— were retained and pushed with varying degrees of vigor. In January 1946 President Truman authorized the extension of the Lend-Lease program for China beyond its expiration date of March 2, to enable transfer of arms and equipment to the Chinese Nationalist forces. It was estimated that the total dollar value of Lend-Lease aid to the Chinese government would have amounted to over 800 million dollars between September 2, 1945, and June 30, 1946. This was 100 million dollars more than the amount provided China during the entire war under the Lend-Lease program. The War Department, with State Department concurrence, was anxious to continue the aid project, and was instrumental in drawing up a China aid act as a legal framework for the purpose after the expiration of the Lend-Lease. The bulk of the money was to be spent in providing logistical support to Chinese forces occupying North China and Manchuria, training Chinese officers and pilots, and giving surplus war materiel to the Nationalist armed forces. Here the basic idea was that such aid would enable the Kuomintang regime to establish a viable authority through most of China and help the country's development as an independent entity.[24]

Such support of the Nationalists, however, would have been compatible with the goal of bringing about a unified government in China through mediation only if they had been militarily successful in their struggle against the Communists, or if they had commanded undisputed support of the Chinese people. Since neither was the case, American policy could give the impression of assisting one group in China against others. This would militate against the policy of encouraging the formation of a coalition government in China representative of all political groups. To offer aid to China unified under the Kuomintang leadership was one thing; to assist one faction was quite another. As events throughout 1946 showed the inability of the Nationalists, despite (some thought because of) American aid, to establish a

[24] See ibid., pp. 724–66.

new representative government, the question naturally arose whether the continuance of such aid served any purpose. If unification in China were not to be forthcoming, American support of Chiang Kai-shek could be justified only in terms of the larger context of American-Soviet relations. At this time, however, the State Department as well as the White House did not believe that the Yalta structure had been so undermined that massive infusion of American aid was required to counter the trend. Such thinking led to a growing disposition on the part of some officials, including General Marshall, to reconsider the policy of mediation. It was not that the United States should withdraw entirely from China; such a stance would only cause further instability in Asian international relations. It was rather derived from the view that the American-Soviet equilibrium in East Asia could afford to live with a situation of disunity and uncertainty in China. Thus Marshall hoped that the China aid bill would not quickly be passed by Congress; a delay would constitute valuable pressure upon Chiang Kai-shek to undertake necessary reforms.[25] In a similar vein, President Truman sent a strongly worded message to Chiang Kai-shek in August, declaring,

> Recent developments have forced me to the conclusion that the selfish interests of extremist elements, equally in the Kuomintang as in the Communist party, are hindering the aspirations of the Chinese people.

Since American criticism of the Communists was nothing extraordinary, the message was a clear warning to the Nationalists that they must undertake drastic measures to bring about a ceasefire and a more representative government if they were to continue to deserve American aid. As Truman wrote,

> There is a growing feeling . . . that the aspirations of the Chinese people are being thwarted by militarists and a small group of political reactionaries, who, failing to comprehend the liberal trend of the times, are obstructing the advancement of the general good of the nation. Such a state of affairs is violently repugnant to the American people.

The statement showed that as far as President Truman and his immediate advisers were concerned the United States was losing its faith in the attainability of a unified China in the immediate future, through the kinds of assistance that America had given that country. The idea of a united and independent China, having been part of American thinking for so many years, was not easy to give up. But if the Chinese leaders were proving themselves incapable of achieving this goal, then the United States would have to reconsider its policy assumptions and think of other ways in which to

[25] Marshall to Carter, July 23, 1946, ibid., p. 753.

promote its own interests. This was the meaning of the concluding passage in Truman's warning to Chiang:

> Unless convincing proof is shortly forthcoming that genuine progress is being made toward a peaceful settlement of China's internal problems, it must be expected that American opinion will not continue in its generous attitude towards your nation. It will, furthermore, be necessary for me to redefine and explain the position of the United States to the American people.[26]

From this time on through the remainder of the year 1946, General Marshall and President Truman failed to observe any evidence to cause them to alter such pessimistic thinking. Even the convening of a national assembly under Kuomintang auspices in November, and the subsequent adoption of a new constitution, did not change the situation, since the Communists refused to participate and the government's popularity continued to decline. Marshall was coming to the conclusion that the presence of Communist forces in parts of China was a military reality that could not be ignored in any attempt to bring about a more unified government. If the Nationalists persisted in treating the Communists as a minor party to be eliminated by force, there could be no peace in the land. As he told Ambassador Stuart in December, he doubted that

> hostilities could be stopped unilaterally since the Government always claims to be fighting in self-defense [and] the Generalissimo is convinced that a policy of force is the only practicable solution as he completely distrusts the Communists and their purposes in getting into the government.[27]

If there were to persist hostilities between Nationalists and Communists, the only possibility would be a prolonged stalemate, a virtual division of China into opposing military camps. Marshall had fondly believed that his presence in China might have some restraining influence upon Kuomintang diehards and force them to undertake reforms as a price for obtaining United States support. But evidently he had failed in his mission.

Under the circumstances, American policy was faced with a choice of leaving China to its own stalemate and internal division, or continuing to support the Nationalists' initiative to unify the country. The third possible alternative, aiding the Communists to bring about unification, was never seriously considered. Marshall was strongly in favor of the first option, not so much because he liked the idea as because he disliked the second alternative the more. Not only did the idea of Kuomintang-controlled China appear to him to be fantastically unrealistic given the Nationalists' ineptitude and

[26] Truman to Koo, Aug. 10, 1946, ibid., pp. 2–3.
[27] See ibid., pp. 573–94.

Communist power, but he considered it unwise for the United States to tie itself to a reactionary regime. He would rather seek to safeguard American national and geo-political interests in Asia through other means than the support of Chiang Kai-shek. Evidently he believed that the cessation of American mediation efforts would not call forth Soviet expansion in China. On the contrary, he seems to have reasoned that the Soviet Union would react strongly if the United States adopted the second alternative and stepped up its aid to the Nationalists. Others, including Ambassador Stuart, however, were exponents of this option. They were convinced that Chiang Kai-shek was still the best hope for a unified and reorganized China and that he was on the right track in his endeavors to bring about that goal. As Stuart told Marshall,

> With a new democratic constitution and a reformed and reorganized government, the government of China would become truly more representative of the Chinese people.

The United States, in his view, should deepen its involvement through increased economic, technical, and military assistance to the Nationalists since such involvement alone would enable it to exert influence on the latter to undertake reforms. Stuart's thinking was clear-cut; by intensifying American support of and influence upon the Kuomintang regime,

> We would be strengthening a democratic form of government as against a Communist form of government . . . we would be exchanging one party tutelage for American tutelage . . . any other course would amount to abandoning China.[28]

Here was an argument that demonstrated that in trying to uphold the Yalta idea of an independent and unified China the United States could end up establishing its "tutelage" over the country.

Marshall was not willing to support such a policy. Nor did he agree with Stuart that unless the United States established its tutelage over China it would be "abandoning" the country. Marshall was eager to retain what power, influence, and interests the United States had in China and to maintain an equilibrium vis-à-vis Russia, but doubted that these objectives could be promoted if the nation tied itself exclusively to Chiang Kai-shek and the latter began to take American support for granted. In his telegram to President Truman of December 28, requesting that he be recalled from China, Marshall frankly stated,

> I can do much to destroy the power of the reactionaries and bring a liberal

[28] Ibid., pp. 594–99.

element into control of the Government by a frank statement [on] the occasion of my arrival in the United States

concerning the frustrations he had encountered.[29] In Washington, Vincent immediately understood the purport of the telegram. Agreeing with Marshall, he wrote that henceforth American policy should concentrate

> on furthering and strengthening our diplomatic and economic relations with China in a manner regardful of our own interests and of our desire to aid China in practical non-political ways, thus leaving it to the Chinese to reach some kind of settlement of their political difficulties.[30]

President Truman had already decided to recall Marshall and to appoint him secretary of state to succeed James F. Byrnes. Marshall issued the intended statement, and thus, at the beginning of the new year, 1947, the American efforts to bring about a unified China through active mediation came to an end. From this time on, as Vincent indicated, United States involvement in China would not take the form of promoting its unity by bringing America's power, prestige, and influence to bear upon Chinese internal politics. Rather, the United States would follow other objectives and establish other criteria for its policy in East Asia. The idea of China as a unified, independent power entered a state of suspended animation as far as American policy-makers were concerned.

What had been destroyed was the Chinese ingredient in the Yalta system. The system had been predicated upon the existence of a more or less independent China not subject to either Soviet or American control. Chinese sovereignty had already been infringed upon by the presence of American and Russian troops, but at least the United States through General Marshall had tried to consolidate the Yalta system by encouraging the emergence of a united and representative government of China. The end of the Marshall mission meant that a new policy would have to be pursued by the United States, a policy in which the idea of a unified and independent China would lose its centrality. How to preserve the Yalta scheme for an American-Soviet balance in such a situation was the challenging question after the end of the Marshall mission.

China Between the Superpowers

In the meantime, the Chinese Communists had begun accusing the United States of interference in Chinese domestic affairs. As the failure of the Marshall mediation efforts became more and more apparent, they came

[29] Marshall to Truman, Dec. 28, 1946, ibid., pp. 661–65.
[30] Vincent to Acheson, Dec. 31, 1946, ibid., pp. 671–72.

openly to insist that the presence of American troops, and even of Marshall himself, in China was an infringement upon national sovereignty. The Communists reasoned that despite Marshall's protestations to the contrary, American presence could only mean support of the Nationalists and frustration for their own efforts to seek a more representative central government and greater regional autonomy. Initially the Communists had welcomed Marshall's mediatory mission, but after the middle of 1946 they lost confidence in America's allegedly neutral stance. Under the circumstances, United States forces in China could only be of benefit to the Nationalists. Moreover, continuation of the civil war could provide justification for keeping American troops in China, who in turn would encourage the Kuomintang to persist in their military campaigns against the Communists, thus further intensifying the domestic turmoil. In short, by its military presence the United States was interfering in Chinese domestic affairs and violating Chinese sovereignty. As *Chieh-fang jih-pao* noted in its editorial of June 7,

> Although we have repelled the Japanese imperialist bandits, we have not gained national independence. We are even being murdered by foreign arms.

Never before in Chinese history had imperialism interfered in China's internal affairs and oppressed the Chinese people's movements for democracy and freedom to such an extent. It was not that the United States as a whole was to blame, the editorial continued, for the reversal of Franklin D. Roosevelt's policy of friendship between the two peoples. It was only a minority of American reactionaries that were obstructing the friendship. They were making a serious mistake, for

> they do not realize that the Chinese people today are not what they were in the past. Now they have great and inviolable strength.

When the China aid act was introduced to Congress, Mao Tse-tung declared that American assistance to the Kuomintang regime was tantamount to armed intervention in international affairs of China, causing continued division, chaos, and poverty in the country and destroying the friendship between the two peoples. Why were the American "reactionaries" so eager to "assist" China, asked a Communist declaration of July 7, and answered its own question by asserting that these reactionaries were aiming at imperialistic aggression. United States imperialism, the declaration said, was even stronger and more dangerous than Japanese imperialism. The survival of the Chinese people was now threatened by the joining of forces of domestic and foreign reactionaries.

Such outbursts made it extremely difficult for Marshall to deal with the

Communists in an effort to mediate between them and the Nationalists. What he called "the Communist picture of misrepresentation and vicious propaganda" gave him added impetus to seek to be relieved of his mission.[31] To the extent that there was intentional misrepresentation on the part of the Communist leadership, this seems to have been due to a desire to put pressure upon American public opinion so as to speed up the withdrawal of United States forces from China. By depicting American policy as imperialistically seeking hegemony all over the world, the Communists undoubtedly hoped to arouse resentment as much inside the United States as outside. As Mao Tse-tung told Anne Louise Strong in August, the United States now controlled the South Pacific, Japan, south Korea, and Kuomintang China. It was planning to extend its hegemony over the British empire and western Europe, in addition to Central and South America. Intervention in China was thus but an aspect of worldwide ambitions of United States imperialism. The Chinese people, therefore, were justified in opposing it, just as much as the American people were. However, Mao and his comrades were desirous of avoiding the impression that they were turning to the Soviet Union for aid, precisely as they accused the Nationalists of relying on American support. Actually, the Communists seem to have been concerned lest continued American presence in China should bring about Soviet counteraction, thus causing direct confrontation between the two super-powers on Chinese soil. Such an outcome would be disastrous. There was all the more reason, therefore, why United States intervention must be ended.

Chinese Communist thinking and strategy were thus to stress the importance of avoiding foreign intervention and of asserting Chinese sovereignty. Only a China free of American military presence and of American-Soviet clashes on its soil would be truly independent. As the Marshall mission came to an end in January 1947, therefore, the Communists not surprisingly emphasized that chances of war between the United States and the Soviet Union were subsiding. According to Lu Ting-i, propaganda chief of the Communist Party, the basic contradiction in the world was not between America and Russia but between the mass of people and reactionaries in the United States. There was no inevitability of war between the two giant powers, but the democratic forces in America, China, and elsewhere would continue their struggle against United States imperialism. Wang Ping-nan, representing the Communists in Nanking, told Ambassador Stuart on the occasion of Marshall's departure that in the past several months there had been "marked improvement" in American-Russian relations.[32] What all these statements indicated was a sense of confidence on the part of the Chinese Communists that their struggle against the Nationalists would now be easier, and chances of foreign intervention less,

[31] Ibid., p. 664.
[32] Stuart to Byrnes, Jan. 10, 1947, ibid., pp. 695–96.

than earlier. All the same, they were making it unmistakably clear that they would continue to oppose foreign encroachment and to view the United States as an imperialist *par excellence* so long as it gave assistance to the Chiang Kai-shek regime.

The Soviet Union, too, did not want large-scale American presence in China or a military clash with the United States in Asia. Russian policy was still conducted within the framework of the Yalta synthesis which to the Soviet Union meant the maintenance of a China that would not be hostile toward Russia. In other words, it was essential to prevent an American take-over of China through intervention in the civil war, which would upset the equilibrium in Northeastern Asia. During the latter half of 1946, as the Marshall mission was apparently proving not quite neutral and the United States seemed to deepen its commitment to the support of Chiang Kai-shek, the Soviet Union began accusing America of partiality and interference in Chinese domestic affairs. Moscow reiterated more and more strongly the Chinese Communists' argument that American imperialism was trying to dominate China and violate its independence. As *Izvestia* stated in December 1946,

American policy in China is inspired by those reactionary circles in the United States who want to turn China into a semicolony and a military-strategical jumping-off ground in the Far East.[33]

In Russian perception this meant that the United States was seriously undermining the Yalta system. To prevent its complete collapse it was essential to insist on removal of American troops from China. At the same time, however, Soviet policy did not contemplate large-scale involvement in China to counterbalance American power. Such a step would heighten the sense of crisis not only in Asia but elsewhere and prematurely bring about a conflict with the United States. Moreover, Russia was still hopeful of utilizing its formal ties with the Kuomintang in such a way as to maximize the advantages it had obtained at Yalta. A complete rupture with Chiang Kai-shek would serve no useful purposes. Thus the Soviet Union avoided overt interference in the Nationalist-Communist conflict and concentrated on trying to reduce American power and influence in China. In this sense the recall of the Marshall mission was a mixed blessing; it ended the period of active American mediation that had been coupled with support of the Kuomintang, but at the same time it could presage a policy of more open intervention in Chinese affairs.

At the beginning of 1947, then, a balance still existed between the United States and the Soviet Union in East Asia. For a time it had looked as

[33] Max Beloff, *Soviet Policy in the Far East, 1944–1951* (London: Oxford University Press, 1953), p. 53.

if the former might be trying to extend its power beyond the limits foreseen at the time of the Yalta Conference, but the withdrawal of the Marshall mission put matters in China back where they had been in 1945 as far as American-Russian relations were concerned. The question now was whether a seemingly hopelessly divided China would still be left alone by the big powers, or whether that country would become embroiled in the Cold War that was beginning to take definite shape in Iran, Turkey, and Greece. As seen already, the United States was responding to crises in these areas within the framework both of power politics—to maintain the Yalta equilibrium, although American power was complementing and gradually superseding British power in Europe and the Middle East—and of ideology—the idea that the United States was standing behind freedom-loving peoples everywhere. Moreover, American national interests were undergoing redefinition in view of the possession of atomic weapons and the growing influence of the military and the service departments within the United States government. American public opinion, too, was once again becoming accustomed to talks of war, not because of the resurgence of German or Japanese militarism but because of Soviet Communist expansionism. There was a sense of frustration that the world had not been restored to a peaceful state and that the much heralded era of good feeling between America and Russia had failed to materialize. Those segments of American opinion which ordinarily would have gone back to isolationism and provincialism were among the most belligerent toward the Soviet Union. They were prone to see in Communist movements in other countries or in Soviet foreign policy decisions a sinister, anti-American design.

In view of the fact, then, that the Cold War was a multi-dimensional phenomenon, there was little unusual about the basic characteristics of American-Soviet relations as they developed in East Asia after 1947. Neither the United States nor the Soviet Union was scheming for worldwide conquest or global expansionism—neither of them was anxious to exchange the Yalta order for something unknown and precarious. They did extend their power, interests, and influence, but by and large driven by balance-of-power considerations, each to deny to the other side opportunities for undermining the position it enjoyed in its spheres of predominance. At the same time, both Americans and Russians had their idealistic visions and were prone to interpret world affairs in ideological terms. Both stood for "freedom," "democracy," and "anti-colonialism" in all parts of the globe and accused one another of violating these principles. Finally, both boasted their armed might, the Soviet Union trying fast to break American atomic monopoly, while the United States retained a sense of superiority in economic power and did not conceal its readiness to use it for political purposes.

All these ingredients of the Cold War could be found in Asia after 1947. Perhaps most important, in terms of long-range consequences, was the disinclination of both Washington and Moscow to redefine drastically the Yalta scheme in the Asia-Pacific region. Specifically this meant that the United States would persist in controlling the occupation of Japan, that in Korea America and Russia would decide to live with a de facto partition, and that neither party would involve itself in a massive scale in the Chinese civil war. These were fairly clear-cut decisions, but the situation became more complex than the decisions indicated because of the intrusion of the other dimensions of Cold War diplomacy. Nevertheless, it is significant to note that the structure of international affairs in the region changed much more slowly than the Cold War rhetoric implied.

Effects of the U.S. Occupation of Japan

For Japan the year 1947 had tremendous significance. In March the new constitution was promulgated, declaring the nation's renunciation of "war as a sovereign right of the nation and the threat of force as means of settling international disputes." Although the constitution had been drafted and imposed by the occupation authorities, it was duly deliberated by the Diet and discussed by the political parties, leaving little room for doubt that the so-called "no-war clause" had widespread acceptance by a people who had experienced fifteen years of war and devastation. The Tokyo military tribunal was coming to an end, as if to symbolize the fate that awaited militaristic imperialism. Here again national opinion was overwhelmingly in support of the trials, although this was clearly a case of "victors' justice." Most important in terms of future developments was the consolidation of the leadership of Yoshida Shigeru, a professional diplomat, who would preside over the country more or less continuously until 1954. He had become prime minister in May 1946. Although he was out of office between May 1947 and October 1948, his ideas concerning Japanese foreign policy remained influential and were beginning to dominate the thinking of the bulk of the bureaucracies and political parties. According to Yoshida, Japan's future lay in economic expansion. In order not to repeat the mistakes of the 1930s and the 1940s, it was imperative to concentrate national energies on promoting overseas trade and other types of economic relations through peaceful means. But in order to do so Japan must regain independence by concluding a peace treaty with its former enemies. Given the fact, however, that the United States was the predominant power in the Pacific and the main occupier of Japan, as well as being the richest country in the world, it stood to reason for Japan to deepen its ties with America and to seek its salvation through special arrangements with the United States. Such thinking in part was derived from a tradition of peaceful commercial expansionism in Japan which, as noted earlier, had existed side by side with more imperialistic types of expansion. Yoshida was urging a return to that tradition which he thought had been thwarted by the military with devastating consequences for the nation. Economically oriented foreign policy also had an Anglo-American bias inasmuch as Japan would be dependent on raw materials, capital, technology, and markets of Britain, the United States, and their territories. The fact that the United States was the main occupation force in Japan was therefore most convenient from such a point of view. The country, Yoshida felt, should take advantage of the situation in such a way as to tie its destiny closely with the United States. Moreover, the developing tension between America and Russia could also be useful; the United States would not wish to expose Japan to the threat of Communist expansion through economic insecurity and political instability, but would do what it could to promote order and welfare of Japanese society. Most important, Yoshida believed that the Cold War could provide an opportunity for inducing the United States to restore Japanese independence, while at the same time maintaining its forces in Japan for security purposes. In other words, Japan would regain sovereignty through a peace treaty, but its national security would be safeguarded primarily through the presence of American forces. Such an idea fitted the "no-war" constitution, reinforced the notion of peaceful economic expansion, and rationalized the strategy of maintaining close economic, political, and military ties with the United States.

Here was a strategy for action that was to remain a guiding principle of Japanese diplomacy for more than twenty years. Yoshida represented those in Japan who before the war had stood for a commercially, as opposed to militaristically, oriented foreign policy and for cooperation with the Anglo-American powers as opposed to the Axis powers or the Soviet Union. The defeat and occupation had resulted in a purge of the pro-Axis leaders as well as the military, and it was no accident that those who came to positions of power were men like Yoshida. Even when he was out of office briefly during 1947–48, his ideas were carried forward by Ashida Hitoshi, foreign minister in the short-lived Socialist cabinet of Katayama Tetsu (May 1947–February 1948) and then prime minister (February–October 1948) before Yoshida returned to power. Ashida belonged to the same generation of professional diplomats and held similar ideas to Yoshida's concerning Japan's immediate needs and future goals. Together they tried to persuade General MacArthur's headquarters to terminate the occupation regime and substitute for it an arrangement for continued presence of American bases and troops in Japan. In other words, they were doing their share to consolidate the Yalta scheme by incorporating Japan into the developing framework of the Cold War. The choice they adopted was to perpetuate America's dominant position in Japan and its environs, at the same time putting an end to the victor's occupation of the land. The only other alternatives would be either the continuation of the occupation or a scheme for neutralizing Japan, both of which Yoshida and Ashida rejected as damaging to national interests.

The Yoshida-Ashida strategy was clear-cut, and in time it found acceptance by the United States government. In 1947, to be sure, no decision was reached by the latter concerning the shape of the Japanese peace treaty; while a committee of the State Department began work on the subject and had produced three drafts by March 1947, there was uncertainty concerning the mode of preparing for a peace conference. Not only was there the increasingly serious question of Soviet reaction to any idea of a Japanese peace treaty, but countries such as Australia, France, and the American republics that had been at war with Japan had to be consulted. Technical procedural matters took up much of the State Department's attention throughout 1947–48. Nevertheless, the fact that American officials began deliberations on a Japanese peace treaty was significant; it indicated willingness to consider an eventual termination of the occupation. This in turn was derived from the assumption that the primary goals of the occupation had been largely accomplished. As General MacArthur stated in March 1947,

> The Japanese nation and people are now ready for the initiation of negotiations leading to a Treaty of Peace—ready in the sense that Japan's war-making power and potential is destroyed, the framework to democratic government has been erected, reforms essential to the reshaping of Japanese lives and institutions to conform to democratic ideals have been instituted, and the people have been accorded the fundamentals of human liberty.[34]

It is less important to ascertain if MacArthur really believed in all these achievements allegedly accomplished in less than two years of occupation, than to note that in his own mind the primary objectives of the occupation had been attained. He was thus giving his authoritative support to a policy of ending the state of war between Japan and its former enemies. It meant that Japan had been sufficiently punished and that it could now be restored as a member of the new international community. As General John H. Hilldring, assistant secretary of state for occupied areas, noted in June, whereas two approaches, punitive and constructive, had existed on the subject of what to do with Japan, the former was declining in influence within the United States government.

> We need not any longer, I am sure, concern ourselves with whether or not we shall advocate a punitive treaty. That is a closed issue.[35]

[34] MacArthur memo, Mar. 21, 1947, *Foreign Relations of the United States 1947* (Washington, D.C.: Government Printing Office, 1972) VI, 454–56.
[35] Hilldring to Atcheson, June 9, 1946, ibid., pp. 461–62.

In line with such thinking, Washington began stressing the desirability of not overburdening the Japanese economy with punitive reparations payments but rather of encouraging Japan's economic reconstruction through industrialization. The War Department was particularly interested in stabilizing social conditions in Japan and advocated unilateral action by the United States to put an end to the dismantling and removal of Japanese factories, ships, and other items for reparation purposes. Survey missions headed by Clifford Strike were sent by the War Department to Japan in 1947, and they advocated drastic reduction of Japan's reparations. Also in the same year, the Supreme Headquarters in Tokyo permitted Japan to resume export trade. The obvious implication was that Japan had to export in order to pay for its vital imports, and that to undertake export trade it must be allowed to manufacture goods over and above what had to be earmarked as war reparations. In this way American policy was beginning to approximate, at least in part, the wishes of the Japanese leaders.

The United States government continued to assume that it enjoyed a dominant position in Japan in accordance with the Yalta understanding. In the absence of overt Soviet moves to challenge that supremacy, it is not surprising that American officials stressed economic recovery as the most practical way of maintaining the Yalta status quo as far as Japan was concerned. At this time, there was no thought that Japan should be transformed once again as a military power. Such a step would be a serious infringement on the framework of American-Russian balance in the Asia-Pacific region and was bound to provoke Soviet retaliation. Actually, the Russians were extremely sensitive to any sign that Japan's demilitarization and eradication of imperialism were not moving fast enough. In 1947 they repeatedly accused the MacArthur administration of having failed to carry out these programs fully and even of planning to resurrect the Japanese army.[36] American authorities were well aware of Soviet accusations; but they, too, did not wish to alter the status quo drastically. If anything, some American officials, including MacArthur himself, believed it possible to reduce and remove ultimately all foreign troops from Japan so that the latter would truly maintain a peaceful existence. In March 1947 MacArthur stated that Japanese security, under the terms of the new constitution, would be

> subject to the justice and good faith of the peace-loving peoples of the world.

It was incumbent, therefore,

> that the Allied Nations for their part . . . undertake to guarantee the neutrality of Japan, with a view to the transfer of such undertaking to the stewardship of the United Nations, where the responsibility properly should rest.[37]

[36] Beloff, *Soviet Policy*, pp. 122–25.
[37] MacArthur memo, Mar. 21, 1947, *Foreign Relations 1947*, VI, 454–56.

This type of idealism was heard only infrequently, and throughout most of 1947 American officials concerned themselves with procedural questions about a Japanese peace conference. Their assumption was that Japan would continue to be a negligible factor militarily but would be allowed to recover economically. Whether United States troops would remain indefinitely in Japan was a debatable question, but few doubted that stability would be maintained with or without them; there would be no serious threat by the Soviet Union.

In this way there was some parallel between American policy toward Germany and Japan, the two former enemies under allied occupation where the eradication of militarism and imperialism had been the main goal of the victorious powers. In Germany, as in Japan, the United States government began stressing economic reconstruction. As George F. Kennan wrote,

> The economic reconstruction of Western Europe is of urgent and primary importance. The restoration of German productivity, if only in a part of Germany, is essential to that rehabilitation. We cannot wait for Russian agreement to achieve that restoration.[38]

The German case was more complicated than the Japanese since it was divided into separate zones of occupation; but at the same time it was easier to see the relationship between economic reconstruction at least of western Germany and that of Western Europe, than to see the place of an economically rehabilitated Japan in a changing Asia. Still, the basic rationale was the same; the United States would encourage "the establishment of stable political and economic conditions" (a phrase in the July 1947 directive by the Joint Chiefs of Staff for United States authorities in Germany) in the former enemy lands under American control.[39] As yet no military measures were involved, either in Germany or in Japan; it was not even clear if United States forces would be long maintained. Rather, the stress was on economic reconstruction so as to foster stability and prevent Soviet penetration and expansion. This was entirely in line with the Yalta system; the United States would seek to prevent a radical transformation of the status quo in Asia as well as in Europe. The Cold War rhetoric, which became accepted by the American people and government in 1947, added an ideological dimension to such a policy, giving the impression that American-Soviet relations were entering a new, critical phase. In fact what was happening was a consolidation of the Yalta system. Just as the United States was taking the initiative in this direction, therefore, the Soviet Union could be expected to respond in kind and solidify *its* power within its spheres of influence. In areas which were within neither power's orbit, however, the

---

[38] Kennan, *Memoirs 1925–1950*, p. 333.
[39] Kolko, *Limits of Power*, p. 353.

American-Russian confrontation would be more ideological than physical. Korea offered a good example of the former situation, and China of the latter.

Status Quo in Korea

In Korea the year 1947 marked the virtual end of any attempt on the part of the United States and the Soviet Union to work together to help create a unified government for the country. The American-Soviet joint commission met for the last time in October, signifying the two powers' lack of interest in a unified Korea if that meant the possibility of one or the other power's extending its control over the entire peninsula. From Moscow's point of view, there was concern that the United States might retain its troops in south Korea indefinitely and give the latter massive economic aid, just as it was on the point of doing in Western Europe and Japan. Such steps would entrench American power in the southern half of the Korean peninsula and threaten the stability of the northern half. The Russian government was suspicious of any American-inspired program for Korean unification, and countered with its own proposals, which took the form of calling for a national assembly composed of equal numbers of delegates from the two halves. Obviously, the Soviet intention was to keep north Korea under its control as a safeguard against the possible expansion of American influence northward.

The United States, on its part, was anxious to prevent Soviet penetration of south Korea. A secret memorandum of February 25 by a special inter-Departmental committee on Korea gives a flavor of official thinking in Washington. In it the authors pointed out that Korea was "the only area where we and the Soviets stand face to face alone." Under the circumstances, unilateral withdrawal of United States forces was premature and unthinkable, since it would surely be followed by south Korea's falling "under Soviet domination." Echoing the then developing rhetoric of bipolar confrontation, the memorandum continued that the effect of such an outcome

> on world power relations . . . would almost certainly far transcend the mere transfer of southern Korea from the U.S. to Soviet control. The loss of U.S. prestige and influence, and the consequent increase in Soviet influence and power, would have prejudicial repercussions not only on U.S. interests in the Far East but on the entire U.S. world position.

It followed that the United States must do all it could to "remain in Korea" until such time as the danger of Soviet take-over of south Korea passed, and to "initiate an aggressive, positive, long-term program" of economic and technical assistance. An economically viable south Korea could in time become the basis for a new unified and independent Korea free of foreign control.[40] Quite evidently, in such a policy memorandum there was no longer any pretense that the United States and the Soviet Union might still work together to effect Korean unification or arrange for a trusteeship, as had been specified in 1945. The stress now was on maintaining the status quo in Korea as part of the global balance between the two super-powers. In Korea the status quo was fairly well defined, at the thirty-eighth parallel, and both the Soviet Union and the United States tried to preserve it through various means—the former stressing evacuation of foreign troops from Korea, and the latter pouring in aid to south Korea.

Indirect Confrontation in China

In China American-Soviet confrontation was much more indirect than in Korea. At the beginning of the year 1947, John Carter Vincent wrote,

> Without sacrificing any legitimate national interest, it is our purpose to prevent China from becoming a major irritant in our international relations, particularly with the U.S.S.R. [A] unified China is, from our point of view, a means toward an end rather than an end in itself. In short, we are following policies in China to achieve a larger objective.

Vincent was reiterating his devotion to the Yalta system; a unified China was a crucial ingredient in the Yalta equilibrium between the United States and the Soviet Union. The reality of the situation, unfortunately, was far otherwise. The civil war raged with greater furor after the recall of the Marshall mission, and any attempt at a coalition government was formally terminated both by the Nationalists and the Communists. Each claimed to speak for China and accused the other of incurring foreign intervention. Moreover, even the objective of American-Soviet balance as basic to a stable international system in East Asia was becoming clouded by the increasingly powerful impact of Cold-War perceptions. Vincent persisted in the belief that stable American-Soviet relations were of fundamental importance in the Asia-Pacific region, and in order to preserve the Yalta system he cautioned against involving the United States too deeply in Asia, which was bound to provoke Soviet counter-expansion. Massive military aid to the Nationalists would only make the latter more determined to push for victory over the Communists and ignore much needed reforms, thus further polarizing Chinese society and contributing to the growth of Communist influence. Here was a vicious cycle, and only American restraint could preserve a degree of stability. As Vincent wrote,

[40] Memo by special committee on Korea, Feb. 25, 1947, *Foreign Relations 1947*, VI, 608–18.

It would be preferable from our standpoint to let the opposing Chinese military forces reach some kind of solution or equilibrium without outside interference.

Although the United States would have to reconsider its position should the Soviet Union intervene materially in support of the Communists, it was unlikely, he asserted, "that the U.S.S.R. wishes to assume a forward position in China." In June he reiterated the argument that

A USSR-dominated China is not a danger of sufficient immediacy or probability to warrant committing ourselves to the far-reaching consequences which would ensue from our direct and large-scale involvement in the Chinese civil war on the side of the Chinese National Government.[41]

Here was a logical case against United States intervention in China. The atmosphere in Washington was such, however, that this type of calm Realpolitik, calculated to perpetuate the Yalta status quo, was becoming less and less popular. Pressure was mounting in and out of Congress, in the press, and even inside the government to view international affairs and civil wars through the lens of Cold-War perceptions. One theme of this was expressed by Navy Secretary James Forrestal, who said that

The United States might as well face the fact that if the United States withdrew its support from the Central [Nationalist] Government, the influence of the U.S.S.R. in China was bound to proportionately increase.[42]

Another was the view of Secretary of War Robert P. Patterson that there was

obviously a continuing community of interest and identity of aims between the Chinese Communists and Soviet-inspired international Communism.[43]

Once these theses were accepted (and it took little imagination to apply a bipolar vision to Soviet-Chinese relations), the kind of realistic power politics which Vincent advocated could appear naive and defeatist.

One of the clearest expositions of the new viewpoints as opposed to Vincent's was a memorandum prepared by the Joint Chiefs of Staff in June. They took it upon themselves to criticize Vincent's formulation of American policy toward China and recommended a frankly more interventionist policy. As they said,

In China, as in Europe and in the Middle and Far East, it is clearly Soviet policy to expand control, and influence wherever possible.

[41] Vincent memos, Feb. 7 and June 27, 1947, *Foreign Relations of the United States 1947* (Washington, D.C.: Government Printing Office, 1972), VII, 789–93, 852–54.
[42] Conference by Secretaries of State, War, and Navy, Feb. 12, 1947, ibid., pp. 795–97.
[43] Patterson to Marshall, Feb. 26, 1947, ibid., pp. 799–803.

Russia already was in a predominant position in Manchuria. This, coupled with the prolongation of the civil war, would result in Communist victory in China. Conditions would then have been created facilitating

> the eventual continued expansion of Soviet power in Asia southward through China and towards Indo-China, Malaysia and India.

Challenging the interpretation that the Chinese Communists were more nationalistic than Soviet-oriented, the memorandum asserted that they

> as all others, are Moscow inspired and thus motivated by the same basic totalitarian and anti-democratic policies as are the communist parties in other countries of the world. Accordingly, they should be regarded as tools of Soviet policy.

Under the circumstances, the "danger of Soviet expansion" must be halted with effective and timely countermeasures. As the Joint Chiefs of Staff noted,

> With a disarmed and occupied Japan, the only Asiatic government at present capable of even a show of resistance to Soviet expansion in Asia is the Chinese National Government.

While the writers of the memorandum recognized the existence of corruption and political shortcomings of the Nationalists, they thought these were of secondary importance. What was far more crucial was their survival so that China under the Kuomintang would

> more effectively . . . resist Soviet expansionist efforts in the Far East and . . . be a stabilizing factor throughout the Far East.

The Joint Chiefs of Staff recommended a program of "carefully planned, selective and well-supervised assistance" to the Nationalists.

It is interesting to note that in this memorandum the concept of American security was given the broadest possible definition. It stated

> A Soviet position of dominance over Asia, Western Europe, or both, would constitute a major threat to United States security. . . . It is to United States military interests that the nations of Eurasia oppose Soviet expansion.[44]

Considerations of power, ideals, and national interest merged in such a way that national security was considered adequately safeguarded only if Soviet expansion were halted and non-Communist regimes maintained everywhere

[44] Joint Chiefs of Staff to SWNCC, June 9, 1947, ibid., pp. 838–48.

in the world. Such a definition was tantamount to altering in a fundamental way United States policy toward China. Instead of viewing it in the context of the Yalta synthesis—leaving the Chinese outside Soviet and American spheres of influence—the new concept suggested that the preservation of the Chiang Kai-shek regime was essential to American security. Thus the United States would have to intervene in Chinese domestic affairs and extend its influence and power so as to ensure Nationalist victory, in effect destroying the Yalta equilibrium.

It was getting more and more difficult to rebut this type of argument in an America that was embracing the far-flung rhetoric of the Truman Doctrine, and to retain the less extreme Realpolitik of the Yalta compromise. As the Joint Chiefs pointed out, President Truman's decision to aid Greece and Turkey implied a policy

> to oppose further territorial and ideological expansion by the Soviet Union.

In such a situation, there was logic to their view that

> If this policy is to be effective it must be applied with consistency in all areas of the world threatened by Soviet expansion. Otherwise, if temporarily halted by our action in Greece and Turkey, the Soviets may decide to accelerate expansion in the Far East, in order to gain control of those areas which outflank us in the Near and Middle East.

Such thinking had an appeal to wider and wider circles of men in the United States, making it extremely difficult for the Truman administration to act within the earlier more limited structure of Yalta. In the duel with the military, Vincent eventually lost out. Even his subordinates, like Arthur R. Ringwalt, chief of the division of Chinese affairs, sided with his critics.[45] Because Vincent personified the older approach, he found himself relieved of his position as director of the State Department's office of Far Eastern affairs and sent abroad to a politically neutral embassy in Switzerland.

In such an atmosphere, it was no longer possible for the Truman administration to espouse the idea of a unified China on the basis of Nationalist-Communist compromise. The rhetoric of the Cold War provided it with no conceptual framework to view the civil war in China except in terms of the struggle between Communism and anti-Communism. Under the circumstances, officials in Washington were compelled to consider giving further aid to Chiang Kai-shek even though his claim to national leadership in China was daily becoming more tenuous. President Truman himself was seriously concerned, and at the end of February asked Secretary of State Marshall

[45] Ringwalt to Vincent, May 5, 1947, ibid., pp. 831–33.

specifically as to whether or not the time had come when we must give the National Government ammunition.

According to Marshall, he

> explained that this presented the most difficult issue before our Government in the present Chinese situation. . . . I told the President that the situation in China was deteriorating, I thought, rapidly and that sooner or later we would have to act. However, at the present instant, overt action on our part would virtually stabilize the Kuomintang Party in its present personnel.[46]

The Wedemeyer Mission

As this exchange indicates, Marshall was still disturbed by the thought that American aid to the Nationalists would tend to perpetuate the reactionaries in positions of power and militate against the idea of broadening the character of government in China, the only way to prevent the anti-Kuomintang Chinese from turning to the Communists. Nevertheless, he recognized that "sooner or later we would have to act." This was not necessarily because Marshall or Truman wanted to give up the professed posture of American goodwill toward the Chinese people's aspirations for an independent, representative government. Rather, it was because of the growing difficulty to separate policy toward China from the Cold War perceptions they were espousing for Europe and the Middle East. The upshot was the decision to permit the sale and shipment of arms to China, the transfer of "obsolescent" American arms and ammunition in the Pacific islands to Nationalist use, and the implementation of other types of programs to modernize the Nationalist armed forces. In July President Truman dispatched General Albert C. Wedemeyer on a fact-finding mission to China to assess the political, economic, and military situation with a view to establishing a realistic basis for further United States commitments to the Chiang regime.

The Wedemeyer mission, however, epitomized the difficulties involved in the application of the Cold-War vision to a country that lay outside the Yalta definitions of the American and Soviet spheres of predominance. Should the dualism of the Truman Doctrine be taken seriously, it would have to be implemented in China by means of large-scale commitments of United States power and resources on the side of a regime that was daily losing ground to the Communists and other dissident groups. The result would be an extension of American power and influence far beyond the limits contemplated at Yalta. Wedemeyer, before his departure, wrote up a draft

[46] Marshall to Vincent, Feb. 27, 1947, ibid., pp. 803–4.

directive for his mission, clearly revealing his understanding of the situation. He suggested that he be

> authorized to state categorically that the United States Government is prepared to assist realistically and immediately a program of rehabilitation and stabilization provided that the Chinese Government stipulates, guarantees and accepts definitive supervisory measures to be maintained by representatives of the United States.[47]

This, however, was further than Marshall and Truman were ready to go at that time. They shrank from giving this kind of mandate to Wedemeyer and instead told him to offer assistance to the Nationalists only if the latter "presents satisfactory evidence of effective measures looking towards Chinese recovery." Clearly, Truman wanted to await the reports of the mission before agreeing to more extensive aid. But General Wedemeyer himself quickly developed second thoughts about the advisability of committing the United States to Chiang Kai-shek's effort to unify the whole of China by force.

Soon after he arrived in China he telegraphed Marshall that

> The Nationalist Chinese are spiritually insolvent. They do not understand why they should die or make any sacrifices. They have lost confidence in their leaders, political and military, and they foresee complete collapse.[48]

He was particularly pessimistic about the Nationalists' ability to regain control of Manchuria; if they moved sufficient troops from North China to Manchuria to fight the Communists, the situation in North China would become precarious. Nevertheless, Chiang Kai-shek seemed intent on military operations in both these regions in the expectation that the United States would come to his rescue. The Nationalists, Wedemeyer reported,

> are familiar with our program in Western Europe and through the Balkans. They sense the fact that we would assist in establishing sound economies and political entities outside the Soviet orbit.

The trouble was that Manchuria was already within the Soviet orbit; as Wedemeyer stated,

> Without participating directly and without providing damaging evidence, the Soviet Communists have created or are in process of creating conditions that strongly contribute to the establishment ultimately of a satellite or puppet state in Inner Mongolia, Sinkiang, Manchuria and throughout Korea.[49]

[47] Wedemeyer to Marshall, July 2, 1947, ibid., pp. 636–38.
[48] Wedemeyer to Marshall, July 29, 1947, ibid., pp. 682–84.
[49] Wedemeyer to Marshall, Aug. 8, 1947, ibid., pp. 712–15.

Under the circumstances, it was hopeless to try to regain Manchuria for the Nationalists unless the United States were prepared to go to war against the Soviet Union. Since this seemed to be out of the question, the best practical solution would be to separate Manchuria from the rest of China. The United States might still help the Kuomintang in China proper, but it would "unquestionably make the suggestion" to the Nationalists that Manchuria be either placed under a guardianship of five powers (the United States, the Soviet Union, Britain, France, and China), or, since Russia would refuse to accept such a solution, referred to the United Nations for the establishment of a trusteeship as had been arranged for Korea.[50]

This was a forthright proposal which reflected Wedemeyer's assessment of the military and political situation in China and East Asia. Its implementation, however—besides being, in all probability, impossible of fulfillment because neither Chinese side would have accepted it—would have militated both against the Yalta system and the Cold War doctrine. By virtually dividing up China into Soviet and American spheres of influence, it would have resulted in the extension of their power beyond the Yalta limits. At the same time, it would have formally put an end to the notion of China as an independent entity which had formed part of the Yalta system. On the other hand, a division of China and the certainty of Communist take-over in Manchuria would have given the impression of American retreat in the face of Soviet expansionism. As Colonel David D. Barrett, assistant military attaché in Peking, wrote,

> A feeble, emasculated, mendicant China, shorn of the area from the Amur to the Yellow River, would be worth nothing to the United States, either as a sphere of economic activity or as a buffer against Soviet domination of all Asia.[51]

For all these reasons, Wedemeyer's final report including the recommendation for the future of Manchuria was suppressed by the State Department and the White House. In doing so the key policy makers in Washington were revealing their bewilderment at the lack of a workable concept toward China. They would not accept any of the three alternative policy proposals that had been made during 1947: Vincent's suggestion for strict adherence to the Yalta equilibrium, the Joint Chiefs of Staff's readiness to commit the United States to the support of Chiang Kai-shek, and Wedemeyer's compromise plan for division of China. Instead the Truman administration offered small-scale assistance to the Nationalists which proved to be of little practical value in the Chinese civil war.

Nevertheless, it is clear that by and large the structure of the Yalta

[50] Wedemeyer memo, Sept. 7, 1947, ibid., pp. 769–70.
[51] Barrett memo, Aug. 6 [3?], 1947, ibid., pp. 707–9.

system remained. Despite the Cold War rhetoric, no massive American involvement in China was undertaken. And there was no thought that there would be frontal confrontation with the Soviet Union in China. Despite their disagreement, Vincent, the military, and Wedemeyer all recognized Soviet preponderance in Manchuria but not in the whole of China. Even the Joint Chiefs of Staff admitted that the immediate objective of Soviet policy would be "limited to the control of the great resources and industrial potential of Manchuria." This, however, had always been foreseen by the United States; in fact such a perception of Soviet desires and intentions had formed a basis of the Yalta accord. Unless the United States were to commit itself on a massive scale to intervene in China, therefore, American-Russian relations on the Asian continent would remain what they had been since 1945: an uneasy equilibrium, shunning direct confrontation in China. Instead of publicizing this fact, the Truman administration was compelled by the logic of Cold-War ideology to lay stress on the survival of a non-Communist government in China and on the need to help the Nationalists. And because these pronouncements were not followed up by concrete deeds, other than programs of limited assistance, there grew a gap between the power-political and ideological components of American policy toward China. This was the characteristic of the Cold War in Asia at its inception: the Yalta system remained in structure but not in vision.

These trends in United States policy provoked counterattacks, again more verbal than physical, by the Soviet Union and the Chinese Communists, further creating an atmosphere of Cold-War confrontation in Asia. Russia continued to accuse America of interference in the Chinese civil war and to demand withdrawal of all American forces. From the Soviet point of view the recall of the Marshall mission did not seem to be bringing about an era of United States withdrawal from China. The sending of the Wedemeyer mission and the tenor of public debate in the United States indicated that the latter was still interested in playing a role in Chinese affairs. Nevertheless, American action was not such as to necessitate a reorientation of Soviet policy in China. No steps were taken by Moscow to side openly with the Communists against the Nationalists. It seems fair to accept the evaluation by the Joint Chiefs of Staff that what the Soviet Union foresaw in China proper was internal chaos.[52] Such chaos would serve Soviet purposes by weakening Chinese resistance to the Russian position in Manchuria and by providing an opportunity for the spread of Communist influence. In the meantime, Soviet policy would concentrate on attacking American infringements on Chinese sovereignty.

The Chinese Communists, too, persisted in their opposition to United States policy, accusing it of trying to take advantage of the civil war to extend

[52] Ibid., p. 839.

its control over China. Their attacks upon Wedemeyer were particularly vitriolic. In August the *Chieh-fang jih-pao* asserted that Wedemeyer had been instrumental in implementing a policy of enslaving the Chinese people, of turning China into a permanent colony of the United States. The October 10 slogan of the Communist Party, celebrating the 1911 republican revolution, called on the Chinese and American people to unite in opposition to the American imperialists' aggression upon China. It also appealed to the other peoples in Asia to join forces in a common struggle against imperialism. On Christmas day Mao Tse-tung stated that the Communists must defeat Chiang Kai-shek since the civil war was in fact a counterrevolutionary war waged by the Nationalists under the guidance of United States imperialism to oppose the independence of China and the liberation of its people. However, he went on, Chiang's reliance on American imperialism was doomed to failure because it was based on the illusion that the United States was all-powerful and that it would fight against the Soviet Union to preserve its hegemony in Asia. But in fact the United States was never that powerful; it was being steadily weakened by an emerging coalition of democratic forces headed by the Soviet Union. Here was as extreme a view as the Chinese Communists had allowed themselves to express, and summarized their perception of international affairs at the end of 1947. In their view the civil war in China would have been ended much earlier but for American intervention; but it was in the nature of imperialism to seek world domination, and consequently the Chinese people, as well as freedom-loving people everywhere, must redouble their effort to defeat it. In their anti-imperialist struggle they could count on Soviet support. As Ambassador Stuart commented,

> Even though the recent months have witnessed heightening attacks on the United States, this is the first time that one of the top leaders of the party has publicly joined the hue and cry.[53]

Mao Tse-tung was thus indulging in his own brand of Cold-War rhetoric. His emphasis, however, was on Chinese sovereignty and independence. His determination to unify China and assert its role in international affairs was destined to challenge not only the American policy of aid to the Nationalists but also the American-Russian scheme for Asian stability that had originated at Yalta.

Finally, Britain's role in the Asia-Pacific region further declined during 1945–47. Even in the overall context of the erosion of British power in postwar world affairs, ultimately resulting in the loss of its empire, there was something precipitous about the phenomenon in Asia. It may be that in Iran,

[53] *United States Relations with China* (Washington, D.C.: Government Printing Office, 1949), pp. 840–41.

Turkey, Greece, and Western Europe, there was a transition period, 1945–47, when Britain gradually gave up its position as a great power and turned to the United States to assume part of its geo-political functions. This brought about face-to-face confrontation between American and Soviet power in Europe and the Middle East and increased Cold War tensions. In Asia and the Pacific, in contrast, there was not even this much transition. As already noted, British officials had all but given up hope of their country's ever recovering its prewar status in Chinese affairs. One can only speculate what might have happened if Britain had decided to interest itself more actively in the domestic politics and foreign affairs of postwar China. General Jan Smuts of South Africa had remarked in April 1945 that the Big Two would welcome the counsel of wisdom born of experience which the British Empire possessed:

> The world would need our maturity and experience in world affairs. There were grave dangers in power suddenly acquired, without experience and a mature sense of responsibility, as had been exemplified by the recent history of Germany and Japan. . . . The future of the world would depend on our being able to pull our weight in partnership with the two other Great Powers.[54]

Britain might have "pulled its weight" in Chinese affairs during the tumultuous years after the war. But it almost totally abstained from the scene, content with carrying on commercial activities where possible and maintaining *de facto* relations with local Chinese authorities where necessary.

The one hope for British aspirations as a great Asian power lay in Southeast Asia, but here the transfer of leadership in London from Churchill to the Labour cabinet under Clement Attlee precluded the possibility that the country would resume a career of a full-fledged colonial power. The transition, to be sure, was not entirely abrupt. In Thailand, for example, London sought energetically to establish some sort of control over the government so as to ensure the security of nearby Burma and India as well as adequate amounts of rice to feed their populations. Despite the often bitter objection on the part of Washington, trying to prevent British suzerainty over Thailand, Great Britain was able to maintain a position of supremacy in Thai affairs for a few years after the war. In Burma, on the other hand, the London government announced the intention, as early as December 1945, that independence would shortly be granted. With the Labour cabinet committed to an eventual independence of India, the whole region was being thrown into a period of turmoil and violence, with Britain less and less inclined to provide a structure of regional stability. Unlike Europe and the Middle East, however, the United States did not immediately replace Britain to redress the balance of power. In fact, there was no balance of power in Southeast Asia to begin with, in the absence of direct American or Soviet

[54] War cabinet minutes, Apr. 3, 1945, CAB 65/52, Public Record Office.

involvement.[55] Although Communist parties were active in parts of the area in independence movements, Soviet policy was disinclined to pursue an active role, its attention being diverted to other parts of the world, and was content with providing ideological leadership for the struggle for freedom from colonial rule. Some of the indigenous revolutionaries, most notably Ho Chi Minh, in fact turned to the United States for support, but the latter, too, was reluctant to involve itself in Southeast Asia. Both America and Russia, then, were still acting within bounds visualized at the Yalta Conference.

[55] See Fifield, *Americans in Southeast Asia*, pp. 86–94.

CHAPTER
FIVE

Toward
a
New
Internationalism

Necessity for a New World View

By the beginning of 1948 certain themes and trends in international relations in the Asia-Pacific region had become clearly established. At one level the Yalta system remained; the United States and the Soviet Union claimed their respective spheres of predominance and were anxious to prevent each other from infringing upon them. By and large they successfully maintained the system; the United States did not openly challenge Soviet power and interests in Manchuria and north Korea, and the latter refrained from forcing a crisis in south Korea or Japan. In China, too, the two powers desisted from confronting one another directly and militarily. In the meantime, the Soviet Union extended its sway over the Kuriles, and the United States over Okinawa, the Bonins, and other islands in the Pacific. In the rest of the region—in the Southwestern Pacific and Southeast Asia—Britain and other European powers were trying to cope with nationalistic movements, creating a region of instability but without overt interference by America or Russia. All these developments were more or less aspects of the Yalta system.

At another level, however, there was a sense that international affairs were entering a new stage, that of the Cold War confrontation between the American and Soviet blocs. The Cold War rather than the Yalta compromise became the way in which men looked at international affairs in general and American-Russian relations in particular. While the Yalta system was specific in its global arrangements, the Cold War was universalistic as a conceptual framework. It defined a reality which was often at variance with actual policy decision, but nevertheless it tended to determine the way in which these decisions were articulated and communicated to the public. The confusion was particularly notable in China where two different principles— power politics and Cold-War visions—produced sharply contrasting influences upon United States policy. These two forces interacted with one another constantly, giving rise to confusion in policy and in perception about events.

The subsequent history of Asian-Pacific relations indicated the gradual erosion both of the Yalta system and the Cold War, in Asia as well as in Europe, although it would only be in the 1970s that a new international order would begin to take shape. A detailed story of the post-1948 phase of the Cold War in Asia cannot be attempted here, but it is hoped that the foregoing discussion has paved the way for comprehending the underlying significance of the multitude of disparate events that took place after 1948. A bare outline of this phase should serve to illustrate the lingering influence of the period 1940–47 upon subsequent developments.

The dialogue between the Yalta structure of power politics and Cold War perceptions continued to characterize Asian-Pacific affairs during 1948–49. Both the Soviet Union and the United States retained their interest and influence in China, but the latter was left essentially to its own people to determine their destiny. The United States officially refrained from massive intervention in China, but the ideology of the Cold War compelled its officials to take certain steps at least to give the impression that the government was not sitting by idly while the Nationalists were being overrun by the Communists. Thus both President Truman and Secretary of State Marshall put an end to the idea that the United States favored the formation of a coalition government in China, including the Communists. In March 1948 Marshall said that

> The Communists were now in open rebellion against the Government and that this matter (the determination of whether the Communists should be included in the Chinese Government) was for the Chinese Government to decide, not for the United States Government to dictate.

Truman agreed and told the press,

> We did not want any Communists in the Government of China or anywhere else if we could help it.[1]

More specifically, Marshall instructed Ambassador Stuart in August that

> The United States Government must not directly or indirectly give any implication of support, encouragement or acceptability of coalition government in China with Communist participation.[2]

Here was a complete and frank retreat from the professed policy of 1945–46. It showed readiness on the part of the United States government to view events inside China in terms of the Cold War. Since the same thinking was producing a European recovery program as well as a policy of containment, it took little imagination to produce a program for aiding Chiang Kai-shek's China. The China Aid Act of 1948 was a stopgap measure adopted to placate those in China and the United States who were critical of American policy for doing nothing to help the Chiang government.

Nevertheless, the basic thrust of United States policy was to refrain from large-scale involvement in China. As Marshall told Stuart in October 1948,

> Underlying our recent relations with China have been the fundamental considerations that the United States must not become directly involved in the Chinese civil war and that the United States must not assume responsibility for underwriting the Chinese Government militarily and economically.

This was the case even though American passivity should bring about the spread of Communist influence in China. Should the United States decide to fight the Communists to ensure the survival of the Nationalist government, it would become necessary for the nation

> virtually to take over the Chinese Government and administer its economic, military and governmental affairs. . . . It would involve the United States Government in a continuing commitment from which it would practically be impossible to withdraw, and it would very probably involve grave consequences to this nation by making of China an arena of international conflict.[3]

This was essentially the language of the Yalta system; the United States would not extend its hegemony over China, nor provoke the Soviet Union to

[1] *United States Relations with China*, pp. 272–73.
[2] Ibid., p. 279.
[3] Ibid., pp. 280–81.

direct confrontation in that country. There was no change in this principle even if "China" in 1948 was different from what it had meant in 1945. In the Cold-War framework China was becoming Communist and therefore turning itself into a Soviet satellite. At the same time, in the Yalta scheme of power politics there was to be no frontal conflict between America and Russia in China. Such dualism created an intellectual and psychological tension, but this was a reflection of the simultaneous existence of geo-political and ideological considerations in United States foreign policy in all parts of the world. The two forces could co-exist so long as the other powers did not challenge these American perceptions.

Such was the case at this time. Neither the Soviet Union nor the Chinese Communists were acting in such a way as to induce the United States to depart from the prevailing policies and attitudes. Until a Communist victory was all but assured in the first half of 1949, Soviet foreign policy remained cautious and maintained diplomatic ties with the National-ist government. As the Communists established de facto regimes in Manchu-ria and north China, the Soviet Union opened up offices in these regions to deal informally with the Communists. There was, however, no departure from the policy of avoiding a rupture with the Nationalists or of refraining from active involvement in China. The most the Russians sought was a confirmation of their Yalta-sanctioned position in Manchuria. There was a chance that this might be achieved through cooperation with Kao Kang, chairman of the newly established People's Government of the Northeast (Manchuria). Kao was inclined to proclaim Manchurian autonomy in close alliance with the Soviet Union. In the end the scheme came to little since the Communist leadership did not approve of regional separatism but wanted to preserve China's territorial and administrative entity. The Soviet Union, at any event, was unwilling to go beyond these political means to implant its influence in parts of China.

At the same time, Russia was developing its own brand of Cold-War ideology. Just as American officials and opinion leaders painted a picture of bipolar confrontation everywhere in the world, their counterpart in Russia subscribed to a new "two-camp" definition of international affairs. The American initiative in Turkey, Greece, and Western Europe in 1947 brought about a Soviet counteroffensive in Czechoslovakia, Berlin, and Yugoslavia. Andrei Zhdanov, the ideologue of the Soviet version of the Cold War, offered a view of the world divided between imperialism and its opponents, the Soviet Union offering the leadership to the latter's struggle for national liberation. Much as the United States government was interested in seeing a foreign country remain non-Communist or anti-Communist, so did the Soviet Union become ideologically intolerant of dissension and neutrality in the ranks of the Soviet-bloc nations. The European Recovery Program was matched by the Council of Mutual Economic Assistance (Comecon). Given such developments, China naturally had special significance to the Russians. It had been pictured by Zhdanov in late 1947 as falling within the orbit of American imperialism; by the beginning of 1949, however, the Chinese Communists were definitely in ascendance and just as fierce as the Russians in their denunciation of the United States and of Yugoslavia which had been expelled from the Communist Information Bureau (Cominform) for Josip Tito's ideological deviation. The Soviet press now gave wide coverage to Chinese Communist utterances and activities at international Communist congresses, which the Chinese were beginning to attend, and to the formation of Sino-Soviet "friendship associations" that were springing out in many parts of China, as if to certify that the latter were authentic members of the Soviet bloc.

The Chinese Communists, too, were relentless in their subscription to the "two-camp" theory. One of the major enunciations of their ideology was Liu Shao-ch'i's essay entitled "Internationalism and Nationalism" which was published in November 1948. In it Liu gave his wholehearted support to the expulsion of Yugoslavia from the Cominform and identified the Chinese Communist movement as part of the worldwide "proletarian internationalism." Such internationalism was alike opposed to "bourgeois nationalism" and to imperialism. It was not enough, he argued, to struggle for national liberation from the yokes of imperialism. The movement must be made part of, and work for the ultimate victory of, proletarian internationalism. The Soviet Union was the leader of this movement, just as the United States was the arch-imperialist. The former was the guiding spirit of the global struggle against imperialism and had as its allies one-quarter of the world's population who had liberated themselves from imperialist oppression. The rest of mankind were directly or indirectly subjugated by American imperialism. The American imperialists, Liu declared, had made plans, as soon as the war ended, to exploit and oppress all peoples in the world. They were now carrying out the Truman Doctrine and the Marshall Plan to place many countries and peoples one by one under their control, establishing military bases and interfering in the domestic affairs of these countries. Their scheme to enslave the entire world, however, was being resolutely opposed by people's democracies in Eastern Europe and by the national liberation movements in China, Greece, Vietnam, Indonesia, Malaya, Burma, and the Philippines, under the leadership of the Soviet Union. In such a dichotomous situation, where the two camps divided nation against nation and class against class, one had to stand on either one side or the other. If one did not choose to be a tool of American imperialism, then one must join the anti-imperialist struggle; one must side with and assist the Soviet Union. It was impossible to maintain neutrality. The stronger and more influential the Soviet Union became, the greater blow would be dealt to American imperialism and its tools in other countries. The Chinese people, therefore, must not only struggle against the reactionary Nationalists or oppose interference by the United States, but they must join the worldwide revolution under the banner of Soviet Communism.[4]

There is reason to believe that this type of total submission to the Soviet Union was rare among the Chinese Communist leadership. Mao Tse-tung and several other Communists were not entirely convinced of the need to identify their destiny completely with that of the Russians. In 1948–49, however, whatever misgivings they might have entertained about Soviet approaches to China had to be subordinated to a larger ideological framework of proletarian internationalism which seemed to explain many acts of United States policy in China and to give hope that the Chinese Communist movement had the support of the global revolutionary forces. As Mao said at about the same time, difficulties still lay ahead before final victory, but the Chinese people and the Communist Party would ultimately succeed because they were no longer isolated; they were part of a revolutionary phase of world history.[5]

The White Paper

The publication in August 1949 of *United States Relations with China* (the so-called *White Paper*) was a milestone in the history of the Yalta system. It showed that at least in official American perception the Yalta framework of Asian international relations had broken down. In his preface to the volume, Secretary of State Dean Acheson underscored the crucial importance the Yalta accord had played in the formulation of American policy in East Asia. As he said, the Yalta agreement and the subsequent Sino-Soviet treaty had

> in fact imposed limitations on the action which Russia would, in any case, have been in a position to take.

The two instruments were a way of defining the limits of Soviet power in East Asia, but Acheson made it clear that the Yalta system had also imposed restrictions upon American action in China. It had been hoped, he pointed out, that the Chinese civil war would somehow come to an end and an independent China would emerge without interference by either Russia or America. But the civil war had continued unabated, and only full-scale intervention by the United States would have stemmed the tide of Nationalist deterioration. But such intervention would have

> required the expenditure of even greater sums than have been fruitlessly spent thus far, the command of Nationalist armies by American officers, and the

---

[4] *Shin Chūgoku shiryō shūsei* (Tokyo: Japan Institute of International Affairs, 1964), II, 325–47.

[5] Ibid., pp. 349–51.

probable participation of American armed forces—land, sea, and air—in the resulting war.

Acheson admitted that such action would have obliterated one important rationale for the setting up of the Yalta system, the independence of China.

It is interesting to note that nowhere in this preface did Acheson explicitly accuse the Soviet Union of violating the Yalta agreement—except once pointing vaguely to "the conduct of the Soviet Government in Manchuria." But Manchuria after all had been assigned to the Soviet Union as its sphere of influence, and at any event Acheson wrote that Russian troops had been evacuated from the region. Nevertheless, he interpreted the impending Communist victory in China as a departure from the Yalta framework. In his words, the

> Communist leaders have foresworn their Chinese heritage and have publicly announced their subservience to a foreign power, Russia, which during the last fifty years, under czars and Communists alike, has been most assiduous in its efforts to extend its control in the Far East.

Since the documents in the *White Paper* did not warrant the assertion that the Soviet Union had systematically sought to extend its power and influence in China, Acheson must have come to such a sweeping conclusion through the medium of Cold-War visions. As he wrote,

> The Communist regime serves not their [the Chinese people's] interests but those of Soviet Russia.

Moreover,

> [should] the Communist regime lend itself to the aims of Soviet Russian imperialism and attempt to engage in aggression against China's neighbors, we and the other members of the United Nations would be confronted by a situation . . . threatening international peace and security.

This type of rhetoric was coupled with a frank admission that

> The ominous result of the civil war in China was . . . the product of internal Chinese forces. . . . A decision was arrived at within China, if only a decision by default.

Furthermore, Acheson expressed his hope that

> However ruthlessly a major portion of this great people may be exploited by a party in the interest of a foreign imperialism, ultimately the profound

civilization and the democratic individualism of China will reassert themselves
and she will throw off the foreign yoke.

Stripped of its embellishment, such passages indicated the disbelief that
anything fundamentally drastic had taken place. China was still evolving its
own history, and the Chinese people could be expected to resent any kind of
foreign domination. These were assumptions of the Yalta system. The duality
of American response to world problems—in terms of the Yalta synthesis and
of the Cold War rhetoric—was nowhere more starkly and vividly revealed.

Neither the Chinese Communists nor the Nationalists helped the
Americans to see the situation any more clearly, as they themselves reacted to
the publication of the *White Paper* as if to underscore the Cold War aspects of
its narrative. To the Chinese Communists, the *White Paper* seemed to provide
further evidence that the American leaders had consistently plotted to
intervene in Chinese domestic affairs to promote their selfish ends. Marshall,
who had earlier been regarded as a man of good intentions, was now
castigated as one of the imperialists, in the same company as Wedemeyer,
Truman, Acheson, or Stuart. The Marshall mission itself was denounced as a
sham; it was an attempt by the United States to control the whole of China
without resort to force. It had been a device to deceive the Chinese people. At
the opening ceremony of the Chinese people's political consultative conference, convened in September, Mao Tse-tung declared that the Communists
had now won victory over the reactionary Nationalist regime which had been
assisted by American imperialism. Now that the Chinese people had risen
against and were on the point of expelling the imperialists, they must
redouble their efforts to promote national independence and revolution. They
must unite with the Soviet Union and other people's democracies.[6] Chiang
Kai-shek, on his part, met with Syngman Rhee of South Korea and declared
their determination to continue the struggle against international Communism. They said that the menace of Communism was nowhere greater than in
the Asia-Pacific region; since mankind could never be half slave and half
free, those who opposed Communism must unite to obliterate it.[7]

On October 1, 1949, the People's Republic of China was officially
proclaimed. Recognition by the Soviet Union soon followed, as did recognition by Poland, Czechoslovakia, North Korea, and Rumania. By then the
Nationalist regime had been driven from the continent to the island of
Taiwan, there to continue to claim legitimacy, while the Communists vowed
to liberate the island. The Chinese Communists, declared an editorial in
Ch'ün Chung (Masses), must liberate the whole of China, including Taiwan
and Tibet. If the imperialists should try to cut these lands off from China
proper, they would only have themselves to blame if their heads were cracked

[6] Ibid., pp. 578–80.
[7] Ibid., p. 567.

by the resolute fists of the people's liberation army.[8] The Soviet press also reiterated the refrain that imperialism had been stopped at the gates of China, and that the Chinese people "have won the freedom and independence of their country." [9] It seemed as if the Communist victory in China were tipping the scale in favor of one of the two camps in world politics.

Chinese independence and sovereignty should have consolidated rather than weakened the Yalta system, based as it had been on the maintenance of a balance between the Soviet Union and the United States, with China in the middle under neither power's control. But at that juncture all interested parties—American, Russian, and Chinese—tended to view the emergence of a China unified by the Communists in the context of a bipolar world. Obviously, a China under Communist control and, *ipso facto*, within the Soviet orbit would introduce a totally new factor to the international system in the Asia-Pacific region. Since such a situation, in Cold War perception, entailed a vast extension of Soviet power on the Asian continent, the Soviet and American spheres of preponderance would come face to face with one another. The Yalta equilibrium would be jeopardized. The United States would have to seek an alternative order of international relations in that part of the world, if it were still to retain a globalistic foreign policy.

Roughly speaking, then, there were three alternative paths open at the end of 1949 as the Asia-Pacific region greeted the birth of a Communist China. The Yalta framework of international relations could continue, on the assumption that Communist China, whatever its ideological affinity with the Soviet Union, would function as a more or less independent, sovereign power as had been envisaged at Yalta. The United States would deal with it, not because it was Communist but simply because it was China, and an independent China was a prerequisite to the larger system of American-Russian balance. Second, viewing events in China as having brought about a redefinition of that balance, the United States would try to strengthen its own position in the areas that had been assigned to it as spheres of predominance —such as Japan, South Korea, and the western Pacific. Third, the United States might launch its counteroffensive and seek to establish a new order in Asia by extending its power to those areas which had not been clearly defined in the Yalta scheme—in particular, Southeast Asia.

The first alternative might have seemed the most sensible in view of the original American commitment to the Yalta status quo. However, in the frenzied Cold War atmosphere of late 1949, which saw the Soviet explosion of atomic devices and the United States decision to develop the hydrogen bomb, it was all but impossible to consider China independent unless it were non-Communist. There seemed to be no such thing as an independent and Communist China. The *White Paper* expressed the wish that the Chinese

[8] Ibid., pp. 569–71.
[9] Beloff, *Soviet Policy*, pp. 68–69.

people might once again come to assert their sovereign rights; it was not assumed that they could do so and retain their Communism at the same time.

New American Perception of the
Role of Japan

Under the circumstances, close adherence to the Yalta system as a framework for dealing with Asian policy was no longer tenable. The United States begun pursuing the other two possibilities. The policy of strengthening its own position within its spheres of predominance, now that China seemed about lost to the Soviet orbit, had become more and more articulate in United States policy toward Japan during 1948–49. As we have seen, Japan had been an area of American preponderance according to the Yalta scheme, and in 1947 a "constructive" phase of the occupation was initiated. But the future role of Japan in the Asian international system had not been clarified, some advocating neutralization and others envisaging a continued presence of United States forces. As George F. Kennan, director of the State Department's policy planning staff, had noted in August,

> We have not yet formulated with any degree of concreteness our objectives with respect to Japan and the Pacific area.[10]

The situation changed after 1948, as American officials came to have more clearly defined objectives in the Asia-Pacific region. Basically, these were related to the erosion of the Yalta system as a result of Communist victories in China. Although certain key officials in the State Department, including Kennan and John P. Davies, were not totally convinced that China was succumbing to the Soviet orbit, virtually all were in agreement that the United States must improve its military position in the western Pacific to prevent further disintegration of the Yalta equilibrium. Obviously, Japan would be a key in any such arrangements, and a new concept of Japanese-American relations had to be developed. In a forthright policy recommendation, Kennan wrote in February 1948 that the United States should

> devise policies toward Japan which would assure the security of that country from Communist penetration and domination as well as from military attack by the Soviet Union and would permit Japan's economic potential to become once again an important force in the affairs of the area, conducive to peace and stability.

[10] Kennan to Lovett, Aug. 12, 1947, *Foreign Relations 1947*, VI, 486–87.

Such a view reflected Kennan's thinking that continued poverty, weakness, and insecurity of Japan would contribute an element of instability to the Asia-Pacific region. It was imperative, therefore, that Japan be permitted once again to become a factor, a power, in the international affairs of the area.[11]

Although Kennan at times felt that a new, stable Japan could eventually be neutralized as part of an American-Soviet understanding, the basic thrust of United States policy was quite otherwise. Japan would be encouraged to regain its economic and military power to the extent necessary to preserve what remained of the Yalta status quo. More specifically, the National Security Council recommended the formation of a 150,000-man national police force in Japan. The State Department, on its part, revised its earlier interest in a Japanese peace conference to be comprised of all its former enemies, and began pushing for a peace treaty with Japan which would amount to an alliance between that country and the United States. By the end of 1949 any idea of the Soviet Union and Communist China joining together with the United States to conclude a peace treaty with Japan was becoming not only unrealistic but undesirable from the American point of view. In order to preserve America's position in the western Pacific, the best strategy seemed to be to put an end to the state of war and then to conclude a military alliance with Japan, enabling the United States to keep its forces on Japanese soil more or less indefinitely. This would perpetuate the existing situation, but it would also mark a departure in that the way would now be opened to Japan's eventually becoming a power, thus cooperating with the United States to maintain what was left of the Yalta balance rather than being a passive captive of the system. Such a policy was in line with the Ashida-Yoshida strategy, mentioned earlier, which had sought to ensure both Japanese independence and security by integrating the country more explicitly into the American security system. A crucial aspect of this policy was the enhanced strategic importance of Okinawa, which would be turned into a major United States base in the western Pacific. General Joseph Lawton Collins, army chief of staff, declared in 1949 that the United States would keep Okinawa "indefinitely," and a fifty-million dollar construction program was begun to install bases on the islands.[12]

Viewed from Moscow, these trends in United States policy might have seemed exactly as events in China were impressing American officials in Washington. The proposed peace treaty with Japan without Soviet and Communist Chinese participation, and public discussions about the desirability of resurrecting Japanese power, might well have struck the Russian leaders as evidence that the United States was pursuing a policy calculated to alter the Yalta status quo by encouraging the resurgence of Japanese

[11] Kennan, *Memoirs, 1925–1950*, p. 381.
[12] Emmerson, *Arms*, p. 160.

militarism and imperialism. Just as the Americans believed the Yalta equilibrium was being eroded through Communist victories in China, the Russians and the Chinese Communists became convinced that Japan was being turned into a tool of United States imperialism. After 1949 they reiterated with increasing frequency that the United States was secretly rebuilding a Japanese army and that the reactionaries and militarists in Japan were scheming once again to invade the Asian continent. As General Chu Teh said in a radio speech commemorating the twelfth anniversary of the outbreak of the Sino-Japanese War (July 7, 1949), Japanese imperialism had been defeated through the heroic effort of the Chinese people and the assistance of "the United Nations, in particular the Soviet Union." In their view the American imperialists had been trying to assist the Nationalist reactionaries to oppress the Chinese people and, when the former proved powerless, to encourage the revival of Japanese militarism to turn Japan into an arsenal for arms and a base for aggressive policies. In order to oppose the ambitions of the American imperialists and the Japanese militarists, the Chinese people must strengthen their friendly alliance with the Soviet Union. Such an alliance was the most important weapon to resist the new aggression in East Asia.[13]

As if to act out such a scenario, Mao Tse-tung left for Moscow at the end of the year, there to stay for over two months before concluding a treaty of "friendship, alliance, and mutual assistance." The treaty specifically mentioned its object: to prevent a

repetition of aggression and violation of peace on the part of Japan or any other State which should unite in any form with Japan in acts of aggression.

In view of trends in United States policy toward occupied Japan, the alliance was clearly aimed at demonstrating the identity of Chinese and Russian interests and intentions against the combined threat of Japan and the United States. Equally significant, and presumably the reason for the prolonged negotiations in Moscow, was an accompanying agreement whereby the Soviet Union renounced most of the rights in Manchuria which it had been assured at the Yalta Conference and which it had actually obtained in the Sino-Soviet treaty of 1945. These rights were to be restored to China at least by the end of 1952, or by the conclusion of a Japanese peace treaty, should it come first.

Such an agreement obviously involved a redefinition of the Yalta system as far as the Soviet Union was concerned. Its hold on Manchuria would be severely restricted, if not completely eradicated, although the independence of Outer Mongolia was not affected by the new agreements.

[13] *Shin Chūgoku*, II, 533–35.

From Russia's point of view the retreat in Manchuria was the price it had to pay to retain some degree of control over the new China, but it should be noted that no similar concessions were made by the Soviet Union in its relations with the people's democracies in Eastern Europe. Actually the whole phenomenon of China's unification by the Communists was something neither the United States nor the Soviet Union had anticipated at Yalta, and for the Russians it necessitated a reorientation of the postwar international order in the region. Just as the United States was seen as intent upon restoring Japan as a power and an ally, the Soviet Union was going to incorporate a unified China into a new scheme of international relations. China would be anti-American, much as Japan was being turned into a bastion of anti-Soviet strategy. In such a situation, it might have seemed to Moscow's leaders that a sovereign China with rights restored would be an important ally worth the price of a change in the Soviet sphere of influence.

Preserving Dominance in a
Modified Yalta System: Korean War

At the beginning of 1950, then, two new factors were being introduced to the five-year old Yalta system. China had been unified and was emerging as a potential power, but not as an independent entity as had been visualized earlier but as an ally of the Soviet Union. Simultaneously, Japan was being turned into an active agent in the Asian balance, closely tied to the United States. There was still an overall framework of American-Soviet equilibrium as the two greatest Asia-Pacific powers, but these new developments were making American and Soviet policies more rigid in seeking to preserve their respective areas of dominance and power.

It was in such a context that the Korean War broke out in June 1950. It may be seen as an aspect of the two powers' continuing desire to consolidate their respective positions in the Asia-Pacific region. It is usually argued that the United States virtually invited the Soviet-inspired North Korean attack on South Korea by publicly declaring its lack of intention to defend the latter country. President Truman, Secretary of State Acheson, and General MacArthur all expressed the view that America's defense perimeter extended only as far as to Japan and did not include South Korea. However, such a stance did not mean that the United States would cease to be a factor in Asian international affairs. On the contrary, by including Japan in its defense system and by building Okinawa up as an advance base of the United States, the latter was clearly revealing its intention to stay and fortify its position in the region. This type of determination was far more crucial than the temporary absence of American forces in South Korea. Only with respect to China, a clear-cut policy had been established; the United States would not deal with the Communist regime, but neither would it foresee a state of conflict with China. There would be no contact with it, friendly or hostile. But after all, the Yalta scheme had not involved American domination over China, and there was no substantial departure from this position in 1950, except that the United States refused to acknowledge the existence of a unified government in China. Outside of China and the Soviet orbit, however, American policy would see to it that the total power of the United States would not only not diminish but increase. The trips to Japan and East Asia undertaken by John Foster Dulles, appointed a State Department advisor on Asian matters, Secretary of Defense Louis Johnson, and General Omar Bradley, chairman of the Joint Chiefs of Staff, in the spring of 1950, gave graphic demonstration of such determination. No commitment of American forces in South Korea had been made primarily because it had not seemed to the strategists in Washington that an all-out invasion of that country would take place in the immediate future.[14] Rather, Washington's vision was the hardening of a modified Yalta status quo, with the Soviet Union and the United States each consolidating its power within its zone of supremacy.

Such a perception was not very far from the views held by Kremlin's leaders, although it is still extremely difficult to ascertain Russian policy at that time. They, too, were apparently convinced of the need to strengthen the Soviet position in Asia. This need was now reinforced by the surrender of the rights in Manchuria to the Chinese Communists. Under the circumstances, it made sense to try to match the totality of American power in the Asia-Pacific region by taking advantage of spots where American power was not fully entrenched. South Korea was a case in point. The Soviet Union did not desire a full-scale war with the United States, any more than the latter expected a conflict at that juncture. But the North Korean invasion of South Korea could conceivably serve useful purposes by bringing the whole of the Korean peninsula under Soviet control through proxy and checking further growth of American power in Asia. Soviet power in Korea would compensate for the loss of Manchuria and would in part offset the impact of a remilitarized Japan. Thus, although the invasion of South Korea was a clear violation of the Yalta scheme which had assigned the country to the American orbit, it may have been an attempt to redress the balance which the Russian leaders believed had tipped in favor of the United States. If so, it was part of an effort to define a new order in the Asia-Pacific region to replace the crumbling structure of Yalta equilibrium.

For American officials, however, the North Korean invasion was a direct challenge to the policy of strengthening the position of the United States in Asia in response to the Soviet domination of China. That policy

[14] Glenn D. Paige, *The Korean Decision, 1950* (New York: Free Press, 1968), p. 75.

faced collapse from the beginning unless the latter showed its will to resist the forceful change in the Korean status quo. Thus within the Truman administration there was no disagreement with John Foster Dulles and his aide, John Allison, when they telegraphed from Tokyo,

> It is possible that the South Koreans may themselves contain and repulse the attack, and, if so, this is the best way. If, however, it appears that they cannot do so, then we believe that United States force should be used.[15]

Dulles had written in the previous May, referring to a sense of crisis enveloping American-Russian relations,

> A series of disasters can be prevented if at some doubtful point we quickly take a dramatic and strong stand that shows our confidence and resolution.[16]

Such a view reflected a sense that the United States and the Soviet Union were searching for a new equilibrium, and that each could consolidate the status quo which it perceived only at the expense of the other. South Korea was a symbol of this contest of will.

America's initial response to the Korean crisis was thus comprehensible within the conceptual framework of the revised Yalta system: to repulse a challenge to the policy of strengthening the American position in the areas of its predominance. As George F. Kennan said with characteristic forthrightness in November,

> Our position had become [similar] to that occupied by the British for a long period in the past and [it was necessary] for us, on occasion, to hold stubbornly . . . to positions which by military logic might appear to be useless.[17]

It was essential not to give up South Korea, not necessarily because its defense was militarily feasible or sensible in terms of the overall global strategy, but because its abandonment would signify a lack of will, determination, and confidence to bolster up the structure of Asian-Pacific international relations which had begun to be redefined by the United States after the fall of China to the Communists.

The Korean War, however, impelled the United States government to go beyond this policy, which was basically derivative of the Yalta system, and embrace an additional approach, the third alternative that was mentioned earlier—to entrench American power in areas that had not been defined as its spheres of predominance. The decision to cross the thirty-eighth parallel

[15] Ibid., pp. 111–12.
[16] Kolko, *Limits of Power*, p. 562.
[17] Kennan, *Memoirs 1950–1963* (Boston: Little, Brown, 1972), p. 32.

and to try to unify Korea militarily was the most striking departure in that direction. North Korea had clearly lain within the Soviet orbit, unchallenged by the United States. By authorizing General MacArthur not only to repulse the North Korean attack on South Korea but also to invade the region north of the parallel, President Truman and his advisers were offering a counter-challenge to the Soviet Union. They were redefining the Asian order fundamentally. Here they were frustrated, however, as the Chinese intervened toward the end of the year, and both the United States and the Soviet Union eventually decided to settle down to a stalemate along the thirty-eighth parallel.

Elsewhere in Asia, the United States was more successful in its attempt to go beyond the Yalta status quo and extend its power in areas that had not been specifically assigned either to the Soviet or the American orbit. Taiwan and Indochina are cases in point. The outbreak of the Korean War brought about a decision to dispatch the Seventh Fleet to the Taiwan Strait in order to prevent forceful unification of the island with mainland China. This was in violation of the Yalta accord which had assumed that the island would revert to China. The reasoning behind the decision was that the fall of Taiwan to the Chinese Communists would result in the island's being turned into an advance base for an anti-American power to the clear detriment of the position of the United States in the region. The United States should, under the circumstances, detach the island from the mainland and safeguard its separate existence. Whether it would be actively used as an American base was not yet explicitly determined, but henceforth it would no longer be considered as lying beyond America's sphere of interest. The status of Taiwan, President Truman declared, would be kept in abeyance to be determined at some future date. Such a policy, envisaging a two-Chinas stand, was contrary to the Yalta image of a unified and independent China and did much to undermine the conceptual foundation of United States strategy in the Asia-Pacific region.

In Indochina, too, the Truman administration acted with dispatch to come to the aid of the French regime as soon as the Korean War started. The State Department, it is true, had already in 1949 adopted a policy guideline:

> It is a fundamental decision of American policy that the United States does not intend to permit further extension of Communist domination on the continent of Asia or in the southeast Asia area.[18]

The French regimes comprising the peninsula—Cambodia, Laos, and South Vietnam—asked for American aid in February 1950, and three months later the United States government decided to grant the request. But before the outbreak of the Korean War there had been no idea that this region would be

[18] Kolko, *Limits of Power*, p. 554.

formally incorporated into the American zone of interest. As Secretary of State Acheson said in January, the decision as to the future of Asia "lies within the countries of Asia and within the power of the Asian people." The whole region of Southeast Asia had lain outside the Yalta system, and before June 25 there had been no indication that the United States would radically alter the situation.

The invasion of South Korea provided impetus for taking bold action to extend American power and influence beyond the limits perceived at Yalta. Although the United States had espoused the idea of a trusteeship for French Indochina before 1945, and after the war withheld interference with the civil war in the country, there was a sense in the summer of 1950 that a new framework of American policy was needed in Southeast Asia to cope with what was believed to be the collapse of the Yalta formula. Externally, there was an image of a global challenge by the Soviet Union to the postwar international system; as the State Department instructed its representatives overseas,

> Possible that Korea is only the first of series of coordinated actions on part of Soviets. Maintain utmost vigilance and report immediately any positive or negative information.[19]

Domestically, the Yalta concept of American-Russian understanding, already under fire after the fall of Chiang's China, came to be condemned as the evil that had brought about the North Korean aggression. As Senator George W. Malone of Nevada declared on the Senate floor on June 26,

> What happened in China and what is now happening in Korea were brought about deliberately by the advisers of the President at Yalta and by the advisers of the State Department since then.[20]

It was not surprising, then, that the Truman administration felt impelled to act in another area of Asia where Communists and anti-Communists were struggling for supremacy. China and the Soviet Union had recognized Ho Chi Minh's North Vietnamese government in January 1950, while the United States had established diplomatic relations with the Bao Dai regime in South Vietnam which had been set up by the French. The situation was similar to Korea, with the crucial difference that the United States had not involved itself in Indochina after 1945. Now, however, it began giving military and economic aid to Bao Dai, to the amount of half a billion dollars per year. The aim was to prevent a Communist takeover of South Vietnam, an aspect of Cold War diplomacy, but also a departure from the Yalta

[19] Paige, *Korean Decision*, p. 134.
[20] Ibid., p. 153.

system. For the first time since 1945 the United States was beginning to entrench itself as a power in Southeast Asia.

The significance of the Korean War, then, lay in the fact that its outbreak coincided with two crucial developments—China's unification by the Communists, and a more vigorous American policy in Asia—and brought about further modification, if not demolition, of the Yalta system. The United States through its responses of 1950 made it clear that it would redefine the structure of Asian-Pacific international relations on the basis of three principles: the revitalization of Japan once again as a power, the extension of American power in Southeast Asia, and the detachment of Taiwan from mainland China. None of these policies had been envisaged in the original Yalta scheme, and they defined a new structure of power relations for the United States. In terms of ideology, such a policy corresponded to the Cold War perception of world affairs in terms of Communist expansion and American response.

And yet one aspect of the Yalta system remained; the United States would not challenge Soviet supremacy· in its spheres of predominance if it contained risk of war between the two super-powers. The invasion of North Korea by United States forces proved to be the exception to this principle, and by recalling General MacArthur, President Truman and the Joint Chiefs of Staff indicated their reluctance to provoke the Soviet Union into open conflict. In Europe, too, the Korean War resulted in a decision by the United States government to step up military strengthening; American forces were sent to Europe, turning the North Atlantic Treaty Organization into a military instrument, and West Germany and Turkey joined that organization. But there was no thought that the United States and its allies would attack the Soviet position in Eastern and Southeastern Europe. As in Asia, the American orbit would strengthen itself, but extreme caution would be exercised lest there should develop a premature war between America and Russia.

The Soviet Union, too, did not desire complications in Asia from which the only outcome to expect might be war with the United States. The Russian government had been willing to encourage North Korea to expand southward as part of an overall response to what was perceived as the American policy of strengthening its position in Asia. It was ready to see the United States humiliated and frustrated in Korea at no particular expense to itself. In and out of the United Nations the Russians castigated the United States for engaging in an aggressive act in what they considered a civil war in Korea. But they, no more than the Americans, were prepared to see the Korean conflict develop into a war between the two giants. Seeing, by 1951, that American troops would not be repulsed from the peninsula without larger-scale infusion of Chinese forces, the Soviet Union was ready to settle for a stalemate. As Kennan, who carried out a secret mission to ascertain

Russian intentions, guessed, the Soviet Union was as reluctant as the United States to trigger a global conflagration out of the Korean conflict.[21]

So there would be no war between the United States and the Soviet Union. But the structure of international relations that had been established in 1945 to ensure the two powers' global equilibrium would undergo change. The Cold War would enter a new phase, with fewer pockets of gray areas between the two power blocs, more and more of which would be filled by either one of them. In Asia, the United States would take the initiative and entrench its power in Taiwan, Indochina, and elsewhere in Southeast Asia. None of these countries directly affected the Soviet zone of power, and there would be no overt conflict with Russia in the area. Instead, underneath the surface balance between the two, other developments were destined to occur and reshape the course of international relations in the Asia-Pacific region.

First of all, the Korean War had the effect of speeding up the conclusion of a Japanese peace treaty and the rearmament of the country. Immediately after the outbreak of hostilities in Korea, General MacArthur directed the Japanese government to create a 75,000-man security force to prevent domestic turmoil in the absence of the bulk of the United States occupation forces that had to be sent to Korea. Simultaneously, President Truman authorized the State Department to initiate negotiations with other governments for a Japanese peace treaty. Although some officials, notably George F. Kennan, urged caution and wanted to settle the Japanese question as part of an overall framework of American-Soviet understanding in Asia, Truman, Acheson, Dulles, and the military advisers were determined not to be delayed in their strategy to strengthen Japanese defenses as part of the American security system. More specifically, they envisaged certain ingredients of the new relationship between the two countries: the rearmament of Japan, continued presence of American forces in Japan, their military alliance, and the retention by the United States of Okinawa and the Bonin islands. In return the United States would remove all restrictions on Japan's economic affairs, and renounce the right to demand reparations and war indemnities. Here was a program for turning Japan from conquered and occupied country to military ally, frankly aimed at responding to the rising power of the Soviet Union and China in the Asia-Pacific region.

The San Francisco System

The San Francisco System—the new regime of American-Japanese relations that resulted from the San Francisco peace conference of 1951—incorporated most of these ideas. The Japanese government under Prime Minister Yoshida Shigeru steadfastly refused to undertake a large-scale rearmament, desiring

---

[21] Kennan, *Memoirs 1950–1963*, Ch. 2.

instead to concentrate on economic recovery and development and to rely on a mutual defense treaty with the United States to safeguard national security. The result was a compromise, the peace treaty being signed simultaneously with a Japanese-American mutual security pact on September 8, and the latter specifying that the United States would have a right to maintain armed forces in Japan and its vicinity in order to contribute to the "peace and security" in East Asia. The preamble to the security pact recognized Japan's right of self-defense, but the country was not obligated to undertake rearmament. From the Japanese point of view, the removal of restrictions on its sovereignty justified the signing of a peace treaty with the United States, coupled with a security pact, although these two instruments were tantamount to identifying Japan's position in Asia as a member of the American security system. The Soviet Union and Communist China could not be expected to countenance such a stand; they refused to accept the legality of the new system and insisted that as far as they were concerned the state of war with Japan still remained.

China, in fact, was not represented at the San Francisco conference. The American view was that there was no international consensus as to the recognized government of China, that at any event the United States could not confer with a country with which it was fighting in Korea, and that Japan should be free to conclude a separate peace treaty with the Chinese government of its choice. But it was evident that Japan really had no choice in the matter, as Dulles exacted a promise from Yoshida that the Japanese government would sign a peace treaty with the Chiang Kai-shek regime in Taiwan. The 1952 peace treaty between Japan and the Republic of China was an anomaly insofar as the authority of the Nationalists was limited to Taiwan and its environs. Japan recognized the situation and succeeded in inserting its view in the official documents that the provisions of the treaty would be applicable only to those areas under control of the Republic of China. In other words, Japan was not recognizing the latter's authority to the mainland. Still, the conclusion of a peace treaty in such circumstances was tantamount to accepting the view that there existed two Chinese governments, one in Peking and another in Taipei. Such a policy was "insane," declared Foreign Minister Chou En-lai in Peking. Japan's signing of a peace treaty with the United States and another one with Taiwan, he said, showed that Japanese imperialism still dreamed of enslaving the Chinese and other Asians in collaboration with United States imperialism.[22]

The San Francisco peace treaty affected American-Chinese relations in another, crucial way. It contained a clause whereby Japan renounced its rights and privileges in Taiwan and the Pescadores. However, nowhere was it specifically stated that Taiwan was Chinese territory. The same was true of

[22] Tai T'ien-ch'ao, *Taiwan kokusai seijishi kenkyū* (Tokyo, 1971), pp. 404–5.

the Japanese peace treaty with the Republic of China. Such an omission was to provide justification to those who would call for Taiwan's independence or autonomy, or for a two-Chinas policy. By the same token, it could be seized by the People's Republic of China as a blatant interference in Chinese affairs and evidence that the United States and Japan were plotting to detach the island from the China mainland. Whatever the merits and demerits of legal issues, the fact remains that by refusing to invite Peking to the peace conference and by inducing Japan to sign a separate treaty with Taiwan, the United States was further revealing its policy of isolating Communist China and entrenching its own power on the island.

As this example showed, American policy in Asia after 1950 began to have serious complications with China, quite apart from American-Soviet relations. China was still considered a puppet of the Soviet Union. As Assistant Secretary of State Dean Rusk declared in May 1951,

The Peiping [Peking] regime may be a colonial Russian government—a Slavic Manchukuo on a larger scale. It is not the Government of China.

The United States might not recognize the legitimacy of the government in Peking, but it was more and more forced to reckon with Chinese power, as witnessed in Korea. Since it was unlikely that the Soviet Union would be involved in an assault on the island of Taiwan, the policy of defending the latter involved a stance of hostility toward mainland China, which in turn demonstrated America's concern with the latter's growing power. This, the increasing tension between China and the United States, was the second byproduct of the Korean War.

The Chinese Communists, on their part, viewed American policy in Taiwan as the major obstacle in the way of China's emergence as a power. American presence on the island was regarded as a symbol of United States hostility toward China, part of the design by the American and Japanese imperialists once again to dominate the Asia-Pacific region. Already on June 28, 1950, Chou En-lai accused the United States of forcefully violating Chinese territory. From the Chinese point of view, Taiwan was part of China, and to deny the island's unification with the mainland was an act of aggression. American interference in Taiwan, he said, was part of an aggressive design to extend its imperialistic control over the whole of Asia, including Taiwan, Korea, Vietnam, and the Philippines.[23] From this time on, the Chinese leadership showed themselves extremely sensitive to the question of Taiwan, and the bulk of their official statements during the Korean War dealt with it. They viewed the liberation of Taiwan from Nationalist rule and its reunification with the mainland as the final stage in their struggle for

[23] *Shin Chūgoku shiryō shūsei* (Tokyo, 1969) III, 129–30.

Chinese independence and power. Taiwan, therefore, had special significance which was not overshadowed even by the dramatic Chinese intervention in Korea. While the Communists decided to send its troops to Korea to demonstrate its solidarity with the North Koreans and to prove that American imperialism was "a paper tiger," their fundamental concern remained Taiwan. This is revealed in the fact that in almost all their speeches and declarations concerning the Korean War, they coupled American intervention in Korea with its "invasion" of Taiwan as simultaneous developments, both evidence of United States policy to try to frustrate the Chinese people's aspirations to enjoy freedom and exercise their sovereign power. Peking insisted time and again that the two issues should be discussed together at the United Nations.

Ironically, the Chinese were less successful in Taiwan than in Korea. While they proved themselves capable of matching American strength in North Korea, forcing the United States to retreat and accept a stalemate, they were unable either to have the United Nations debate the American "invasion" of Taiwan or to liberate the island by themselves. As if to compensate for the lack of success, the Communist leadership stepped up their propaganda campaign to keep the Taiwan question always in full view of world opinion. As Wu Hsiu-ch'üan, sent from Peking in November to attend the United Nations Security Council meetings, said, there had been Chinese in Taiwan even before Columbus got to America, and it had always belonged to China. The Communists had now established themselves as the sole government of the Chinese people. Under the circumstances, American intervention in Taiwan, five thousand miles away from the United States, was an act of provocation to involve China in war. In a speech Wu prepared for delivery but was not permitted to give at a session of the United Nations, he alluded to Japanese rearmament and the preparations being made for a Japanese-American peace treaty. These, he said, were part of a plan to encircle China and undertake a frontal assault on the People's Republic. The Chinese people, however, had a long history of anti-imperialist struggle, and they were determined ultimately to liberate Taiwan and stop America's direct and indirect aggression upon China.[24] The focus in such declarations was on Chinese-American relations, rather than the broader framework of Soviet-American relations, and the tension involving Taiwan indicated that conflict between China and the United States was emerging as the critical factor that would determine the future shape of Asian international affairs.

The third crucial development after 1950 was the extensive United States involvement in Indochina and other parts of Southeast Asia. This was related both to the broader Cold War perception, calling for a reactive response to any Communist movement, and to the emergence of Japan and

[24] Ibid., pp. 191–231.

Taiwan as key ingredients of American Asian policy. In order to incorporate these two countries into the American security system, it was necessary to develop a comprehensive program of policy and strategy that would serve as the framework for the new American zone of power. Specifically, the United States signed treaties with Australia, New Zealand, and the Philippines to guarantee their security, while control over United States forces in Taiwan and the Philippines was placed under the commander in chief of the Pacific Fleet. This new command, which hitherto had rested with the commanding general of the United States forces in Japan, had a focus on the Southwestern Pacific and Southeast Asia, and reflected the view that a fresh crisis could arise at any moment in such areas as Taiwan and Indochina. Of these two, Taiwan was more securely guarded through the stationing of the Seventh Fleet, whereas South Vietnam, because of its geographical closeness to China and the strength of Ho Chi Minh's North Vietnam, was considered to be in greater danger. But the danger in either case, it should be noted, was perceived to lie in the potential threat of Communist China to extend its power to these regions. It was China, rather than the Soviet Union, that was the crux of American strategy. As Secretary of State Acheson told Foreign Secretary Anthony Eden in early 1952, the United States was determined

> to do everything possible to strengthen the French hand in Indo-China. On the wider question of the possibility of a Chinese invasion, the United States Government considered that it would be disastrous to the position of the Western powers if South-East Asia were lost without a struggle.[25]

In such a perspective, United States involvement in Southeast Asia was part of the new definition of its position and power in the Asia-Pacific region. It was to extend the limits of its power in order to keep China in check. Such a policy was considered necessary because of the decline of British and European power in the colonial areas, which was creating a power vacuum in Southeast Asia.

Southeast Asia had not initially been seen as falling within either the American or the Soviet sphere of influence. It had been assumed that the region would undergo a long period of uncertainty as a result of the interactions between European governments and indigenous populations. But Great Britain and, to some extent, France and the Netherlands had been expected to provide some kind of tenable framework for regional stability on the whole. By 1950 it was clear that the European powers would no longer play the key role. Those accustomed to view the Asia-Pacific region in terms of the Yalta system of power politics readily concluded that the vacuum would have to be filled by a non-European power. Earlier, Chinese expansion into this region might have been accepted with equanimity—especially when

[25] Anthony Eden, *Full Circle* (Boston: Houghton Mifflin, 1960) p. 92.

China was pictured as friendly toward the United States. But the possible penetration of Southeast Asia by Communist China was another matter. Such an eventuality, in Cold War perception, would only be upsetting the American-Soviet balance in Asia and encouraging the steady advance of international Communism. It was necessary, from the American point of view, to counter this trend, prevent the rich land mass and its combined resources from falling under hostile control, and protect the sea routes connecting the eastern part of the Indian Ocean with the Southwestern Pacific, the vital cornerstone of the postwar American security system in East Asia. The United States, in short, would have to act as the stabilizer of Southeast Asia.

Through an ironical twist of history, Japan reentered Asian international politics at this juncture, as the United States encouraged it to play a role in Southeast Asia. It will be recalled that the Pacific War had been brought about by the struggle between Japan and America for control over Southeast Asia and the Southwestern Pacific. Less than ten years after Pearl Harbor, the rivalry between the United States on one hand and China and the Soviet Union on the other provided Japan with an opportunity denied it earlier. American policy makers well understood that Japan, Taiwan, Southeast Asia, and the United States all fitted like pieces of a puzzle into the whole framework of Asian-Pacific affairs. As Richard Nixon said in 1953,

> Why is the United States spending hundreds of millions of dollars supporting the forces of the French Union in the fight against communism? If Indo-China falls, Thailand is put in an almost impossible position. The same is true of Malaya with its rubber and tin. The same is true of Indonesia. If this whole part of Southeast Asia goes under Communist domination or Communist influence, Japan, who trades and must trade with this area in order to exist, must inevitably be oriented towards the Communist regime.[26]

Because of the identification of its foreign policy with the United States, the Japanese government recognized that Japan could not revive the kind of close trade relations with mainland China that it had maintained before the war. Southeast Asia would provide a substitute market and source of raw materials. The more stable the region became due to American power, and the more American aid funds were poured there, the more favorable the situation would be for Japan. The San Francisco peace treaty paved the way for establishing diplomatic relations with the countries of Southeast Asia, and the Japanese government began energetically to negotiate reparations agreements with them. Once the thorny issue of reparations was solved, it would become feasible for Japan to re-enter the area openly. Even before such agreements were signed, however, Japan benefited from United States

[26] Kolko, *Limits of Power*, p. 685.

aid to Indochina and other countries through the practice of "off-shore procurement"—that is, they would purchase goods and supplies in Japan, using American funds. In this way, Japan's economic recovery and prosperity were intimately linked to the new United States strategy. It was part of the Asian-Pacific order which the United States was endeavoring to construct as a substitute for the Yalta scheme.

Twenty years after the Korean War, in the early 1970s, the United States was still trying to define an international order in the Asia-Pacific region. But the original conception had become progressively modified, and it was far from clear what sort of equilibrium, if at all, would in the end emerge. But one thing was certain: the Yalta system which had defined postwar international relations in this region and which had survived the initial phase of the Cold War, had been superseded by subsequent developments, and could no longer define the reality or serve as a conceptual framework—except insofar as the United States and the Soviet Union had managed to prevent the outbreak of a third world war.

The Cold War in Asia entered a post-Yalta phase in the mid-1950s, when American-Russian relations came to be seen as those of "peaceful coexistence," and were overshadowed by developments in China, Japan, and Southeast Asia. Peaceful coexistence with the Soviet Union did not produce its equivalent in Chinese-American relations, and the People's Republic of China replaced the Soviet Union as a self-conscious, primary opponent of the United States in world politics. In terms of Realpolitik the Big Two maintained the Yalta understanding with respect to their respective spheres of influence, whereas China rejected such a definition of global balance and challenged both American and Soviet hegemony in international affairs by conceiving of its role as the champion of the rights of smaller nations—as the leader of a new worldwide coalition of all peoples alike opposed to United States imperialism and to Soviet "revisionism."

The United States responded to the challenge by stepping up its assistance to the French in Indochina and, after their defeat in 1954, to the South Vietnamese. The Southeast Asia Treaty Organization was created to provide for collective security against the Chinese threat, and mutual defense pacts were signed with both Japan and Taiwan. The policy of separating the latter from mainland China was continued, the offshore islands were turned into a bastion of American strategy. As earlier, the United States considered Taiwan and Indochina as part of the same picture, but now they were systematically incorporated into a regional framework of collective security. Taiwan gave full support to the policy of the United States to intervene in Vietnam by force. Already in the mid-1950s the bulk of American military and economic aid was being shifted from Europe to Asia, in particular Taiwan and South Vietnam, and in the next decade American energies and resources were spent in trying to maintain the power of the United States in these areas, a policy which was justified as a way to promote regional stability against the disruptive influences and tactics of Communist China.

In the meantime, Japan started on its path to economic recovery, prosperity, and expansion. The country enjoyed America's "nuclear umbrella"—according to the Japanese-American mutual security treaty of 1960

> Each Party recognizes that an armed attack against either Party in the territories under the administration of Japan would be dangerous to its own peace and safety and declares that it would act to meet the common danger in accordance with its constitutional provisions and processes.

Thus assured of military protection by the United States, the Japanese redoubled their effort to promote their economic interests. There was a near-total consensus that "economism" should define their foreign policy; the country would undertake economic expansion at home and abroad without involving itself in complex diplomatic questions and power politics. Trade and investment activities grew phenomenally in Southeast Asia, steadily undermining the position of the Western powers in the economic life of the region. While no such step was yet taken toward the People's Republic of China, de facto relations already existed between the two countries, and semi-official trade delegations periodically paid their visits to Peking.

All these developments were bound to put an end to the period of close Sino-Soviet relations, both as a reality and as a perception produced by the Cold War confrontation. China was beginning to act as an independent and assertive power to an extent never visualized either in the Yalta system or in the post-Yalta phase of the Cold War. Its foreign policy would no longer be tied to the Soviet Union, although there was serious disagreement among the Chinese leaders as to the desirability and practicability of antagonizing Russia. But they pushed ahead with nuclear armament, and stressed more than ever before the uniqueness of the Chinese Communist experiment. With respect to the Soviet Union, Chinese policy was determined by the need to maintain the security of the long common border and to prevent American-Russian rapprochement at the expense of China. By the late 1960s, Russia rather than America was emerging as the greater perceived threat to China's existence as a power.

By the early 1970s, then, the Cold War, either in its earlier or post-Yalta phase, could no longer serve as a framework of Asian-Pacific international relations. Whether an alternative structure would in time be constructed remained to be seen. The United States and the Soviet Union now had to reckon with the resurgence of Japanese power and the achievement of a near super-power status by China. Both of them were multilateralizing their foreign relations, departing from the earlier dependence on one of the Big Two. They were competitors with the United States and the Soviet Union for worldwide influence, economic expansion, or regional power. Whether these four could somehow cooperate, as another foursome had tried to do in the 1940s, and build a stable regional order was a key question of the 1970s.

That there would have to be developed a new framework of power relations was clear. The United States, the Soviet Union, China, Japan and others in the Asia-Pacific region would have to redefine and clarify their mutual rights, interests, and spheres of influence as a basis for stability and equilibrium. The spectacular Nixon and Tanaka trips to Peking in 1972 were a step in this direction. Both the United States and Japan recognized the People's Republic of China as a great power, a key factor in the Asian international system with which it was necessary to come to terms in any attempt at regional order. By the same token, the Chinese leaders decided to accept the fact that despite ideological differences they must deal with these countries as powers if China were to play a role as a member of the system and to prevent its own isolation. The historic meetings of February and September 1972 showed that the three powers were willing to view each other as members in a new balance of power.

The balance of power, however, would remain unstable unless it were accompanied by a new internationalism. The internationalist aspect of the Yalta system had visualized an era of cooperation between the United States and the Soviet Union. When no such cooperation developed, there emerged a concept of fundamental opposition between two ideologies and ways of life. But at least the Cold War rhetoric provided an ideological underpinning for the balance of power between the two super powers, whereas earlier, a structure of international relations had not always been accompanied with a clearly recognizable vision. Whether the emerging new order of the 1970s would be able to develop a realistic vision, a new internationalism, remains to be seen. Both American and Soviet leaders have once again begun to stress the theme of cooperation. The word was used with almost monotonous regularity by President Nixon and the Soviet leader, Leonid I. Brezhnev, when they met in the United States in June 1973. It was a sign of changing times that Brezhnev talked most frequently of "economic cooperation" between the two countries as a desirable end and a basis for "mutually advantageous relations between our two countries."

The Cold War, he told a group of American business leaders in Washington,

> put the brake on the development of human relations, of normal human relations between nations, and it slowed down the progress and advance of economic and scientific times. And I ask you gentlemen, as I ask myself, was that a good period? Did it serve the interests of the peoples? And my answer to that is no, no, no, and again no.[27]

[27] *New York Times*, June 23, 1973.

He was harking back to the spirit of the wartime alliance, back to the time of the Yalta Conference when the great powers had seemed about to usher in a period of international cooperation. In a similar vein, Henry Kissinger declared in a New York address in April 1973,

> We must identify interests and positive values beyond security in order to engage once again the commitment of peoples and parliaments. We need a shared view of the world we seek to build.[28]

This, too, was going back to the language of Yalta internationalism. It was as if the great powers were back where they started, at the beginning of the road where they had jointly sought to establish a framework for postwar cooperation.

The new internationalism in the Asia-Pacific region, however, will be if anything even more difficult to envision and actualize than Big-Two cooperation. "A shared view of the world we seek to build" will be extremely elusive to define if only because the countries and peoples of the region are so different culturally, ideologically, socially, and economically. Unlike the European powers in the nineteenth century, which shared a common civilization, or unlike even the United States and the Soviet Union, which at least built a balance-of-power structure despite ideological differences, "cooperation" in Asia and the Pacific must embrace China, Japan, Korea, Southeast Asia, Australia, New Zealand, and other countries as well as America and Russia. They represent incredible complexity and diversity. For this very reason, however, a shared vision of peaceful international order in the Asia-Pacific region would be a prerequisite if stability were ever to be achieved. If such a vision should develop, and if the peoples of these lands should join others in trying to create a peaceful and prosperous international order, they would have made a signal contribution to history, proving that peoples of divergent cultures and backgrounds could work together in their common interests.

[28] *New York Times*, Apr. 24, 1973.

Bibliography

In 1967, I published *Across the Pacific: An Inner History of American-East Asian Relations* (New York: Harcourt, Brace & Jovanovich). The book traces the history of United States-Asian relations primarily in terms of mutual images among the Americans, Japanese, and Chinese. In its bibliography, I mentioned some of the important works that had appeared on the subject, and an interested reader may turn to it as a guide for further reading. The following discussion is confined, with a few exceptions, to publications since 1967. There has been an impressive amount of literature in the last few years, dealing with the Cold War and United States involvement in Asia. The following is just a partial list, and includes only those items that have been useful in the preparation of this book. For a more extensive annotated bibliography, the reader is referred to Byron Dexter, ed., *The Foreign Affairs 50-Year Bibliography* (New York: R. R. Bowker, 1972).

THE HISTORICAL BACKGROUND

The study of American diplomatic history has seen something of a revival in recent years, as historians have tried to develop new conceptualizations and raise refreshing and often disturbing questions about the nature of American interactions with other countries. United States expansionism, imperialism, and colonialism have been subjected to searching scrutiny, and no student of the Cold War can ignore the recent studies on these subjects. To understand the way nineteenth century Americans viewed and rationalized their expansion, for instance, it is imperative to read such books as William H. Goetzmann, *Exploration and Empire* (New York: Knopf, 1966); Frederick Merk, *Slavery and the Annexation of Texas* (New York: Knopf, 1972); and James A. Field, *America and the Mediterranean World, 1776–1882* (Princeton: Princeton University Press, 1969).

The expansionism of the 1890s, which ushered in the age of world politics for American diplomacy, has been particularly well-explored by recent monographs. Most of them deal with American opinions and attitudes, reflecting the historian's fascination with the intellectual, emotional, and psychological sources of imperialism. Most notable in this connection are Ernest R. May, *American Imperialism: A Speculative Essay* (New York: Atheneum, 1968); William Appleman Williams, *The Roots of the Modern American Empire* (New York: Random House, 1969); David Healy, *United States Expansionism: The Imperialistic Urge in the 1890s* (Madison: University of Wisconsin Press, 1970); Robert L. Beisner, *Twelve Against Empire: The Anti-imperialists, 1898–1900* (New York: McGraw-Hill, 1968); and E. Berkeley Tompkins, *Anti-imperialism in the United States, 1898–1920* (Philadelphia: University of Philadelphia Press, 1970). Although discussing tiny segments of American public opinion, the following two books make interesting observations that are pertinent to the question of the country's relations with colored races in the world: George P. Marks, *The Black Press Views American Imperialism, 1898–1900* (New York: Arno Press, 1971); and Daniel B. Schirmer, *Republic or Empire* (Cambridge, Mass.: Schenkman, 1972).

More formal aspects of United States diplomacy in the late nineteenth century have been explored by three excellent studies of military thought: John A. S. Grenville and George B. Young, *Politics, Strategy, and American Diplomacy* (New Haven: Yale University Press, 1966); Peter Karsten, *The Naval Aristocracy* (New York: Free Press, 1972); and Richard Challener, *Admirals, Generals, and American Foreign Policy, 1898–1914* (Princeton: Princeton University Press, 1973).

The number of books on the history of American-East Asian relations has increased dramatically in the last several years. The most recent surveys include Warren I. Cohen, *America's Response to China* (New York: Wiley, 1971), and its companion volume, dealing with American-Japanese relations, by Charles E. Neu, soon to be published by the same press. Ernest R. May and James C. Thomson, eds., *American-East Asian Relations: A Survey* (Cambridge: Harvard University Press, 1972) gives a detailed listing and analysis of the existing literature, and it would be meaningless to recapitulate it here. Those who are interested in American images of China in the nineteenth century should consult two first-rate monographs: Stuart Creighton Miller, *The Unwelcome Immigrant: The American Image of the Chinese, 1785–1882* (Berkeley: University of California Press, 1969); and Clifton Jackson Phillips, *Protestant America and the Pagan World: The First Half Century of the American Board of Commissioners for Foreign Missions, 1810–1860* (Cambridge: Harvard University Press, 1969). Turn-of-the-century American-Chinese relations have been studied by Paul A. Varg, *The Making of a Myth: The United States and China, 1789–1912* (East Lansing: Michigan State University Press, 1968); Thomas J. McCormick, *China Market* (Chicago: Quadrangle, 1967); Robert McClellan, *The Heathen Chinee* (Columbus: Ohio State University Press, 1971); Jerry Israel, *Progressivism and the Open Door: America and China, 1905–1921* (Pittsburgh: University of Pittsburgh Press, 1971); and Marilyn B. Young, *The Rhetoric of Empire: American China Policy, 1895–1901* (Cambridge: Harvard University Press, 1968). United States relations with Japan have been analyzed by Charles E. Neu, *An Uncertain Friendship: Theodore Roosevelt and Japan* (Cambridge: Harvard University Press, 1967); William R. Braisted, *The United States Navy in the Pacific, 1909–1922* (Austin: University of Texas Press, 1971); and Akira Iriye, *Pacific Estrangement: Japanese and American Expansion, 1897–1911* (Cambridge: Harvard University Press, 1972). On the Philippines, the best study is Peter Stanley's *A Nation in the Making*, a monograph to be published by the Harvard University Press, which examines the interaction between Philippine politics and American colonialist thought.

There are a few English-language studies of Chinese and Japanese foreign relations in the nineteenth and early twentieth centuries. Among them are Ssu-yü Teng, *The Taiping Rebellion and the Western Powers* (Oxford: Clarendon Press, 1971); John E. Schrecker, *Imperialism and Chinese Nationalism: Germany in Shantung* (Cambridge: Harvard University Press, 1971); Mary C. Wright, ed., *China in Revolution: the First Phase, 1900–1913* (New Haven: Yale University Press, 1968); Shumpei Okamoto, *Japanese Oligarchy and the Russo-Japanese War* (New York: Columbia University Press, 1970); and Douglas Hurd, *The Arrow War: An Anglo-Chinese Confusion, 1856–1860* (London: Collins, 1967). Conspicuously absent have been detailed studies of Sino-Japanese relations. The only good if small recent publication, utilizing both Chinese and Japanese sources, has been Madeleine Chi's *China Diplomacy, 1914–1918* (Cambridge: Harvard University Press, 1970), which traces the interaction between Chinese politics and imperialist policies during World War II.

On President Woodrow Wilson's foreign policy and its impact on Asia, see Norman Gordon Levin, *Woodrow Wilson and World Politics* (New York: Oxford University Press, 1968); Arno J. Mayer, *The Politics and Diplomacy of Peacemaking* (New York: Knopf, 1967); Carl Parrini, *Heir to Empire: United States Economic Diplomacy, 1916–1923* (Pittsburgh: University of Pittsburgh Press, 1969); and Arthur S. Link, *The Higher Realism of Woodrow Wilson* (Nashville: Vanderbilt University Press, 1971). These books should be supplemented by monographs dealing with the European powers in the Asia-Pacific region. Among the most recent are Ian Nish, *Alliance in Decline: A Study in Anglo-Japanese Relations, 1908–1923* (London: Athlone, 1972); and Peter Lowe, *Great Britain and Japan, 1911–1915* (London: Macmillan, 1969).

For the interwar years, the most interesting publication is Dorothy Borg and Shumpei Okamoto, eds., *Pearl Harbor as History: Japanese-American Relations, 1931–1941* (New York: Columbia University Press, 1973). The volume contains contributions by American and Japanese historians, who originally wrote their essays for a binational conference held in Japan in the summer of 1969. The conference itself was a main event in intellectual communication across the Pacific. It is to be hoped that similar multinational undertakings may develop not only between Americans and Japanese but also among British, Chinese, Russian, and other historians. The above volume may be supplemented by James W. Morley, ed., *The Dilemma of Growth in Prewar Japan* (Princeton: Princeton University Press, 1971), which contains suggestive essays on various aspects of interwar Japanese society. For a more sensational account, see David Bergamini, *Japan's Imperial Conspiracy* (New York: Morrow, 1971). Also useful is James Crowley, ed., *Modern East Asia: Essays in Interpretation* (New York: Harcourt, Brace & Jovanovich, 1970), which includes chapters on Japan's road to war.

On United States diplomacy before World War II, no comprehensive accounts of American policy in the Asia-Pacific region have been published since the publication, in 1964, of Dorothy Borg's *The United States and the Far Eastern Crisis of 1933–38* (Cambridge: Harvard University Press). However, a number of books have done much to illuminate aspects of American foreign relations during the 1920s and 1930s. They include Joan Hoff Wilson, *American Business and Foreign Policy, 1920–1933* (Lexington: University of Kentucky Press, 1971); Peter G. Filene, *Americans and the Soviet Experiment, 1917–1933* (Cambridge: Harvard University Press, 1967); Robert J. Maddox, *William E. Borah and American Foreign Policy* (Baton Rouge: Louisiana State University Press, 1969); and Arnold A. Offner, *American Appeasement, 1933–1938* (Cambridge: Harvard University Press, 1969). Among works dealing with United States policy in East Asia are Thomas H. Buckley, *The United States and the Washington Conference, 1921–1922* (Knoxville: University of

Tennessee Press, 1970); Russell D. Buhite, *Nelson T. Johnson and American Policy toward China, 1925–1941* (East Lansing: Michigan State University Press, 1968); and Manny Koginos, *The Panay Incident* (Lafayette, Indiana: Purdue University Studies, 1967).

The opening of British archives has resulted in an outpouring of excellent discussions of London's policy toward Asia. The most thorough in documentation and analysis is Christopher Thorne, *The Limits of Foreign Policy: The West, the League, and the Manchurian Crisis, 1931–1933* (London: Hamish Hamilton, 1972). Less detailed but equally stimulating are Roger Louis, *British Strategy in the Far East* (Oxford: Oxford University Press, 1971), and Bradford A. Lee, *Britain and the Sino-Japanese War, 1937–1939* (Stanford: Stanford University Press, 1973). See also a highly personalized but provocative narrative by Captain Malcolm D. Kennedy, *The Estrangement of Great Britain and Japan, 1917–1935* (Berkeley: University of California Press, 1969).

For the Chinese scene, easily the most interesting recent publication is Vera V. Vishnyakova-Akimova, *Two Years in Revolutionary China* (Cambridge: Harvard University Press, 1971), which is a recollection of the author's involvement in the Soviet-Chinese alliance, 1925–27. See also James Claude Thomson, *While China Faced West, 1928–1937* (Cambridge: Harvard University Press, 1969), and relevant chapters in Oliver E. Clubb, *China and Russia: The "Great Game"* (New York: Columbia University Press, 1971).

THE PACIFIC WAR

Official histories of the Second World War continue to be published by the United States, the Soviet Union, Great Britain, Japan, and other countries. They need not be listed here, but obviously they are the basic material for any study of wartime diplomacy. I will only mention Llewelyn Woodward's *British Foreign Policy in the Second World War*, II (London: Her Majesty's Stationery Office, 1971), as particularly pertinent to the study of the origins of the Pacific War.

For a general introduction to the military history of the war, the best recent work is B. H. Liddell Hart's *History of the Second World War* (New York: Putnam, 1971). The Pacific War is well surveyed by Charles Bateson, *The War with Japan* (East Lansing: Michigan State University Press, 1968). For the diplomatic background preceding the war, see Esmond M. Robertson, comp., *Origins of the Second World War* (London: Macmillan, 1971), which is a collection of historiographical essays, and Peter Calvocoressi and Guy Wint, *Total War: Causes and Courses of the Second World War* (New York: Pantheon, 1972).

Concerning American policy just prior to the Pacific War, Warren F.

Kimball, in *The Most Unsordid Act: Lend-Lease, 1939–41* (Baltimore: Johns Hopkins, 1967), chronicles the growing sense of common destiny tying together Britain and the United States. In the same vein is a well-written narrative of the Atlantic Conference of 1941 by Theodore A. Wilson, *The First Summit: Roosevelt and Churchill* (Boston: Houghton Mifflin, 1971). There are also two first-rate studies of American opinion in this period: Mark L. Chadwin, *The Hawks of World War II* (Chapel Hill: University of North Carolina, 1968); and John P. Diggins, *Mussolini and Fascism: The View from America* (Princeton: Princeton University Press, 1972). The latter, in particular, is an historiographical landmark, showing how to study the interaction between mass opinion, elite opinion, and official perceptions. On German-Japanese-American relations in 1940–41, see Saul Friedländer, *Prelude to Downfall* (New York: Knopf, 1967).

Among recent treatments of the origins of the war in the Pacific are the biographies of Generals Douglas MacArthur and George Marshall: Dorris Clayton James, *The Years of MacArthur*, I (Boston: Houghton Mifflin, 1970) and Forrest C. Pogue, *George C. Marshall: Ordeal and Hope, 1939–1943* (New York: Viking, 1966). Also informative are John M. Blum, *Roosevelt and Morgenthau* (Boston: Houghton Mifflin, 1970); and James MacGregor Burns, *Roosevelt: The Soldier of Freedom* (New York: Harcourt, Brace & Jovanovich, 1970). Among autobiographical writings that are relevant, especially notable are George F. Kennan, *Memoirs, 1925–1950* (Boston: Little, Brown, 1967); Charles E. Bohlen, *Witness to History, 1929–1969* (New York: Norton, 1973); William Averril Harriman, *America and Russia in a Changing World* (Garden City, N.Y.: Doubleday, 1971); Oliver Harvey, *The Diplomatic Diaries of Oliver Harvey, 1937–1940* (New York: St. Martin's, 1970); and Sir Alexander Cadogan, *The Diaries of Sir Alexander Cadogan* (New York: Putnam, 1972).

There is still a dearth of specialized studies of the Sino-Japanese War, although John H. Boyle's *China and Japan at War, 1937–1945* (Stanford: Stanford University Press, 1972) has done much to fill the historiographic gap. See also Gerald E. Bunker, *Peace Conspiracy, 1937–41* (Cambridge: Harvard University Press, 1972). On America's role in China, on the other hand, there have been several interesting studies. For instance, Kenneth Shewmaker's *Americans and the Chinese Communists, 1927–1945* (Ithaca: Cornell University Press, 1971) traces the encounter between American journalists and the Communists in China, while Russell Buhite, in *Patrick J. Hurley and American Relations with China* (Ithaca: Cornell University Press, 1973) provides the best treatment to date of the controversial figure whose perception of events in China was an important aspect of the origins of the Cold War. Another good biography is Barbara Tuchman's *Stilwell and the American Experience in China, 1911–1945* (New York: Macmillan, 1970). Although not as thorough as the standard three-volume study of the Stilwell mission, done for the War Department by Riley Sunderland and Charles F. Romanus (1953,

1956, 1960), Tuchman succeeds in recapturing the flavor of wartime American-Chinese relations. Excerpts from Gen. Joseph Stilwell's diary, incidentally, which were originally published in 1948, have been reissued, *The Stilwell Papers* (New York: Schocken, 1972). Among other Americans who became involved in the maelstrom of wartime Chinese politics, John S. Service, in *The Amerasia Papers* (Berkeley: University of California Press, 1971), and John P. Davies, in *Dragon by the Tail* (New York: Norton, 1972), have written personalized accounts. They are both careful and detached (perhaps too much so, considering the dramatic nature of what the two men went through after 1945) analyses of the authors' views on the Kuomintang-Communist rift in China and American policy in Asia.

On wartime American diplomacy, the last few years have seen intensive monographic work and efforts at reinterpretation, especially on the part of younger writers who have tried to go beyond earlier standard accounts. The publication of Gabriel Kolko's *The Politics of War, 1943–45* (New York: Random House, 1968) was a major historiographical event, ushering in a period of reappraisal of wartime diplomacy. The author's main concern is with delineating the impact of American policy upon domestic social forces in various parts of the world. This is an extremely worthy aim, but his tendency to rely on secondary sources when describing foreign countries, and to impose a rigid interpretative structure on the narrative detracts from the value of the book. It should be read in conjunction with more conventional accounts such as, for instance, Robert Beitzell's *The Uneasy Alliance: America, Britain, and Russia, 1941–1943* (New York: Knopf, 1972).

Neither of these authors uses Russian documents, a serious shortcoming in any study of wartime American-Soviet relations. The study of Soviet diplomacy has been left to Russia specialists, whose recent publications include Adam B. Ulam, *Expansion and Coexistence: The History of Soviet Foreign Policy, 1917–1967* (New York: Praeger, 1968); and Louis Fischer, *The Road to Yalta: Soviet Foreign Relations, 1941–1945* (New York: Harper & Row, 1972). The most balanced account to date, and about the only monograph by a specialist in American diplomatic history using Russian material, is Diane Shaver Clemens, *Yalta* (New York: Oxford University Press, 1970). See also an excellent monograph on wartime Soviet-Japanese relations by George Alexander Lensen, *Strange Neutrality* (Tallahassee: Diplomatic Press, 1972).

The study of international affairs toward the end of the war inevitably merges into the historiography of the Cold War. There have been some notable accomplishments recently in the field of American policy with respect to the peace—preparations for ending the war, blueprints for postwar reconstruction, and visions of world politics after the defeat of the Axis powers. Robert A. Divine, in *Second Chance* (New York: Atheneum, 1967), traces the emergence of new internationalist thought as a prevailing strain in American thinking after 1943, while Lloyd C. Gardner, in *Architects of Illusion,*

1941–1949 (Chicago: Quadrangle, 1970), stresses the highly subjective and selfish nature of such images. The economic aspect of American diplomacy, in particular, has been a subject of strong concern among historians, and they differ in assessing its origins and impact. Bruce Kuklick, in *American Policy and the Division of Germany* (Ithaca: Cornell University Press, 1972), sees in the policy toward the German question a classic example of economic "multilateralism," a vision of the postwar world in which American capital would play the predominant role. George C. Herring, in *Aid to Russia, 1941–1946* (New York: Columbia University Press, 1973) emphasizes other factors in trying to understand the issue of aid in the context of the estrangement between the two allies.

THE COLD WAR

Some of the books listed above deal with the question of the origins of the Cold War. This has been a fascinating issue, involving historians' ideologies, trainings, and Weltanschauungen which are shared with contemporaries, as each seeks to expand his reading of the ever-increasing quantity of available documents. The heat which the subject has generated, perhaps prematurely, may be seen in the publication in 1973 by the Princeton University Press of Robert J. Maddox's *The New Left and the Origins of the Cold War*, and the instantaneous furor it created among specialists. At this point in the rather primitive state of the literature, one looks for less dramatic but more dispassionate scholarship. Good examples of it are John Lewis Gaddis, *The United States and the Origins of the Cold War, 1941–1947* (New York: Columbia University Press, 1972); Herbert Feis, *From Trust to Terror: The Onset of the Cold War, 1945–1950* (New York: Norton, 1970); and Lisle A. Rose, *After Yalta* (New York: Scribner, 1973).

The best short history of the Cold War is Walter LaFeber, *America, Russia, and the Cold War: 1945–1971* (New York: Wiley, second edition, 1972). Recent examples of "revisionist" literature—although there is so much diversity among "revisionist" writers that the label is not quite useful—include Joyce and Gabriel Kolko, *The Limits of Power, 1945–1954* (New York: Harper & Row, 1972); and Richard Freeland, *The Truman Doctrine and the Origins of McCarthyism* (New York, Knopf, 1972). Among more conventional writings are Louis J. Halle, *The Cold War as History* (New York: Harper & Row, 1967); Paul Seabury, *Rise and Decline of the Cold War* (New York: Basic Books, 1967); and Paul Y. Hammond, *The Cold War Years: American Foreign Policy Since 1945* (New York: Harcourt, Brace & Jovanovich, 1969). Thomas G. Paterson's *Cold War Critics* (Chicago: Quadrangle, 1971) contains fascinating portraits of men who sensed the need to develop an alternative image of international politics at the onset of the Cold War.

Some policy makers have speculated about the origins and characteristics of the Cold War in their autobiographical writings. In addition to the
memoirs by George F. Kennan and Charles E. Bohlen, noted earlier, one
finds especially illuminating Dean Acheson, *Present at the Creation: My Years in
the State Department* (New York: Norton, 1969); George W. Ball, *The Discipline
of Power: Essentials of a Modern World Structure* (Boston: Little, Brown, 1968);
and Townsend Hoopes, *The Limits of Intervention* (New York: McKay, 1969).
See also David Halberstam's *The Best and the Brightest* (New York: Random
House, 1972), for a highly impressionistic but excellent portrait of American
leaders with typical Cold War perceptions.

American foreign policy has always been intimately connected with
domestic politics, and this was particularly true of the immediate postwar
years, when politicians and the public, opposed to long years of Democratic
rule and New Deal policies, turned on the Truman Administration to attack
its foreign policy, while the latter, in response, stepped up its anti-Communist
campaign inside and outside the country. The story is told in growing detail
in various recent monographs, including Freeland's book, mentioned above;
Bert Cochran, *Harry Truman and the Crisis Presidency* (New York: 1973); Athan
Theoharis, *The Yalta Myths, 1945–1955* (Columbia: University of Missouri
Press, 1970); the same author's *Seeds of Repression: Harry S. Truman and the
Origins of McCarthyism* (Chicago: Quadrangle, 1971); Alan D. Harper, *The
Politics of Loyalty, 1946–1952* (Westport, Conn.: Greenwood, 1969); and Robert
Griffith, *The Politics of Fear: McCarthyism and the Senate* (Lexington: University
of Kentucky Press, 1970).

There has been surprisingly little recent publication on American-
Asian relations in the immediate postwar years. Tang Tsou's *America's Failure
in China, 1941–1950* (Chicago: University of Chicago Press, 1963) is still the
basic work on the subject. John F. Melby, *The Mandate of Heaven: China,
1945–1949* (Toronto: University of Toronto Press, 1968) is an eyewitness
account. Three useful books deal with aspects of postwar Japanese-American
relations: Martin Weinstein, *Japan's Postwar Defense Policy, 1947–1968* (New
York: Columbia University Press, 1971); Richard Minear, *Victor's Justice: The
Tokyo War Crimes Trial* (Princeton: Princeton University Press, 1971); and
John K. Emmerson, *Arms, Yen and Power: The Japanese Dilemma* (New York:
Dunellen, 1971).

On the Korean War, the best treatment is Glenn D. Paige, *The Korean
Decision* (New York: Free Press, 1968), an excellent study of the decision-
making process. Soviet motives and policies are discussed in George F.
Kennan's *Memoirs, 1950–1963* (Boston: Little, Brown, 1972); and Adam B.
Ulam's *The Rivals: America and Russia since World War II* (New York: Viking,
1971). Foster Rhea Dulles, in *American Policy Toward Communist China,
1949–1969* (New York: Crowell, 1972) goes over the familiar ground and
offers little that is interesting or new. The impact of the Korean War upon

American policy in Southeast Asia is analyzed by Russell H. Fifield, *Americans in Southeast Asia: The Roots of Commitment* (New York: Thomas Y. Crowell, 1973). This is an admirable book, well documented and balanced, that should serve as a standard survey of the history of American involvement in Southeast Asia. Together with George M. Kahin and John W. Lewis, *The United States in Vietnam* (New York: Dial Press, 1967, rev., 1969), it offers the basic background material for any discussion of United States policy in Asia in the 1970s.

WORKS IN NON-ENGLISH LANGUAGES

The above list may give the impression that most scholarly contributions in the fields of American foreign policy and Asian international relations have been made in the English language. This is far from the truth. Russian, Chinese, Japanese, and other countries' writers have published a great deal, discussing these subjects as well as their countries' foreign policies. Unfortunately, few of their works have been translated into English, and historians in the United States have tended to argue among themselves rather than with their scholarly colleagues abroad. Obviously, there is need for a more serious interchange of ideas among scholars of many countries, especially when dealing with emotion-charged issues like the origins of the Cold War.

Russian historians have always been interested in Asian international relations and have published numerous studies of different periods of this history. Their writings have been noted by a multilingual approach. Many of them use Chinese and Japanese, as well as Western-language material, and this gives their works a comprehensive and even cosmopolitan outlook sometimes lacking in American publications. However, there is a great deal of conceptual monotony among Soviet writers, and they usually adopt a rigid interpretative framework. In the study of Asian-Pacific international relations, for instance, E. M. Zhukov's *Mezhdunarodnye otnosheniia na Dal'nem Vostoke, 1870–1945* (Moscow: Politicheskoi Literaturi, 1951), a massive volume, still seems to offer the standard formulation for the discussion of the subject, although the author's liberal use of quotes from Stalin and Molotov may be considered inappropriate today. Concerning the Pacific War, Zhukov writes that it was prosecuted, from the Anglo-American viewpoint, in order to snatch Japanese colonies and spheres of influence. After Japan's defeat, he says, Britain and the United States intensified their competition for markets, with the latter trying to give power to the bourgeoisie and semi-feudal elements in the defeated country. In the meantime, the Soviet Union played a crucial role in bringing the war to an end, and the now enhanced power of Russia was needed to further the national-revolutionary movements in China, Korea, and elsewhere. Postwar Asia, then, was divided between two camps, with the Soviet Union standing for peace, democracy, and freedom, and the United States obstructing the attainment of such goals.

Such an interpretative framework has been followed by most Soviet historians. Among their recent publications are A. M. Dubinskii's study of the Soviet role during the Pacific War (*Osvoboditel'naia missiia Sovetskovo Soiuza na Dal'nem Vostoke, 1941–1945*; Moscow: Mysl', 1966); Kh. T. Eidus' survey of Soviet-Japanese relations after the war (*SSSR i Iaponiia*; Moscow: Nauka, 1964); and a history of postwar Soviet-Chinese relations by O. B. Borisov and B. T. Koloskov, *Sovetsko-kitaiskie otnosheniia, 1945–1970* (Moscow: Mysl', 1971). A leading diplomatic historian, Viktor V. Israelian, has written a number of accounts of wartime and prewar diplomacy, including *Antigitlerovskaia koalitsiia, 1941–1945* (Moscow: Mezhdunarodnye otnosheniia, 1964), and *Diplomatiia agressorov* (Moscow: Nauka, 1967). This latter, coauthored with L. N. Kutakov, has been translated into English as *Diplomacy of Aggression* (Moscow: Progress Publishers, 1970). Kutakov is also a prolific writer, specializing in Soviet-Japanese relations. In 1962 he published a survey, *Istoriia sovetsko-iaponskikh diplomaticheskikh otnosheniia* (Moscow: Mezhdunarodnye otnosheniia). In 1972 he wrote a book in English: *Japanese Foreign Policy on the Eve of the Pacific War: A Soviet View* (Tallahassee: Diplomatic Press).

There are also numerous accounts of American foreign policy by Soviet writers. For instance, L. I. Zubok, *Ekspansionistskaia politika SShA v nachale XX veka* (Moscow: Nauka, 1969) traces United States foreign relations at the turn of the twentieth century, dealing with all parts of the world. Its conceptual scheme is not very different from the "Open Door" school of American historians, who stress economic and cultural expansionism as a key theme in the country's external affairs. But Zubok uses Tsarist archival materials and discusses Russian perceptions of American expansion. For the interwar years, covering American responses to the Bolshevik regime, V. K. Furaev's *Sovetsko-Amerikanskie otnosheniia* (Moscow: Mysl', 1964) is informative and well balanced. And for New Deal diplomacy, a recent book by D. G. Nadzhafov, *Narod SShA protiv voiny i fashizma, 1933–1939* (Moscow: Nauka, 1969) stresses the American people's "struggle against war and fascism." While the author is critical of the American leadership for failing to recognize the power of the anti-fascist movement by "progressive" citizens, V. B. Vorontsov is more lenient toward President Roosevelt. His book, *Tikhookeanskaia politika SShA, 1941–1950* (Moscow: Nauka, 1967), is one of the more recent studies of America's Asian-Pacific policy during the 1940s. Like Zhukov, he does distinguish between progressive forces and reactionaries in the United States, and tends to portray Roosevelt as leaning toward the former's more "realistic" attitude vis-à-vis the Soviet Union. After Roosevelt's death, the reactionaries are depicted as having taken over the control of American policy, intent upon reestablishing Japanese power in the service of the nation's monopoly capitalism. Whatever the merit of such a sweeping interpretation, the book abounds in bibliographical references and offers a useful guide to Soviet historiography.

Unfortunately, Chinese scholarship has not been very notable with respect to the Pacific War and the immediate postwar period. Publications in China—both the mainland and Taiwan—have been extremely scanty, probably reflecting the still highly sensitive nature of wartime and postwar foreign relations. Little scholarly work has been published in the past several years on these subjects, and most writings that deal with Chinese politics and foreign affairs during the war are very polemical. The only valuable source of information that I have been able to find has been autobiographical writings by Chinese leaders who reminisce about the 1930s and the 1940s. Valuable in this respect have been Ch'en I-yün, *I-yün hui-i* (2 vols., Taipei: Chuan-chi Wen-hsüeh Ch'u-pan she, 1968); and Kung Te-po, *Hui-i-lu* (3 vols., Taipei: Hsin-wen T'ien-ti she, 1964).

There are many more pertinent publications in Japanese, although in Japan, too, the best and most useful monographs have tended to concentrate on the prewar years. Since 1971 alone, for instance, a number of studies have appeared that shed light on Japanese relations with China, the United States, and other countries in the 1920s and the 1930s. They include Yoshii Hiroshi, *Shōwa gaikō-shi* (Tokyo: Nansōsha, 1971); Usui Katsumi, *Nit-Chū gaikō-shi* (Tokyo: Hanawa shobō, 1971); the same author's *Nihon to Chūgoku* (Tokyo: Hara shobō, 1972); Banba Nobuya, *Manshū jihen e no michi* (Tokyo: Chūōkōron, 1972); Miwa Kimitada, *Matsuoka Yōseki* (Tokyo: Chūōkōron, 1971); and some articles in Uchiyama Masakuma, *Gendai Nihon gaikō-shi ron* (Tokyo: Keiō University Press, 1971). Miwa's biography of Foreign Minister Matsuoka is an interesting attempt to examine an aspect of prewar Japanese attitudes toward the United States, a very complex phenomenon. He shows that one basic approach to the subject is through individual biographies, a method that is also used by Hagihara Nobutoshi in his analysis of an earlier figure: *Baba Tatsui* (Tokyo: Chūōkōron, 1967). Japanese-American relations have begun to be explored by Japan's specialists in American history and literature, and the projected publication of a three-volume series on "Japan and America: A Study in Comparative Culture," edited by Saitō Makoto, Homma Nagayo, and Kamei Shunsuke shows the maturing of the field. The first volume, entitled *Ishitsu bunka no shōgeki to hadō* (Tokyo: Nan'undō, 1973) contains essays on the impact of American culture on Japanese society.

There continue to be published autobiographical and biographical accounts of men who were active in prewar and wartime Japanese relations with China. Among the most interesting are Shōda Tatsuo, *Chūgoku shakkan to Shōda Kazue* (Tokyo: Daiamondo, 1972), which deals with the controversial Nishihara loans during World War I; Tsunoda Jun, *Ishihara Kanji shiryō* (Tokyo: Hara shobō, 1968), a collection of essays and lectures by an architect of the Manchurian crisis; and *Hiroku Doihara Kenji* (Tokyo: Fuyō shobō,

1972), which tries to portray Doihara, another army strategist of long involvement in China, in a sympathetic way.

For the Pacific War, recent surveys include Ienaga Saburō, *Taiheiyō sensō* (Tokyo: Iwanami, 1968); and Imai Seiichi, ed., *Taiheiyō sensō* (2 vols., Tokyo: Aoki shoten, 1972–73). See also personal recollections such as Tomioka Sadatoshi, *Kaisen to shūsen* (Tokyo: Mainichi shinbun, 1968); and Higuchi Kiichirō, *Attu, Kiska gunshireikan no kaisōroku* (Tokyo: Fuyō shobō, 1971). There have, however, been relatively few monographs on Japanese diplomacy during the Pacific War. This is partially attributable to the dearth of first-hand official documents, most of which were destroyed toward the end of the war. The official history of the Foreign Ministry—*Gaimushō no hyakunen* (2 vols., Tokyo: Hara shobō, 1969)—contains but a few pages on wartime foreign affairs. But scattered and fragmentary materials do exist, and it is to be hoped that Japanese policy during the war will be given the kind of detailed treatment American historians have been giving to United States diplomacy.

For the postwar period, too, there have been few solid monographs. Among the exceptions are some of the essays contained in a two-volume study of Japanese-American relations: The International House of Japan, ed., *Nichi-Bei kankei no kenkyū* (Tokyo: Tokyo University Press, 1970). On Prime Minister Yoshida's perceptions of world affairs, see Kōsaka Masataka, *Saishō Yoshida Shigeru* (Tokyo: Chūōkōron, 1968). Most writings on postwar foreign relations have focused on the foreign policies of other countries, and they have frequently been partisan and polemical. Shinobu Seizaburō's study of the Korean War—*Chōsen sensō no boppatsu* (Tokyo: Fukumura shuppan, 1969)—is a good example, where the author relies heavily on a certain genre of American writers. It is still extremely difficult to transcend Cold War frameworks in Japanese academic writings, and it remains to be seen how the events of the 1970s may affect the treatment of postwar international relations. Matsumoto Saburō, *Chūgoku gaikō to Tōnan Ajia* (Tokyo: Keiō University Press, 1971), a study of Chinese policy toward Southeast Asia, is a notable accomplishment in this respect, and it is to be hoped that more such monographs, analytical and free of polemics, will be published in the years ahead. Only then will it become possible for scholars in Japan and the United States, as well as elsewhere, to conduct a meaningful exchange of ideas.

Index